PELICAN BOOKS

# MUSICAL INSTRUMENTS THROUGH THE AGES

### The Editor

Anthony Baines was born in London in 1912. He was educated at Westminster School, and Christ Church, Oxford, where he took a degree in chemistry. His musical enthusiasm, largely for wind instruments, eventual

scientific amb the bassoon playing with (commissione remained an began to condu fessional exper vation of wind music among the young, and both he and his wife teach instruments in schools.

A founder member of the Galpin Society, he took over the editorship of its journal from 1955 to 1963. His own chief published works, apart from various musical editions, are *Woodwind Instruments and Their History* (1957) and *European and American Musical Instruments* (1966).

# Musical Instruments
## THROUGH THE AGES

EDITED BY
## ANTHONY BAINES
FOR THE
GALPIN SOCIETY

**PENGUIN BOOKS**

Penguin Books Ltd, Harmondsworth, Middlesex, England
Penguin Books Inc., 7110 Ambassador Road, Baltimore, Maryland 21207, U.S.A.
Penguin Books Australia Ltd, Ringwood, Victoria, Australia
Penguin Books Canada Ltd, 41 Steelcase Road West,
Markham, Ontario, Canada
Penguin Books (N.Z.) Ltd, 182-190 Wairau Road, Auckland 10, New Zealand

—

First published 1961
Reprinted 1963
Reprinted with revisions 1966
Reprinted with revisions 1969
Reprinted 1971, 1973, 1974

—

Copyright © Penguin Books 1961, 1966, 1969

—

Made and printed in Great Britain
by Cox & Wyman Ltd,
London, Reading and Fakenham
Set in Monotype Baskerville

# Contents

# CONTENTS

# List of Plates

26c Bass trombone. Ehe, Nuremberg, 1732 (*Vienna, Kunsthistorisches Museum*)

  d Trombone, Neuschel, Nuremberg, 1557 (*property of Dr René Clemencic*)

  e Trombone, modern, with F attachment, Conn, Elkhart, U.S.A.

27a Trumpeters and kettledrummer, from an anonymous eighteenth-century German engraving

  b Slide trumpet, Harris, London

  c Modern valve trumpet, Besson, London

  d Three silver natural trumpets: Michael Nagel (Nuremberg, 1657); Anton Schnitzer (Nuremberg, 1581); Johannes Leichamschneider (Vienna, 1725). (*Vienna, Kunsthistorisches Museum*)

28a Helical horn, Dresden, late seventeenth century (*Historical Museum, Dresden*)

  b Single-coil trompe in C, probably French, *c.* 1685

  c Orchestral horn with crooks of early type, probably English, late eighteenth century (*Horniman Museum*)

  d Cor solo, with E♭ crook, by Courtois Frère, Paris, 1816 (*property of R. Morley Pegge, Esq.*)

  e Horn with Vienna valves, Uhlmann, Vienna, *c.* 1855 (*property of R. Morley Pegge, Esq.*)

  f Double horn, F/B♭, Paxman Bros., London, modern (*property of R. Morley Pegge, Esq.*)

29a Serpent, Milhouse, London, *c.* 1800

  b Upright serpent or *Serpent basson*, very early type

  c Bass horn, English, *c.* 1800

  d Key bugle, Ellard, Dublin, *c.* 1820

  e Ophicleide, C. Sax, Brussels, *c.* 1830

  f Cornet, two-valve, Collin, Paris, *c.* 1830

  g Flugel horn, Zetsche, Berlin, *c.* 1840

  h Four saxhorns – soprano in E♭, contralto in B♭, alto in E♭, baritone in B♭. All by Adolphe Sax, Paris, except the alto, which is by Bartsch, Paris

# List of Text Figures

# Editorial Preface

To judge by the accepted meaning of 'instrument' as a popular crossword clue, our title may contain one word more than it need. But if 'instruments' suggest music to the minds of most of us, we are inclined nevertheless to take them for granted, able perhaps to recite many of their names, yet uncertain about the shape and sound of more than a few. This is certainly not the fault of the existing literature on instruments, to which we would not now be adding without having something fresh to offer. I have assembled a symposium, reviewing the field through specialist knowledge and experience of the different classes of instruments. This they really demand; among all professional tools those of the musician are the most highly specialized, each one normally providing a lifetime's occupation for its player. Hence it is virtually impossible for any single author, encyclopedic though his knowledge may be, to understand every instrument with that intimate feel for it in performance which makes the bond between the instrument and its part in music, and to be able to relate questions of design and technique to musical experience and intention – present and also past. The last is very important, and brings us to the Galpin Society, whose book this is, both by commission and by corporate authorship.

This Society was founded in London in 1947 by a group of people who had long been seeking to understand and bring back to life older forms of musical instruments, continuing the work of the late Canon F. W. Galpin (1858–1945) The work has concerned not only instruments which became obsolete after the eighteenth century – many of these now revived through the hands of Arnold Dolmetsch and those who have followed him – but also the older forms and older fittings of instruments today in normal use. Galpin and others have shown that in their sonorous character the older forms belong very much more closely to the music of their day than musicians have generally realized: that the true comparison of an instrument of (say) Bach's day with its modern form is similar to a comparison of the styles of musical composition across the same interval of time, the older bringing immense intensity and variety of expression within a field of techniques that today may appear a relatively narrow one. It may seem odd that anyone should ever have thought otherwise, but until quite recently most people did, condemning antique designs on the authority of one or two superficial and disparaging remarks by old critics (although just such remarks are often made of playing today) or after a mere glance at museum specimens that have not been in playing condition for a century or more.

Times have now changed. A new evaluation of the musical character of the older designs is taking its place beside analogous reassessments of old musical sources, styles of performance, and so on, to bring us very close to the true spirit of earlier music. In some cases it has even begun to show its influence on instrument building.

The approach adopted for the chapters of this book is therefore mainly historical, relating the history of each instrument or group of instruments to its music over the period covered by today's musical programmes, that is to say, roughly the last four or five centuries. In addition, it would not be in keeping with present musicological trends to omit consideration of earlier phases of these histories illustrated by the primitive and folk instruments, even though space obliges us to treat these very briefly. On the other hand, two groups of instruments have been deliberately omitted. One comprises the mechanical musical instruments, in which the player merely turns a handle or winds up clockwork – barrel organs, automata, musical boxes, and clocks – although their music is often charming and its value sometimes considerable as a record of past musical tempi, ornamentation, etc. The other group, electronic musical instruments, must be passed over, even though some of these have already come into limited use and others may well enter widely into music in days to come.

Their technology is so utterly different from that of the traditional instruments, being related rather to that of radio and of sound recording and reproduction, that their description, with the numerous graphs and circuits it involves, must be left to others. Some specialist works on the topic are cited in the Bibliography. So are some leading authorities on musical acoustics, a subject which is gradually progressing from an experimental stage to one of constructive usefulness. But, even with traditional instruments, our book does not set out to be an encyclopedia, and though no reader is likely to lament the omission of the *epigoneion* (whatever it may have been), the Eunuch Flute, and the Bumbass, we hope not to cause disappointment through any other minor omissions forced upon us by considerations of space.

Perhaps a word should be said about certain old authorities, mentioned in the Bibliography and referred to many times in the ensuing chapters. Virdung's work (1511) is the earliest known Tutor for instruments, dealing especially with the keyboard, the lute, and the recorders. It was soon followed (1528) by that of Agricola, amusingly written in rhyming couplets; and by Ganassi's Tutors for recorders (1535) or for viols (1542). By far the most precious of the old books on instruments is that written by Michael Praetorius (1571–1621), director of music to the Duke of Brunswick at Wolfenbüttel. His younger French contemporary Marin Mersenne (1588–1648), a Minorite scholar, provides amplification of Praetorius and a view of what was going on a few years later in France. The rest of the seventeenth century is disappointing (the derivative and credulous Kircher is less often quoted today than formerly) until towards its close, when Daniel Speer in 1687 initiated a useful series of German Tutors and commentaries which ran right through into the early nineteenth century. We also possess the manuscript notes on instruments *c.* 1697 by James Talbot, a Cambridge doctor of divinity, who collected highly detailed information from the leading London musicians of Purcell's time. The eighteenth century has left us the important specialist works

of Quantz (on the flute and on the orchestra), Leopold
Mozart (on violin-playing), and C. P. E. Bach (on keyboard-
playing); but no general survey of instruments approaches
Praetorius in value until we reach Berlioz's *Instrumentation* of
1848, with which the modern literature of our subject
begins. It is a reflection of the growing interest in the historical aspects of instruments that most of these works are
now available as facsimile or scholarly reprints.

*

It remains for the Editor to express his grateful appreciation
of the generous spirit of cooperation and patience, steadily
maintained over a lengthy period of preparation, shown by
the colleagues who have written this book, and his debt to
Prof. Thurston Dart, who laid the foundation of its plan.
We all hope to have contributed towards a deeper understanding of the instruments we love and of the part they
have played in the history of our music. For permission to
reproduce illustrations of instruments the Editor would also
like to thank the Rijksmuseum, Amsterdam; the Historical
Museum, Basle; the Belfast Museum; the B.B.C.;
Boosey & Hawkes Ltd; Arnold Dolmetsch Ltd; Len
Hunt & Co.; Faber & Faber Ltd; J. & A. Hill; Henry
Potter Ltd; the National Trust (Fenton House Collection);
the Horniman Museum; the Royal College of Music, Lon-
don; the Victoria and Albert Museum; Isaac Stern, New
York; the Visitors of the Ashmolean Museum, Oxford;
Christ Church College, Oxford; Madame Thibault de
Chambure; Leblanc et Cie, Paris; the Conservatoire de
Musique, Paris; the Louvre, Paris; the Kunsthistorisches
Museum, Vienna; and the Folger Shakespeare Library,
Washington, D.C. Also Mr Christopher Bradshaw for
valuable help, Mrs Audrey Besterman, Mr Benjamin Sands,
and Dr R. F. A. Dean for making the drawings, and L. G.
Aubin for his equal skill in taking many of the photographs.

*

## *Letter Names of Musical Notes*

In this book, notes given in roman capitals, as C, G, etc., are to be understood in the ordinary way, no particular octave pitch being necessarily implied. Notes given in *italics* both capital and lower-case and whether with or without ticks, as *C, g''*, have specific octave pitches according to the system which is nowadays prevalent and is explained in the chart below.

*London, 1961*                    ANTHONY BAINES

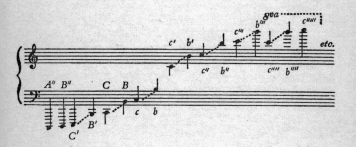

# 1. *The Primitive Musical Instruments*

KLAUS P. WACHSMANN

THE general concept of evolution does not in itself imply a continuous progression of improvement: some early forms of things have survived almost unchanged, others have required modifications, while yet others bear the full record of development. The evolution of musical instruments is similar, and the purpose of this chapter is to describe not merely the instruments of which we possess the earliest records, but also those which are in use today in their original simplicity and those which appear to be the fore-runners of the complex and perfected types with which we are familiar.

While considering them, it must be borne in mind that the effectiveness of a musical instrument can only be measured by the degree of satisfaction its sound gives to the people who use it. Resonance, trueness of pitch, and other acoustic excellences may take second place to the retention of some particular quality of musical sound, and that quality may even seem to us to be unpleasant and unfortunate. On the other hand, while we might expect craftsmanship to be a secondary consideration, it is remarkable how often the simple instruments are made with devoted skill.

The historian of musical instruments is under the disadvantage that the records available to him are fragmentary and inconclusive. The gaps in the historical record make it impossible to classify the early instruments in the sequence of their invention, though attempts to do so have been made. The late Curt Sachs, by a careful interpretation of the pattern of distribution of instruments throughout the world, and by taking into account the migrations of people, trading and cultural contacts, and all the accidents likely to affect development, decided that distribution might have taken place from a few important centres, and he accordingly arranged the whole gamut of instruments in twenty-three successive strata.

Of these, the first five correspond with Palaeolithic stages of culture, the next seven with Neolithic, the next seven above these with the Metal Ages, followed by four strata corresponding with the Middle Ages. It will be necessary to refer to the strata from time to time in this chapter, but Sachs's classification is really for the specialist. For our purposes the instruments will be grouped according to the three familiar principles of percussion, string, and wind, which is convenient – this is the approach adopted, for instance, by Scholes's *Oxford Companion to Music* – though of course it must not be allowed to bring to mind the modern orchestra and modern orchestration. For the instruments now in question, this simple approach is not necessarily inferior to the other, because, owing to the paucity of exact data, there is most doubt about the earlier of Sachs's strata, and it has been suggested that the developments shown in those strata may be a part of man's universal heritage, which has caused groups of men isolated from each other to produce similar instruments for themselves and not to acquire them from the postulated centres of distribution. Other classifications are possible. Sachs has also divided the instruments according to the action required to sound them, and accordingly distinguished beating and shaking, concussion and scraping, rubbing and plucking and blowing. André Schaeffner has proposed a classification based on the physical properties of the material which gives the sound. This is interesting as a new way of thinking about instruments and, possibly, as an approach to the primitive: the two main sources of instrumental sound are vibrating solid bodies and vibrating air, the former being subdivided into those that are rigid, those that are flexible, and those that are tensile.

It is not difficult to find reasons for instrumental music being *rhythmic*, for rhythm is inherent in all bodily movement. The rise of *melodic* performance on instruments is more difficult to explain. The human voice is capable of an infinity of gradations within its range, but similar gradations can be achieved by few of the many classes of instruments, and melody implies selection. There are three points to bear in mind when reflecting how notions of pitch, interval, and timbre could have been applied by accident or design. The first is the contrast between 'light' and 'dark' sounds that may emerge when two or more instruments of different quality are used together. The second is the imposition of some extra-musical standard of reference in the tuning or making of an instrument; examples include the cutting of a flute to the length of a sacred standard in ancient China, and the spacing of the fingerholes on flutes in many countries by fingers' span or breadths. Thirdly, there is the fact that many instruments have been used at one time or another in their development to reproduce speech – literally to talk – and this must have added a stimulus to the exploration of the realm of pitch, interval, and timbre.

Finally, percussion and melody may be combined by using a series of percussion devices. The xylophone, the lithophone, and an instrument consisting of tuned metal tongues that are plucked – the *sansa* – are a few of the many examples that could be quoted. The pianoforte is of course another.

PERCUSSION INSTRUMENTS

The elementary use of percussion is associated with the dance, in which the sound is made in response to, or to emphasize, bodily movement. The dancers – or their audience – may stamp the ground gently or violently or clap their hands or slap resoundingly on their bodies. Reliefs show ancient Assyrians beating their throats as if to obtain some sound effect, and in most parts of Africa today the mouth is tapped in ululation; although the apparatus of the human voice is used, no consideration of speech or song enters into the performance, the effect being purely instrumental.

These noises made by the body without either tools or

instruments offer a narrow range of possibilities, which is immediately extended when the performer, instead of hitting his bare thigh, hits the solid leather of his breeches or the soles of his boots, as in the *Schuhplattlertanz* of Upper Bavaria. Fundamentally this is the same in principle as fixing to the legs of the dancer, or to some other part of his body or clothing (Fig. 1), rattling devices of one kind or another – dry seed shells, strings of bones and teeth, snail shells, or twigs. If the rattling vessel is taken into the hand and shaken, there is still no new principle involved.

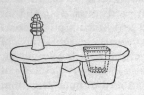

FIG. 1.
Rattling objects enclosed in the heel of clogs, Celebes (after Kaudern)

## Rattles and Scrapers

Rattles may serve to introduce the connexion between music and magic. They have often a magico-religious significance and are frequently part of the equipment of the witch doctor. In tropical South America the gourd rattle *maraca* is identified with the head of a supernatural being in whose service it is used. Rattles show a great variety of forms. In all of them objects are made to strike against each other, the objects ranging from seeds or stones contained inside a sonorous gourd or a tube or basket to particles of bone and wood strung together on a cord like a necklace. Instruments of advanced design like the *sistrum* also belong to the rattle group (Fig. 2); the rattling objects are here suspended in a frame which is shaken by hand like a baby's rattle. The sistrum is known from Ancient Egypt, Rome, Ethiopia, Mesopotamia, the Caucasus, West Africa, Malaya, and with two American tribes. In rattling vessels like the maraca, the percussive sound of objects striking against

FIG. 2.
Sistrum, Brazil (after Izikowitz)

each other is supplemented by a hissing noise caused by the friction against the walls of the container, not unlike the noise of a receding wave on a shingle beach, and it is precisely this scraping motion and noise which captured man's early imagination, as it did also in scrapers.

A simple scraper has a corrugated surface which is rasped with a stick. Bone was found to be an ideal raw material for it, since the corrugations could be easily and permanently carved. Moreover, the bone, as part of an animal previously hunted, had magical power which could be activated by the scraping as part of the ritual preceding the hunt. Every continent has contributed to the lore and magic of the scraper and added to its large range of shapes. Scrapers have survived into modern times, for instance in the folk music of Venezuela, where the *guiro* or *charrasca* is made from a bull's horn, or in the rumba bands of Cuba and the fashionable Western world which use a scraping gourd, also known as *guirol*. In Mesopotamia, Java, India, Cuba, and Europe, the scraper appeared at a later stage in a mechanized form: the cor-

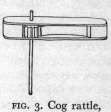

FIG. 3. Cog rattle, Cuba (after Ortiz)

rugated surface took the shape of a wooden cog-wheel fixed to a handle and set into a frame, the scraping-stick became the wooden blade of a ratchet (Fig. 3), and the motion of scraping was provided by whirling the frame around the handle. In the Middle Ages ratchets could be heard in the week before Easter in the churches – a function well in keeping with the magical powers attributed to scrapers in tribal ritual, and foreshadowing their role as a gas warning in the last war.

## Improvised percussion instruments

The discovery of new materials has ever been exploited in the making of rattles and contributed new forms. It is common in Africa to see an old shoe-polish tin filled with stones to form an improvised rattle. Pellet bells ('jingle bells'), too, are rattling vessels known in all five continents, and are executed in brass or iron, though the working of metal introduces the specialist craftsman upon whom the manufacture of instruments of any degree of complexity depends, but who is not essential for most of the instruments mentioned earlier. Indeed, primitive sound instruments are often merely objects of everyday use. Women beat their skin aprons as if they were skin drums, or tap the mouth of a water pot with the bare hand or a fibre pad; aborigines in Australia beat boomerangs together, men clank their bows against their spears, children drum on a log of wood; a rhythm is tapped out on a stick leaning against the wall of a hut, hoe-handles are rubbed against a sleeping board producing a sound like that of a trumpet; and, perhaps most strikingly, herd boys take the hunting bow between their teeth and perform on it as if it were a 'musical bow' – an instrument described later.

This strong element of improvisation shows itself in so many forms that its musical intent is not always obvious. Thus, at a dance, it may be impossible to say whether the metal pendants on a woman's girdle are meant to please the eye or the ear. Observers are often at a loss to know what to record as music. The isolated and backward inhabitants of Tierra del Fuego know of no instruments expressly designed for sound, let alone music. Instead, they blow into the windpipe of a newly killed duck, or at the death dances they stamp the ground with pairs of long thick poles, or drum upon a rigid rolled-up piece of hide. Their men bellow into the hollow of their hands placed against the earth, knock sticks and branches against the frame of the festival hut for rhythm, or simply beat the floor of the hut with bare fists.

*Ground instruments*

The earth itself plays an important part in the earlier phases of man's music-making. Frequently the very ground on which the musician stands or sits is utilized in the construction of the instrument. This might have been done originally for magical reasons, but it was no doubt also convenient, though the association with the ground renders such instruments less permanent than others. The mere fact of placing a beam on the ground where edible termites have nested makes the soil an accomplice; the song which goes with the drumming on the beam is about the termites in the ground, and communicates with the spirit of the insects who controls them. Percussion beams occur sporadically in all continents except Europe; stamping pits have been described from the Solomon Islands; friction boards, of the kind already mentioned, are sometimes placed over a trench in the ground; and the Yoruba of West Africa, the Alur north of Lake Albert, and the Uitoto of Columbia play a xylophone mounted over a pit. It is not only percussion instruments that use the ground in this way. Wind and stringed

FIG. 4. Ground zither, Uganda

instruments may also do so. In Ethiopia a narrow, tapering hole is made in the ground and howled into; the vernacular name of this instrument means 'lion's call'. Zithers are constructed, the earth being used as a base upon which to build up the instrument and to form the resonator cavity, in Indonesia, Malagasy, the Nile–Congo watershed (Fig. 4), and on Fernando Po, and ground bows are commonly made by children in Uganda. In the example shown, the central post stands on a stone slab covering a resonance chamber hollowed in the ground; the string is beaten with twigs by two or more players. In short, the earth itself, the dancing ground upon which man's feet stamp, is a favourite component of musical instruments.

## Stones and tuned percussion instruments

The use of stone is close to the use of the earth. Recent studies have revealed many instances of slabs of rock being used as if they were drums. There 'rock gongs', as their discoverers called them, occur in Africa mainly north of the equator, in Europe, and in Asia. They consist of natural features of the geological formation left *in situ*, so that the site itself becomes the 'orchestra theatre', and they are surrounded in the minds of the local people with legends and ancient religious rites. Not every ringing slab need necessarily win favour: in more than one instance, stones with a clear ringing note which would have pleased European taste were found to have less appeal for the indigenous folk, who preferred slabs with a low, muffled note comparable to the sound of a low-pitched xylophone bar. A set of tuned stone slabs which possibly represents the oldest preserved tuning-pattern was found in 1949 in Indo-China (Fig. 5, in which thickened lines show the edges most obviously altered for tuning purposes). No local tradition exists to throw light

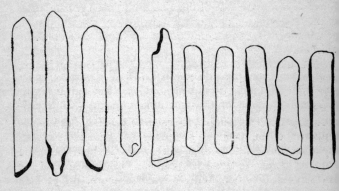

FIG. 5. Prehistoric lithophone (after Schaeffner)

on its usage but in 1958 three stone slabs, the remnant of a larger set, were found to be in actual use in the same region. The players, seated on the ground, placed the slabs across their thighs – just as in a few rare cases of xylophone playing in Northern Melanesia, Celebes, Malagasy, and Dahomey. The surfaces show the typical flaking technique of Stone Age man, but archaeologists are unable to state the age of the finds. Sets of tuned stone slabs with smooth surfaces are in use in Annam, China, Korea, and Somoa; Chinese sets of this type were tuned to what F. Kuttner described as 'a Pythagorean system, 400 to 500 years before the Pythagorean school' in Ancient Greece.

Sachs has observed that these 'Neolithic stones and stone chimes had their counterpart in the Bronze Age *bells* and bell chimes'. The realization of musical scales through tuning occurs in bell chimes. China is their classical home, and Chinese legend and literature often refer to them. We are accustomed to bells made of metal, but they can be made of many other materials, including seed shells, the carapace of tortoises, animal horns, and carved wood, and their clappers may be sticks or the ribs of an animal. Bells are rarely employed for musical purposes; their task is magico-religious – to protect the wearer from harm, or to signify special function, as in the case of the sacred bull calves of the ruler of the East African kingdom of Bunyoro – or else utilitarian, as when bells are hung on hunting dogs and other domestic animals.

The most familiar member of the tuned percussion group, and one that is still actively used, is the *xylophone* of Africa (Pl. 32b), with its offspring the *marimba* of Central America, brought across the Atlantic by the slave trade, and its counterparts in Indonesia, the *gambang kayu* and the 'metallophones' of the *saron* and *gender* types. Whereas the metallophones can be dated – the saron to not much before A.D. 900 and the gender to not later than A.D. 1157 (Kunst) – the ancestry of the xylophone is quite obscure. An archaic two-slab form used mainly for signalling is found in places as far apart as Columbia, New Britain (Melanesia), and Liberia. Schaeffner investigated the possible development of the xylophone from the primitive 'pounding tubes', which in their cruder forms are hollow pipes of bamboo or gourd, whose ends are tapped against the ground or the thigh to give a muffled sound. In a more advanced stage, tubes of different lengths are pounded upon a tree trunk placed on the ground. The African and the Indonesian instruments of the xylophone type have much in common: certain structural details are identical, and there are similarities in tuning and in the form of the music played on them, but the question herein raised, namely, what link is responsible for the similarities? still remains unanswered. It is widely believed by musicologists that nothing short of personal contact through commerce or migration can provide the explanation.

Perhaps the most expressive instrument whose invention has been credited to Africa is the *sansa* (Fig. 6). A set of

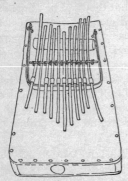

long, thin iron tongues is clamped on to a soundboard in such a way that each can freely vibrate. The playing action consists of depression and release by the thumbs and forefingers of the free ends of the tongues. Occasionally, and especially in the northern part of the sansa area, slivers of bamboo or cane are used instead of metal tongues. The securing of the tongues is adjustable, and it is therefore possible quickly and easily to alter the length of the

FIG. 6. Sansa, Uganda

free ends and thus to adjust their tuning. In this respect the sansa is far in advance of any other tuned percussion instrument. For its ancestry no pedigree has as yet been suggested. It appears in travellers' reports for the first time in 1586, already with the hall-marks of a perfect tool. Its day is by no means over; it is the popular instrument of the common man, and will continue to be so unless the import of Western instruments puts an end to its use.

In contrast to the sansa, whose tuning mechanism shows a concern with musical melody, the so-called *slit drums* (Fig. 7) of America, Oceania, and Africa are percussion instruments often devoted to the rendering of speech elements for signalling purposes, and hence called 'talking drums' occasionally. Their less prosaic magical functions can still be traced in some places where they represent the power of the chief or the spirit of the moon, or where they personify the tribe. A slit drum is rather like a dug-out canoe that has been made with its gunwales almost touching. It is made by hollowing out a tree trunk through a

FIG. 7. Slit drum, Cameroons

narrow slit, and the edges of the slit are intentionally made different in thickness so that, when they are struck with a beater, they produce the different pitches that are necessary for the creation of the impression of speech patterns.

## Drums

Drumming and percussion are often thought of as synonymous, and there is some justification for this. The examples already given of the instruments improvised by stretching skins over the legs or the mouth of a pot point to a course of development of the drum: by first making a frame or resonator, and then finding a method of fixing the skin so that it is maintained permanently in a flexible, stretched condition.

Drums have retained their original magical associations with great tenacity. Reports of travellers are full of tales which stress their extra-musical functions. Their manufacture is often surrounded by ritual, sacrifices are made to them and they are given food, charms are placed inside them or suspended from their sides, and great care is taken to house them properly. An example of the social importance they sometimes assume is provided by one African kingdom, where the power of the ruler is considered to be unlimited except in one way: he cannot silence the royal drums. After his death the drums at the shrine which his spirit is to inhabit, and where his court continues to be maintained, beat the words 'I am now free', to convey the fact of his release from their dominion.

The shape and material of drum vessels and the methods employed in fixing the skin are remarkably diverse. For a

T – B

short classification, four main divisions can be made: (a) single-skin drums; (b) double-skin drums; (c) frame drums (of which the tambourine is our familiar example, and which may either have one skin or two); and (d) friction drums. Of the first class, the cylindrical or tubular drum and the gourd drum are the most elementary types, and are both placed as early as the sixth (lowest Neolithic) stratum in Sachs's sequence. They occur mainly on the west and east coasts of Africa and in a few places in between, and in Malaya, the South Seas, and Central America. The single-skin hourglass-shaped drum, a member of Sachs's tenth stratum, is reported from East and West Africa, Siam, Melanesia, and Micronesia, often with a handle placed at its waist. The cup-shaped or goblet drums are placed in Sachs's thirteenth (lowest Metal Age) stratum, and are widely known in Africa and Asia. The *darabuka*, found mainly in North Africa and Anatolia and the most popular drum in Egypt today, is also a cup-shaped drum, made in clay and covered with painted patterns.

The kettledrum is of special interest to Western musicians on account of its role in the modern orchestra. It belongs to Sachs's most recent stratum. Two types can be distinguished: the medium-sized or small shallow drum which was imported into Europe during the Crusades (*nakers*), and the large instrument mounted on the backs of horses, mules, or camels, which came to the West as late as the fifteenth century (see Chapter 14). In the ethnological chronology, the kettledrum cannot claim great antiquity. The first evidence for the smaller type is in a Persian relief of A.D. 600, and for the larger type in a Mesopotamian miniature from the twelfth century A.D. Sachs has observed that this representation of the larger type shows a flat bottom, and concludes that this points to an earlier and indeed primitive pottery drum. A most important agent for the distribution of the kettledrum was Islam: wherever the influence of Islamic culture was felt, the kettledrum followed. It also spread even farther afield. Europe is one example; Negro Africa, where the form is slightly different, may be another.

Both small and large kettledrums are recognizable in the interlacustrine kingdoms of Equatorial Africa, where their social functions, their occurrence in couples, their vernacular names, and their close association with the royal trumpets all suggest links with the kettledrum proper. The royal drums are always beaten with sticks, but in popular ensembles the kettledrums are often beaten with bare hands. An interesting musical development of the kettledrum can be mentioned here: in Ethiopia, as well as at the court of the Kabaka, sets of small drums are tuned and used as if they were the bars of a xylophone. It is remarkable that even in this arrangement the drums remain tied together in couples. In Buganda three large kettledrums are added to the ensemble of twelve tuned drums; these large drums show the characteristics of royal instruments: they are known by individual names and kept separate from their more common fellows.

Double-skin drums are placed in the Metal Age strata of Sach's sequence. The term 'barrel-shaped drum' draws attention to the bulging body, but there are representatives of this group with comparatively straight sides which make their classification difficult. Both braced and nailed types occur, the former in China, South India, ancient Egypt, and a small area in West Africa, and the latter in East Asia, including Siam and the Celebes. The double-skin hourglass-shaped drum occurs in Africa in two areas, from Sierra Leone to the Cameroons (Fig. 8), and north of the Zambesi. In Asia it is found in ancient Mesopotamia, Persia, Turkestan, and from Ceylon and Java to Japan. With so wide a distribution, it is natural that details of design and playing methods should vary greatly. Noteworthy is a West African technique of pressing the lacing which joins the two skins and which, owing to the hourglass shape of the body, can be

FIG. 8. Hourglass-shaped drum, Cameroons

tightened by the arm to introduce rapid changes of pitch over a range of intervals which depends on the physical strength of the drummer, but can well reach an octave.

Frame drums also include a wide range of forms, with instruments as different from each other as the huge drums of ancient Sumeria, the 'Shaman drums' of Siberian tribes, Eskimos, and North American Indians, and the European tambourines. Africa accepted the frame drum with Islam as indispensable for the recitation of the Koran in very recent times, but has also a non-Islamic form obtained from the Zulu in the South. Sizes vary greatly. The frame may be round or square, and may have a handle, while the fitting of one or of two skins, as well as variation in the method of playing, make for further difficulties in classification. Double-skin frame drums are also occasionally used like rattles, having stones or seeds enclosed between the two skins ('rattle drum').

Friction drums are more closely related to the friction or rubbing boards mentioned earlier than to drums proper. With the friction board, a hole in the ground provides the resonance cavity, while the board placed across it serves as friction surface. With the friction drum, a vessel and skin replace the hole and the board respectively; in other words, the friction instrument gains a flexible surface instead of a rigid one, and becomes portable. Instead of friction with the ends of large sticks or hoe handles, a piece of hide may be rubbed against the drum skin; the Ewe of Togoland sprinkle charcoal on its surface to prevent it from becoming slippery – an addition also use with the rubbing boards. But usually the rubbing is done with a moist hand on a stick or string fixed upright into the drum skin, or the stick itself remains loose and is rubbed to and fro on the skin. Friction drums also survive in Europe, for example in Rumania, where one is used in New Year celebrations. The Dutch friction drum is well known through Franz Hals's painting *The Man with the Rommelpot*.

### STRINGED INSTRUMENTS

The discovery of the principle of the hunting bow must have changed life in the Stone Ages profoundly. It probably took place in North Africa between 30,000 and 15,000 B.C. at a time when the Sahara was still a fertile land, a period corresponding to the Upper Palaeolithic in Europe. In Daryll Forde's apt phrase, the technique of the bow is 'the first method of concentrating energy'.

Amongst the wall paintings in the cave Les Trois Frères in the south-west of France, dating from approximately 15,000 B.C., there is a scene in which, according to the Abbé Breuil's later views which Kirby persuaded him to adopt, a bow is shown in use. Here it is not, however, the hunter's weapon in the act of shooting, but a musical instrument sounded during a religious ceremony. A man disguised under a bison skin holds the bow to his face, as if playing on it as a musical bow.

At the close of the last century Henry Balfour, in his study *The Natural History of the Musical Bow*, concluded that the archer's bow was the progenitor of the musical bow. Twenty years later the Swiss anthropologist Montandon took an opposite view and derived the hunting bow *from* the musical bow. More recently, in 1929, Sachs put forward a theory which could resolve this impasse, suggesting that the genesis of the musical bow was entirely independent of the hunting bow. He traced its ancestry to the percussion beam through an intermediate form, namely the 'ground zither'. Hornbostel called this Sachs's most important hypothesis, and himself proceeded to show how the musical bow became in the course of its development 'assimilated in shape to the aboriginal hunting bow'. From the point of view of classification, musical bows belong to the zither group. A 'zither'. according to Sachs, is 'an instrument with neither neck nor yoke, the strings being stretched between the two ends of a body, whether this body is in the usual sense a resonator itself, or whether it requires an attached resonator'. This definition, however, does not provide for a crude and early stringed instrument like the 'ground bow' which in view of its construction must be assigned to the harps.

The ground bow (Fig. 9) is simple indeed. A pit is dug to serve as a resonance cavity or sound bowl, and close to it a wand is stuck into the ground with a string tied to its free end. The other end of the string is knotted into a piece of bark or similar material, which is placed over the pit like a lid over a pot and is weighted down by a ring of stones or earth. The wand and lid are then adjusted to create sufficient tension to keep the string taut. In playing, the musician's interest in melody asserts itself. He takes the tip of the wand between the thumb and forefinger of one hand so that he can easily alter the tension of the string. By this technique, the musical range

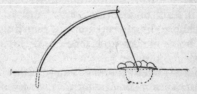

FIG. 9. Ground bow, Uganda

of a fifth can be obtained. The players, however, are not content with this range and employ an additional method for further effects: the left hand is frequently taken off the tip of the wand to stop the string by holding it lightly between forefinger and thumb. The string is meanwhile set in vibration by a steady to-and-fro plucking motion of the straightened forefinger of the right hand. Pygmies in the Congo prefer a more percussion-like sound, and employ a second player to drum with two sticks on the cover of the pit. The distribution of the ground bow is probably far wider than travellers have reported, because it looks like a game trap and is quickly improvised. More important still, because it is a children's toy in many parts, it is easily overlooked.

The element of percussion can be traced in a remarkable number of stringed instruments. Musical bows are tapped –

not only with plain sticks but also with the thin handles of seed-shell rattles – and harps are accompanied occasionally by drumming on their sound tables with two hooked beaters to which rattles have been fixed. It seems that in this kind of music two currents are continually competing, the one melodic and the other rhythmic, and that their integration is not encouraged or emphasized, but avoided.

The sound effect of the action on some primitive stringed instruments built into the earth is certainly very much like that of percussion. But the hitting of the string of a musical bow, held close to the mouth, is supplemented by a further action which involves deliberate selection of the different harmonics of an instrumental sound. At first sight this 'mouth bow' appears to be even more rudimentary than the ground bow. It looks like an ordinary hunting bow, held so that either the string or the stick is as close to the open mouth as possible. Sometimes a tuning noose encircles both string and bow, and can bring them closer together. It also divides the string into two sections of unequal length, giving notes of different pitch. But this is less important than the association of the vibrating string with a resonance cavity – the player's mouth – whose resonance characteristics can be changed with complete freedom. The mouth need only move as in forming words to cause one harmonic of the string after another to sound at the expense of the fundamental and other harmonics, which remain faint. The string is set in vibration by tapping with a twig or stroking with a plectrum, both motions retaining the percussion effect of crisp rhythmical sound. The relation of pitch to speech, combined with the element of percussion, recalls the slit drum.

The technique of the mouth bow is not as rare and exotic as it may appear to Western musicians. The music of the Jew's harp, or *guimbarde*, also imposes the intricacies of oral resonance upon acoustic energy derived from an external source. But instead of drawing this energy from the vibrations of a string, as in the mouth bow, the player of the guimbarde plucks a thorn or blade fixed in a frame – an instrument that may look like a comb with a single tooth. It is held close to the mouth with one hand, the other hand plucking, the method varying in different areas, as do also the design and raw material. With tribal musicians over most of the world, wood or bamboo is common. In Austria at the beginning of the nineteenth century, silver was in great demand by young men who serenaded their sweethearts on this instrument. So popular was the custom and so discreet and persuasive the sound of the guimbarde (*Maultrommel*) that female virtue was endangered and instruments were repeatedly banned by the authorities. Guimbardes, although now made of iron, are still used in Austria for serenading.

## Zithers

In the zither group exploration of melodic music continues. First there are zithers whose construction is integral, strings and all: each string is a thin strip of bark cut loose from the bamboo stem in such a way that its ends are not severed entirely; it is held away from the stem by bridges (Fig. 10). Such 'idiochord' strings are often used singly, and

FIG. 10. Idiochord zither, Serbia (after Kunst)

their percussion character is prominent even to the point of their being played with sticks or beaters like a dulcimer. But the idiochord tube zithers of Malagasy, ancient Cambodia, Malacca, and also of the Carpathians and Serbia (of maize), have several strips of bark thus made into strings, spaced like the spokes of a folded umbrella around its stick. Since the tuning of these strips of bark is difficult, auxiliary bridges are introduced on the tube zither to divide the strings into sections and create further notes.

To the modern string player, an idiochord zither must appear a clumsy instrument. The semi-tensile and semiflexible strips of bark are a far cry from the strings of a violin. Other zithers, however, are strung with tensile strings of fibre or sinew in place of the strips of bark, bringing new qualities to the instruments. Another method of mounting the strings occurs in board and trough zithers, and in some musical bows: a single length of string is laced across a frame several times, through holes or notches. It is then possible, by avoiding an even distribution of tension over the whole length of the string (or in the musical bows by having sections of different length), to tune the individual parts, the tuning being maintained by the friction of the string against the edge of the holes or notches, and alterable at will by redistribution of the tension. The method is dependent on the tensile quality of the string; if this is poor, as in the case of rattan, auxiliary bridges like those of the tube zither must be used.

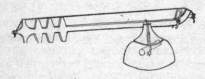

FIG. 11. Bar zither, Uganda

Melodic differentiation in zithers can be aided by yet another device, namely frets. The 'flat-bar zithers' of Africa and of the Far East (Fig. 11) are carved with projections which mark the positions in which the fingers are to stop the strings. The use of auxiliary bridges opens up yet further possibilities for the layout of the strings. In the harp zithers of the Dyak of Borneo, of South India, and West Africa, and in the harp lute of West Africa (all of them multi-stringed), the bridge consists of a stick with a notch for each string, like the teeth of a saw blade, wedged upright against the bow or the sound-box. This notch is, according to Hornbostel, 'ethnologically the essential hallmark' of both the harp zither and the harp lute. These instruments need not be discussed in detail; it must suffice to note the word 'harp' common to both these last descriptive terms.

## Harps

In contrast to zithers, harps are instruments with a neck and with the strings arranged in a plane perpendicular to the sound-board. It is on this account that the primitive ground bow might conceivably be called a harp. The earliest picture of a harp proper occurs on the fragment of a vase from Sumeria of approximately 3000 B.C. It represents an arched or 'bow' harp. A complete specimen from ancient Egypt has fortunately survived (Fig. 12) to reveal in its

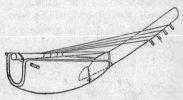

FIG. 12. Arched harp, Egypt (after Hickmann)

internal structure a close parallel to the tribal harps of East Africa. The neck of the Egyptian specimen pierced the skin table (which has not been preserved) and rests against the inside of the sound-bowl like a spoon in a cup. The strings run from the neck to the sound-table where each string pierces the skin and passes through its own hole in a tail-piece and is there knotted to prevent it from slipping. The tailpiece, which is a flat strip of wood, is pulled tightly against the inside of the skin by the tension of the strings. The instrument is remarkably small; yet modern tribal instruments which use a tortoiseshell as a sound-bowl are no larger. Harps of this construction are found today in one area of the world only, namely to the north of Lake Victoria, and no further south. There is, however, a seemingly primitive instrument of four or five strings in use today in the mountains of the Hindu Kush which should be mentioned here: the 'Kafir' harp of Afghanistan. This instrument

shares with the harp type just described the loose attachment between bow-like neck and resonator, and the bow
pierces the skin table without becoming firmly fixed to the
sound-bowl itself, just as does the neck of the tribal harps
near Lake Victoria (Fig. 13). But here the similarity ends,
because in the Kafir harp the lower end of the bow reappears
above the skin a few inches further away from the point where
it entered – like a needle pinned twice through a piece of
cloth. This end, a stump rising above the skin, becomes the
string holder, pierced with the holes through which the
strings are knotted. In short, the entire bow, like a true
musical bow or zither, provides the arch across which the

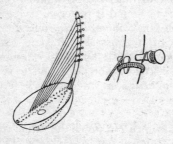

FIG. 13. Arched harp, Uganda

strings are stretched and carries the resonator somewhere
along its curvature; and like a musical bow it is capable of
sound even if the resonator be removed. The Kafir harp is
no isolated freak: Afghanistan is in the area of the ancient
culture of Gandhara, and in a recent description the instrument has been compared with a harp depicted in some
Gandhara sculptures about 1,900 years old. The peoples of
Central Asia must have played the harp extensively, though
not all Asiatic harps are of this primitive type.

Two observations may be added, one in reference to
tuning, the other to timbre. Primitive harps are on the whole
rather deep in pitch. It is obvious that this must be so if
one considers the flexible nature of the bow-like neck, which,

unsupported by a pillar, so easily yields to the tension of the string. The lower the pitch the more difficult it becomes to identify variations in pitch, yet in spite of this difficulty, exact and consistent tuning patterns are produced on primitive harps, provided, of course, that the folk music which they serve is cognizant of, and attaches value to, a consistent pattern. In primitive music the attitude to fixed tuning patterns varies to an astonishing degree from tribe to tribe.

The question of timbre or quality of sound has to be approached along similar lines. A tribe has its own conception of 'true' sound, and this may be different from that of the neighbouring tribes. Instruments are designed to suit tribal tastes. If a jingling, rattling timbre is the most acceptable, or a buzzing sound is preferred, suitable devices are produced. The sansa, for example, may have metal cuffs that slip over the tongues (Fig. 6), and harps may have rings of skin against which the strings can vibrate (Fig. 13). The desire for special timbres accounts to some extent for the variations in design, as we find also in lyres.

## Lyres

Lyres are instruments in which the strings run from a yoke supported by two arms to a tailpiece (Fig. 14). Again

FIG. 14. Bowl lyre with bridge, Uganda

ancient Mesopotamia provides the earliest examples. A buzzing timbre is secured by letting the strings run close to the skin table without using a bridge, or, if this should be impracticable, by the insertion of a rattling raft between strings and skin. The use of a bridge, possibly on feet, is an indication that jingling sounds are not wanted, since it enables the strings to vibrate without touching the soundtable. Tuning pegs capable of being turned, characteristic of modern African harps, do not occur in lyres, which, as in ancient Greece, are equipped with tuning bulges. For each string a strip of cloth is wrapped round the yoke, and after a few turns the string is included. The resulting 'bulge' is the equivalent of a tuning peg. In Abbyssinia twigs are tied to such bulges to act as levers – just as on a lyre from Ur in the British Museum.

A words must be said about lyre-tuning. In Ethiopia and close to the Northern shores of Lake Victoria, where lyres are well developed, their strings are not tuned in a scale of notes moving from low to high pitch in uninterrupted succession, but are invariably arranged in some irregular scheme. As a result, tunings offer a sequence of large and small intervals, for instance *c′ d′ e′ d c g e b* on the *endongo* of Ganda and Soga and *d b e′ d′ g a e g a b* on the *baganna* of Ethiopia. In this respect the accordatura of the ancient Greek lyre, *e′ b a e*, mentioned by Nicomachus, is similar. Today two forms of lyre are still played in Ethiopia, and by a small Nilo-Hamitic tribe to the south, the Sebei: one is the lyre with box-like body, which corresponds to the ancient Greek *cithara;* the other is the lyre with bowl-shaped body (in Fig. 14 a tortoiseshell), an equivalent of the *lyra*. The remainder of the lyre area, that is, the region of the Upper Nile and to the north and east of Lake Victoria and the Nile-Congo watershed, knows only the bowl-lyre.

## Lutes

The last family of stringed instruments to be discussed here is the lute family. Lutes – in the ethnologist's sense – are instruments with strings carried on a handle firmly attached to the body, the plane of the strings being parallel with the sound-table or belly which covers the body. They are subdivided into two groups, plucked lutes, and bowed lutes or fiddles. It is interesting to note that in Sachs' sequence these groups occur very late, no member being placed earlier than the Metal Age strata, while the majority are included in the highest medieval strata of the sequence. Nobody knows how old the harp is, but lutes definitely belong to the historical era and not to the prehistoric background of most of the instruments treated so far.

The bow lute is the earliest. Several sticks are fixed to the lower edge of a sound-box, each of them serving as neck or tension rod to one particular string. When played, it is held like a harp, giving it the impression of being a harp in which each string has a separate neck (Fig. 15). The French word *pluriarc* coined by Montandon expresses this well. Differences in length and curvature of stick and of string tension contribute to the tuning possibilities. But since the plane of the strings is not perpendicular to the sound-table, the bow lute would not fit the definition given above of the harp family.

According to Sachs, true lutes originated in the vicinity of the Caucasus. Assyrian reliefs depict a lute, and ancient Egypt imported this from Assyria. North-west Africa borrowed it from Egypt and kept many of the original features.

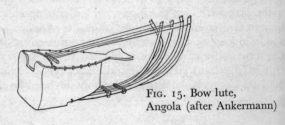

FIG. 15. Bow lute, Angola (after Ankermann)

The body is oval or boat-shaped; the neck passes for support into and out of the skin belly and reaches almost to the far end of the body. The skin does not completely cover the body; the end of the neck inside the latter remains in sight, so that the strings can be tied to indentations in it. At the other end of the neck the strings are attached to leather thongs which encircle the neck and are so firmly knotted that they cannot slip. This kind of lute is still much played in parts of the Northern Sahara, in Senegambia, and further south in the Cameroons. Of the wealth of Asiatic lute forms it must suffice to say that primitive forms like that of the Dyak in Borneo may be regarded as having been derived from the civilizations of Asia.

The central problem of the development of the bowed lutes or fiddles is whether or not the use of the fiddle bow originated in any known *primitive* musical practice. In Africa, although fiddles are played in the north, west, and east, there is no evidence that the instruments are indigenous. In one area where it is possible to make prolonged investigations it was found that the 'tube fiddles' so popular in the area were created by the amalgamation as recently as 1907 of two prototypes, one native (the ground bow) and the other imported (a fiddle brought to the East African coast probably by the Arabs). The term 'tube' draws attention to the short cylinder which serves as a resonator. One end of this is covered by a skin, the other is open. The neck consists of a stick which pierces the cylinder as a toothpick pierces a cocktail sausage (cf. Fig. 56, p. 216). Where it emerges below the resonator the neck has a knob to which the single string is tied. The other end carries a tuning peg. It is played with a short, almost semicircular bow in E. Africa, for instance, but elsewhere comparatively long and shallow bows also occur. At present it is safe to say that knowledge of the fiddle cannot be assumed before the ninth century A.D., when it appeared in the records of the civilized world (see Chapter 9).

## WIND INSTRUMENTS

Wind instruments fall into three groups: flutes, trumpets, and reed instruments. They are sounded by blowing, except for certain instruments which may be classed as 'wind machines', such as the bull roarer, whirled round at the end of a cord, and the Hottentot *gora*, which Professor Kirby terms a 'stringed wind instrument'. In the gora a piece of quill, slit open and flattened out, is knotted between one end of the string and the tip of a bow. The player, without touching it, places the quill between his lips, and by breathing in and out with great force sets the quill and the string in vibration. According to Kirby, pitch differences are produced by variations in breath pressure. Its sound is said to be like that of an Aeolian harp (an instrument of strings and sound-box, suspended so that the strings are set in vibration by the wind).

## Flutes

Of all areas in the world, South America has paid most attention to flutes. In a standard work on the primitive musical instruments of South America, Izikowitz claims that 'every known type of flute in the world was [also] known to the Indians'. As for the whistles and reed instruments native to British Columbia, the late Canon Galpin found their 'ingenuity and originality' worthy of a detailed study. Flutes are very strongly associated with magical ideas. Kirby's description of the flutes of South Africa is a veritable catalogue of magic beliefs. Even in the small area around Lake Victoria the following roles are played by flutes: preventors of storms, makers of rain, encouragers of the flow of milk from the cow's udder during milking, symbols of defloration, givers of life to the divine ruler, and voices that are personal possessions and must not be imitated. It is no accident that the Iron Age bone flute found at Malham Moor, Yorkshire, in 1951 belonged to a ritual or token burial.

The rise of melodic possibilities on the flute has been attributed by some to the influence of the panpipe. Panpipes are made up of a number of tuned tubes, stopped at their lower ends and joined in raft fashion (though the whole set is sometimes carved in stone or wood). Flutes with finger-holes may be of more recent origin that the panpipes, tuning by holes on a single tube being assumed to be an adaptation of the principle of the pipes: firstly, it is an obvious economy; secondly, flutes with four or more holes are much commoner than those with fewer holes – one-holed flutes are rarely used for musical purposes, but serve as signalling instruments. Melodic possibilities do not depend solely on fingerholes. Flutes may be used in couples, one larger than the other, either joined together permanently as in some early flageolets, or separate and played by two persons. In the latter case, one flute is regarded as male and the other as female. In an example from Uganda (Mount Elgon), each flute has two holes and the player of the female instrument increases the range of his flute by adding his hollowed fist to its length. In signalling flutes with one fingerhole, as with the Nilotic animal-horn whistles, the angle at which the instrument is put against the lips is considerably changed during performance to add to the melodic range.

The technique of 'overblowing' may increase the melodic possibilities. This consists in sounding harmonics for the instrument to sound in higher registers. In most primitive flutes, overblowing appears to be inevitable, the fundamental note being so difficult to produce, that, especially in the rapid style of playing used by tribal flutists, it can be of no practical use at all. It is not uncommon to find that a player mixes grunts with the notes of his instrument to make good the deficiency of the lower range. The low notes are anyhow very 'breathy', and hence the grunts may not stand out very noticeably in the flow of a tune. Clearly, low notes are considered desirable, and it is only reluctantly that the lower registers of the flute are left unused. Flutists often also supplement the notes of the instrument with notes which they sing.

This brief survey of melodic techniques on flutes has taken us well ahead of classification. Flutes are tubular or globular (such as the ocarina), and the former are either end-blown or side-blown, often with the nostril instead of the mouth. What seems to be of greater importance, however, is the arrangement for sounding the flute. The earliest type is the 'fipple' flageolet, which makes use of the block, somewhat as in a recorder. The flutes from Mount Elgon are 'notched flutes' in which the breath is directed against a U- or V-shaped notch cut in the upper rim of the instrument. These enjoy a very wide distribution, across the African continent from Ghana to Kenya, and in the Far East, the South Sea Islands, and South America. In the tribal music of Africa

their gentle timbre is particularly striking, and against the
Western musician's common impression of tribal music as
savage drumming, the music on notched flutes can come as
a sweet surprise, even as did the trio of recorders that Pepys
heard and described in his diary ('The wind-musick when
the angel comes down was so sweet that it ravished me').
Next there is the straight-cut, sharp rim of the upper end
of the pipe, with its deceptive simplicity, for it is neither
early nor crude. Transitional forms between these types are
too numerous to list fully here. They include a flute with an
'outside flue' (Fig. 16) used by North American Indians and

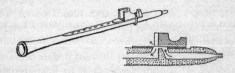

FIG. 16. Flute, Iroquois Indians (after Izikowitz)

shown in the codices of the Mayan period of Central
America. The player blows into the main tube, but his
breath is forced to make a detour through a channel along
the outside of the flute, which in turn directs it against a
sharp edge.

No exposition of primitive flutes can afford to disregard
the theory of 'blown fifths'. The first part of the theory
depends on those norms of measuring length that have
already been mentioned (see p. 25 above) as the origin of
standard pitch. Standard measurement of this kind was
sacred in Sumeria, Egypt, and China, and not illogically the
notes of tubes cut to the sacred lengths signify more than
mere sound. The standard lengths can be allowed to govern
the proportionate lengths of the tubes of a panpipe, and each
of its stopped tubes is cut to two-thirds of the length of the
preceding pipe, the sacred standard length forming the
starting point. It is then postulated that the overblown
twelfth of the longer tube – the third harmonic, for a stopped
tube will not sound the second – is identical with the funda-

mental note of its shorter neighbour. From this point the theory is difficult to follow, since it depends on intervals of fifths (i.e. twelfths with one note transposed an octave) that are assumed to be 'shorter' than ordinary Pythagorean fifths. Controlled experiments do not, however, confirm the existence of these 'short' fifths, and the theory is perhaps most worth noting for its contribution of the idea that primitive music may not be devoid of fixed conceptions of tone material, which may be different from those of the modern West.

## Trumpets

Whereas in flutes the lips of the player are not directly responsible for generating vibrations, in trumpets they are applied to the instrument to become active parts of it. Used in the ethnologist's sense, the word 'trumpet' embraces the whole range of trumpets, horns, conches, etc., regardless of the shape and position of the embouchure hole, and irrespective of the material used, be it animal, vegetable (e.g. gourd), or mineral. There are some primitive instruments which have the outward appearance of trumpets, but no lip vibration in the usual brass-player's sense is involved in them. Such instruments serve as vessels into which the performer may hum, sing, or speak, pitching his voice to the resonance frequency of the vessel. This is important. According to Caldwell P. Smith, the resonance frequency, once set into vibration, is likely to stimulate a corresponding frequency of lip vibration in the player and thus a first step is taken towards trumpet-playing proper. In north-west Australia the aborigines lower the end of the *didjeridoo* into a hole in the ground, no doubt with some acoustic effect.

Most primitive trumpets are straight and are end-blown, like ours, though some have the embouchure hole in the side, among them the beautifully-carved ivory trumpets of the Congo and West Africa.

Like that of the flute, the literature of the trumpet is full of references to its magico-religious functions and associations. In spite of its early association with voice and speech, with few exceptions the trumpet did not develop this association beyond calls for communal functions such as hunting, dancing, or an armed foray, whereas the flute cultivated it even to the point of conversation by flute language (in modern Uganda flute pieces are identified by the verbal pattern of their tunes). Nor have primitive trumpets shared in the development of melodic possibilites by exploitation of harmonics or extensive use of fingerholes on the surface (like those of the cornett). The initial steps were taken, and no more: some side-blown trumpets make use of a hole in the tip as a fingerhole to vary the note of the instrument, or are overblown to replace the fundamental by a higher note, or the hand is slipped into the bell.

Obviously the melodic principle of the panpipe would be difficult to realize in trumpets. Trumpet *sets*, however, both of single-note instruments and of those with one fingerhole, flourish extensively in Negro Africa and Ethiopia. The melodic method which they exploit is that of the 'Russian horns' of former times: each player has one instrument and produces one or two notes. An analogy is met in the sets of stopped flutes known from Lake Albert through the Western Rift Valley to South Africa, which are in effect panpipes dissolved into their component tubes, each tube being played by one flutist. Where such trumpet sets are part of the royal regalia, and especially where they are associated with the worship of cattle, sets made of gourds, wood and hide, and animal horns are attached to the royal drums. Whether or not these royal bands date back to an early Arab source as may the kettledrum, or to what extent they may owe their existence to tribal custom, it is impossible to decide. It must suffice to mention Vasco da Gama's reports of his reception by trumpets when he landed on the African shores of the Indian Ocean, and the Janissary bands which are pictured as late as the 1820s in Constantinople with a set of nine trumpets and their drums.

*Reed instruments*

The third group of wind instruments consists of those that

are sounded by a vibrating reed. Its first and truly primitive representative – the 'ribbon reed' – is reminiscent of a stringed instrument: a ribbon is stretched between two points like a string, but it is excited by a stream of breath. The ribbon is more easily excited if it is held in a hollow or tubular frame which makes a channel for the breath, much as children everywhere in Europe stretch a blade of grass in their cupped hands. Thus the Venda and Tonga of South Africa mount a vibrating ribbon between two troughs of wood which are kept pressed rim to rim by a tight outer cover of hide.

Lastly in this brief survey we reach the family of reed instruments proper, of which two main modern groups are most familiarly represented by the clarinet and the oboe. In clarinets a 'single reed' beats against the edge of the opening over which it is mounted; in the older form of single reed the vibrating blade is cut down the side of a short length of cane closed at the top end, and in the West it is still so made for the drones of bagpipes (cf. Fig. 70 h, i, p. 234). In oboes, two reed blades beat against each other, or, in more primitive oboe-like instruments, the reed consists merely of a hollow stem pinched flat so that the two opposite sides can beat against each other.

Hickmann describes an Egyptian figurine of a musician playing a 'double clarinet' dating from 2600 B.C. or even earlier, but there are other single-reed instruments which, according to Sachs's time scale, still belong to the Stone Ages. It is an interesting coincidence that the earliest example of an 'oboe' – the silver double pipes of cylindrical bore that were found in the royal cemetery of Ur – should be separated from the first representation of the 'clarinet' by only one or two centuries. Almost three millennia later, another 'oboe' is documented on Jewish coins of the second century A.D., which show the characteristic new features surviving widely today: the conical shape of the tube, and, outside Europe, the disc below the reed, which supports the player's lips. Widely spread with Islamic culture, the shawm can today be heard along the fringes of Africa north of the equator from the Guinea coast to Mombasa, and in Asia from Arabia to the Far East. Bartók thus described its sound as he heard it in Algeria in 1913:

> Its tone is much stronger than that of the lowest notes of the oboe; throughout its registers the tone remains equally piercing and shrill, and indoors it almost bursts one's eardrums. The players know how to maintain long notes at will without interruption. Apparently they breathe in through the nose, store air under pressure between extended cheeks from whence the air is fed into the instrument, and thus they avoid pauses for taking breath.

The disc keeps the player's lips well away from the reed, and so assists in maintaining the tension of the inflated cheeks. In West Java, instead of the disc, 'large coconut wings', as Kunst calls them, are attached to the mouthpiece, forming a crescent which reaches from ear to ear, like a slice of melon across its eater's face, to support the extended cheeks. In ancient Greece a bandage, *phorbeia*, was at times worn over the mouth; it was pierced at the centre to allow the reeds to pass through, and it covered the cheeks, supporting them in a similar way. In Europe, Sachs thought to discern 'a last vestige of the oriental lip-supporting disc' in oboes made early in the eighteenth century. So wide is the horizon revealed to the student of musical instruments.

Naturally a survey of such brevity as this cannot be anything but incomplete, and the choice of instruments and of associations must perforce be arbitrary. The aim of the present choice has been to convey the atmosphere that surrounds man's early making of instrumental music.

# 2. *The Organ*

## CECIL CLUTTON

Six hundred years ago Guillaume de Machaut described the organ as 'the king of instruments', and the name has stuck. But so strange a position does it hold in the musical world of today that it would be almost more appropriate to call the organ 'the brontosaurus of instruments'. It evoked the most noble instrumental music of the Baroque era, but since 1750 it has very rarely attracted composers of the front rank, and this is because it is fundamentally alien to the romantic idiom. With ponderous effort the organ acquired a stock of 'romantic' tricks – but in truth it had become an unwieldy giant that outlived the climatic conditions in which it had prospered. However, so great was the vitality of the organ that it survived the conditions which threatened to exterminate it. Today the romantic style itself is *vieux jeu*, and in a musical world still seeking new forms of expression the organ is coming into its own again. Its idiom is well attuned to some of the most healthy manifestations of modern musical thought, as one or two notable composers have already discovered. It is against this background of fluctuating fortunes that the history of the organ has to be studied.

It is very remarkable that so complicated an instrument should have survived with no basic alteration for over two thousand years. But before this long history is begun, it is necessary to understand what an organ consists of and how it works. Both these are, of course, far too complex matters to be dealt with in full in a book of this nature; the following outline is confined mainly to those points which most directly bear upon the instrument's musical history up to the present.

Nearly all new English organs have electric actions. That is to say, depressing a note merely closes an electrical circuit, energizing an electro-pneumatic motor which opens a valve or 'pallet', letting wind into the appropriate pipes. All this, together with many other electrical operations, makes the modern organ superficially complicated. But as these operations only replace functions which were carried out for many centuries by a very simple mechanism, it is quite easy to understand the basic workings of an organ without delving into the mysteries of electricity.

In order to be capable of dealing with the bulk of legitimate organ music, an organ must have at least two manuals, or keyboards, and a further keyboard, or more accurately pedalboard, which the player operates with his feet. Each keyboard controls a department, almost a separate organ, of its own. In the very smallest organs the pedal department has only one set of pipes, but each manual department has more than one set, known as 'ranks' or 'stops', which may be used separately or together by drawing the appropriate stop knobs at the keyboards or console. With certain exceptions to be discussed later, each stop has one pipe to each note, the pitch of the pipe being determined by its length. An open-ended pipe giving $c'$ is two feet long. For $c$ it is four feet long; for $c''$ one foot long, and so on. The practical limits are about thirty-two feet in the downward, and half an inch in the upward direction. Fig. 17 is a cross-section through a fairly conventional small organ with one pedal stop and with three stops on each of its two manual departments. It has a purely mechanical, or 'tracker', action and may thus be considered as a basic organ. The drawing is purely diagrammatic and not to scale; much detail, including the coupling mechanism, has been omitted for greater simplicity. With this much understood, it may be said that any larger instrument is merely a multiplication of units, with the interpolation of electric relays between player and pallet.

The Greeks, and subsequently the Romans, had a quite highly developed organ, named *hydraulus* because the air reservoir was constructed on the principle of a gasometer, with a water-seal. It had a balanced keyboard and up to four stops, with sliders much like those in use today. The

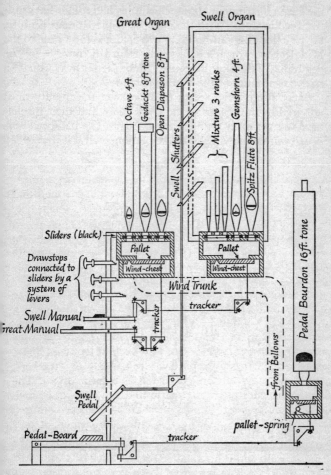

FIG. 17. Organ, generalized scheme

hydraulus was used at public entertainments, such as those
connected with lions and Christians, and it is therefore
understandable that the early Christians found no liturgical

use for an instrument about which they had somewhat sensitive recollections. With the collapse of the Roman Empire, the practice of organ-building was confined for a time to the Middle East, whence it began to return to Europe by the beginning of the eighth century. Since then it has formed an essential adjunct of the Christian liturgy.

Sheer brute noise seems to have been the quality most admired in the organs of the Dark Ages, and their mechanism was certainly crude in the extreme. The balanced keyboard was unknown, and the key action, such as it was, called

FIG. 18. Portative organ

for a blow with the clenched fist. Not for nothing was an organist called the *pulsator organum*. Side by side with these music mills grew up smaller organs known as portatives and positives. The portative was a very small organ slung round the neck. It was blown with one hand and played with the other (Fig. 18). Portatives were used in processions and chamber music, and survived into the sixteenth century. Positives were rather larger, standing either on the floor or on a table; they continued to be made until the nineteenth century, and are now being revived for use in small churches. The keyboard developed slowly, but by the fourteenth century it had reached a point where the blind Italian organist and composer Francesco Landini could acquire widespread fame as an executant. By the fifteenth century the keyboard had become the close prototype of the modern arrangement. In the meantime, the large organs had been undergoing refinement, and at Halberstadt, near Brunswick, in 1361 there were three manuals and pedals, although there were still no stops. In default of individual stops, multiple manuals were, of course, the only means of using separate ranks or groups of ranks; but the stop mechanism appeared during the fifteenth century.

Nor was development confined to the mechanical side of the instrument. The big medieval monastic organ was one huge 'mixture' of pipes. A 'mixture', in the organ builder's sense, denotes a special organization of pipes in one stop, by which each note played on a keyboard is automatically sounded by several pipes tuned to various harmonic intervals above the note actually represented by the key that is struck. Such special 'mixture stops' are described later. The larger medieval organ, however, was itself built as a mixture; on striking a key, the player sounded pipes at different pitches including the actual note of the keyboard ('unison pitch'), the octave above, and also 'quints' – pipes sounding one or more actaves plus a fifth (e.g. a twelfth or a nineteenth) above the 'unison' pitch, and no doubt suggested by the singing of organum. Later, fauxbourdon may have suggested the addition of third-sounding ranks (at the seventeenth, etc., above unison).

Until the invention of stops, there was no incentive to develop varied tone qualities. These were introduced in rapid profusion during the fifteenth and sixteenth centuries. The basic organ pipe or 'flue' pipe closely resembles a penny whistle. If its diameter or 'scale' is small, it will be bright in tone. If its scale is wide, the tone will be dull. It is an 'open pipe'; but if a stopper be inserted in its open end, it will sound an octave lower ('stopped pipe'). If an open pipe be overblown, it will jump to its octave, but a stopped pipe overblown will jump a twelfth; by suitable adjustment it can be made to sound the fundamental or 'unison' tone and the twelfth simultaneously. Other variants may be produced by pipes of conical shape with only a small opening at the top, and so forth. Reed instruments, widely known in the Middle Ages, were adapted to the organ in the fifteenth century. Organ 'reed' pipes are normally of inverted conical shape, but using a cylindrical resonator has the same effect on a reed as stopping has on an open flue pipe, causing it to sound an octave lower. Some reeds had very short resonators indeed, and these were called 'regals'. Small portable organs were also made with one rank of regal pipes only, and this type of instrument was itself called a regal. In larger organs, regal stops were developed to produce a wide range of tone qualities, and were much admired despite extreme pitch instability, which called for frequent tuning. The modern *vox humana* stop is in fact a regal.

Thus, by the fifteenth century the organ was fully developed with two or more manuals, pedals, separate stops and a great variety of tone colours produced from flue and reed pipes. A mechanism had also been developed for coupling two manuals at will, so that playing on one would also pull down the keys on the other. Fifteenth-century composers, with their highly developed taste for contrasted tone colours, were not slow to write music for such a medium. Music had been written for the organ as early as 1325–50 (the presumed organ pieces in the 'Robertsbridge manuscript' in the British Museum), but as an identifiable art form, organ music dates from the second half of the fifteenth century. Paumann, Isaac, Schlick, and Hofhaimer were the pioneers. Variations on a plainsong theme gave ample opportunities for a variety of stop combinations, while the slow-moving theme was often assigned to the pedals. This form of composition, now known as a chorale prelude, has always been a favourite form of organ music.

It is a most remarkable fact that the late medieval organ as it developed in North Germany in the late fifteenth cen tury was essentially baroque in outlook, destined to develop into the highest peak of organ-building, the richest product of the High Baroque. It had little in common with the Renaissance, with its essentially *a cappella* idiom. More truly 'renaissance' organ music was produced in England than in any other country, which is the more remarkable since the Renaissance never gained a very secure foothold here. But English organs during the sixteenth century were thoroughly renaissance in outlook, with only one manual, no pedals, and a handful of stops with little or no tonal variety. Similar organs were built in Italy and Spain, but those countries seem not to have produced the wealth of true renaissance organ music which is found among the work of the Tudor keyboard composers from Redford and Tallis to Byrd and Bull. This may, with some justice, be regarded as organ music in its purest form, since it makes no mechanical demands in the way of registration (combining stops in different octaves, etc.) or contrasted tone colours. English organs never recovered from this unusual start, followed as it was by the almost complete destruction of church organs during the Commonwealth. Even afterwards England lagged behind the Continent; pedals were only introduced during the eighteenth century, the manual departments were not much better developed, and it was not until the height of the Romantic period that the English organ began a tardy but spectacular growth, much of which has been of lasting value.

During the sixteenth century the continental organ was steadily improved, refined, and to some extent standardized, in North Germany, France, and the Netherlands. But the sixteenth century, so far as the organ is concerned, was really one of preparation, and it was not until the High Baroque, the century between 1650 and 1750, that the instrument reached its greatest popularity and artistic importance. There were two great schools of organ-building at this time: the French on the one hand, the German and Dutch on the other. The French organs were highly standardized and stylized, as befitted the music of Daquin,

Couperin, and their contemporaries. The German and Dutch school was at once more varied and more robust, and has proved to be of more lasting worth and influence. It was for such instruments that Bach and Buxtehude composed, and their organ music cannot be fully understood or appreciated without some understanding and preferably actual experience of surviving specimens. Many of these survive in Germany and Holland.

It is usual to talk of the baroque organ as a well-defined type of instrument, but in point of fact the various national schools differed to a tremendous extent, as did the music written for them. Also, the technique of voicing (i.e. determining the tone colour of a rank) changed fundamentally about 1700, so that there is a further distinction between organs of the seventeenth and eighteenth centuries, although both are technically baroque. The aesthetic of the baroque organ is so fundamentally different from the romantic organ, which is almost the only kind that now survives in England, that it can best be described by a certain amount of reference to the modern English romantic organ. The romantic organ is designed for simulating crescendo and diminuendo. For this purpose its stops are graduated from very soft to very loud, and to enhance the illusion of expressiveness, some of them are enclosed in a swell box, with movable shutters on one side under the control of the organist. Opening and closing the shutters makes the sound louder or softer, which is the nearest an organ can get to 'expressiveness'. In the last century, when orchestras were comparatively rarely heard, while no front-rank romantic composers were writing music in any quantity for the organ, organists acquired some cheap popularity by playing 'arrangements' of orchestral compositions, and to assist them in this, organ builders developed stops to imitate as many orchestral instruments as possible, including even the strings. The more closely the organ approached to being a one-man band, the better it was thought to be, and by the end of the century the approximation had become very close indeed in the most debased examples.

Such was the romantic organ at its height, but the baroque organ builders had no such problems. 'Expressiveness', in the form of crescendo and diminuendo, has no place in baroque organ music, which relies on clear-cut contrast. The baroque organ was devised to afford a considerable range of well-balanced contrasted effects, which may be divided into the two main categories of 'solo' and 'chorus'. An organ chorus consists of a number of ranks of roughly the same tonal quality and power, sounding at many different pitches, both unisons and quints. Because choruses cannot be built up from extreme tone colours (particularly at extreme pitches), choruses were always made up of ranks of diapason or principal tone, which is the basic organ tone, lying midway between the extremes of dull and bright. Such stops have unrivalled blending qualities, and if properly treated the various ranks become almost one sound. The mixture stop, too, was an essential ingredient of the baroque chorus, and although it survived in an attenuated form in the romantic organ, its function there was superficial and many builders left it out altogether. As we have seen, a mixture has more than one pipe to each note; frequently as many as six or seven. Its purpose is to add brightness and definition in the bass, where the tone tends to be dull and indefinite, and to maintain power and fullness in the trebles, which tend to be weak and thin. To achieve this, a mixture 'breaks' at several points in the compass. A typical mixture, having four ranks to each note, might be arranged thus: at bottom C the ranks would sound at intervals of a 19th, 22nd, 26th, and 29th (i.e. two quints and two unisons) above the unison tone. At the C above there would be a 'break' to the 15th, 19th, 22nd, and 26th, and so on, one rank dropping to a lower interval at each C until, in the top octave, the composition might be 5ve, 12th, 12th, and 15th. To provide additional power in the treble, a mixture might take on extra ranks as it went up the compass, increasing from four in the bass to six in the treble. In that case, the stop just considered would have all its ranks doubled in the top octave, sounding 8ve, 8ve,

12th, 12th, 15th, 15th. If a scale is played right up the keyboard on a mixture stop alone the effect is distinctly bizarre, but they were never intended for use alone and the foundation stops completely covered the breaks. Thus the baroque builders ensured that their organs had not only melodic ability but also – helped by the high-pitched ranks low in the compass – polyphonic clarity. This last vital quality they enhanced by imparting a very smart attack to their pipes, which spoke with a barely perceptible 'spit' like the bite of a bow on the string, or the effect of a flute or horn player's tonguing. Romantic organs seldom have much attack, and this, coupled with their usually ponderous tone colour, makes them singularly lacking in the essential characteristic of clarity. A good baroque chorus is bright, clear, and ringing, and is fairly powerful, though neither so loud that it rapidly palls nor so bright that it screams. It was for such a chorus that Bach wrote his great organ preludes and fugues.

There was a complete chorus on each manual of the baroque organ, and an independent chorus on the pedals. For the episodes in a Bach fugue, the player would transfer from the primary manual to another of sharper but not appreciably softer tone. When he returned to the main keyboard it might be with an added mixture stop, but this was the only point at which changes in registration were generally effected. The modern practice of making Bach's music sound as 'romantic' as possible consists of starting a fugue on a single soft stop, then building up to a crashing fortissimo, the episodes being treated as though they were echo effects. This makes nonsense of the music. Bach's climaxes are thematic and they do not rely upon mere volume of sound, which, far from enhancing the climax inherent in the music, actually detracts from it by the purely artificial effect of super-added notes. It is said by some that Bach would have revelled in the modern organ, and would have used its resources to the full. This may be true, but he would have written quite different music for it. The music he did write was for the organ as he knew it, and to argue that it sounds better played in the romantic idiom amounts to a complete misunderstanding of Bach's process of musical thought. There is as much emotional content in the music of Bach as in that of any 'romantic' composer, but this is not to be confused with mere sentimentality. Players lacking true feeling for music of the Baroque era seek to mask their deficiency by constant stop changes and use of the swell pedal, but the attempt is sterile.

Quite distinct from chorus music was that in which each of the different voices was played on a different manual, each with a well-contrasted combination of stops. Bach's six trio-sonatas are the outstanding examples. For these contrasted effects the baroque organist did not have to rely on single stops of strongly individual character, but upon the combination of stops of fairly neutral tone and at different pitches. The regal stops afforded important colour, as also did stops sounding at intervals of a 12th, 15th, 17th, 19th, or 22nd above the unison. The latter were called 'mutation' stops, and by combining them in different ways a number of highly colourful, quasi-synthetic effects were achieved. It was, of course, important that these effects should balance against each other, and to this end all the stops of a baroque organ were fairly similar in power. Thus, a combination of any three stops on one manual was certain to balance any three on another, and so forth. Such balanced effects are extremely difficult and often impossible to produce on a romantic organ, but without them baroque organ music cannot be performed intelligibly.

What has been said so far has clearly been derogatory to the romantic organ, but this has only been by comparison with the baroque organ *for the purpose of playing baroque music*. Expressiveness is the essence of romantic music, and most of the great romantic composers dismissed the organ's laborious simulation of expression as being unworthy of their attention. Yet the few great organ works of Liszt and César Franck show how fine a medium the romantic organ might have become under suitable direction. One of its great weaknesses as a romantic solo medium is that the works of Liszt

and Franck, and of Reubke and such late romantics as
Reger, Jongen, and Elgar, rely upon a very large instrument with at least twice the number of stops which can do
justice to the whole vast repertory of Bach and his predecessors. Curiously enough, Mendelssohn's six organ sonatas
sound at least as well on a baroque as on a romantic organ,
and, with a handful of exceptions, the greatest works in the
repertory were all composed for the baroque organ.

The great strength of the romantic organ, however, was
an accompanimental instrument to the church liturgy, and
it was its success in this connexion which ultimately ensured
its survival throughout the Romantic era. In this context,
even such a questionable expedient as the swell box takes on
an artistic quality.

In the third quarter of the last century, before the
romantic organ entered upon its period of decadence,
English organ builders had arrived at a remarkably good
general-purpose organ, with complete and balanced choruses
as well as enclosed reed choruses and other legitimate organ
effects (as distinct from those which merely ape the orchestra). Throughout the present century the English organ has
mostly followed a rather timid policy of compromise, slightly
tempering the worst excesses of the romantic organ with a
minimum of badly-balanced and rather insipid choruses.
The use of solo mutation stops has also, to a limited extent,
been rediscovered.

On the Continent, especially in Holland and Scandinavia,
there has been a wholesale return to the baroque organ,
completely free of swell boxes or other romantic manifestations. There has also been a return to the use of tracker
action, which is facilitated by the spacious locations of these
organs upon a west gallery (cf. Pl. 1). In England, our
cramped and awkwardly shaped organ chambers often make
the use of electric action unavoidable. But there is no doubt
at all that rhythmic playing with sensitive phrasing and
accentuation of the highest artistic order demands tracker
action; on this the leading artists, both here and abroad,
increasingly agree. Belgium, Holland, and the Scandinavian

countries are developing a style of modern music consistent with this conception of the organ, although no masterpiece has yet resulted. The French are aiming at a more general-purpose organ, but the greatest strides in this direction have been made in America, with organs combining well-balanced and contrasted manual and pedal choruses with sufficient mutation stops, and also one or two enclosed departments with accompanimental effects and reed choruses. Such instruments can do justice to the music of all schools and centuries. Until very recently we have had no example of this general-purpose organ in England, but the organ completed in 1954 for the Royal Festival Hall in London first made good the deficiency, and after a slow start the movement is now spreading very rapidly indeed. The popularity of the Festival Hall instrument shows that the musical public has not been slow to appreciate its merits as a solo instrument.

Among contemporary composers of the front rank, Hindemith, Schoenberg and Messiaen have written major works for the organ, but it still remains to be seen whether it can regain something approaching its position in the seventeenth and eighteenth centuries as the unchallenged 'king of instruments'.

# 3. *The Clavichord*

THURSTON DART

FOR more than four hundred years the clavichord (Pl. 2a) held a place of honour among keyboard instruments, and its revival during this century has once again made its delicate expressiveness familiar to discerning musicians. Its mechanism is very simple. A brass blade (the 'tangent') is set upright at the far end of each key. When the key is depressed, the blade rises, strikes the string close to one end, and remains in contact with it until the key is released. The sound is necessarily very soft, for the tangent is light and travels only a very short distance. Since the string is in effect struck at one extremity, every harmonic is theoretically present, and the tone quality is therefore rich. Moreover, a slight increase in finger-pressure increases the tension of the string and consequently raises the pitch of the sounding note. The resources available to a good player on a good instrument thus include a most expressive vibrato, the so-called *Bebung* (a gentle reiteration of the note), an astonishing control of dynamics, great beauty of tone, and an unbroken repertory extending from the earlier years of the fifteenth to the last years of the eighteenth century, and including fine contemporary music by Howells, Hessenberg, Ridout, Hadlinott and others.

The early history of the clavichord is somewhat obscure. There seems little doubt that it derived from the *monochord*, a laboratory instrument perhaps invented by Pythagoras (*c*. 550 B.C.) and certainly in existence during his lifetime. The monochord, as its name suggests, consisted of a single string of gut or metal, stretched between two bridges resting on a soundbox. A third movable bridge could be placed at any one of a number of mathematically determined positions between the other bridges, and the string segments so formed demonstrated the fundamental laws of harmonics and the construction of the diatonic scales. Such instruments were used throughout the early Middle Ages for teaching music and singing. Many representations of them appear in early manuscripts, and the pitch-letters of the Guidonian scale or gamut of medieval music (*G–e''*, diatonic, with *b♮* and *b'♭*) were often shown on the side of the sound-box, corresponding to the various set positions of the third bridge. The addition to the monochord of a primitive key action was the next step. It grew out of the use of the organ in the West between about A.D. 800 and A.C. 1200 and of the hurdy-gurdy (*organistrum*). Both instruments were still only melody instruments, capable of playing nothing more than the notes of the gamut, one at a time; their key action was simple but efficient, and it could be transferred to the monchord without alteration. A keyed single-string monchord with the compass of the gamut is described in the *Novellus musicae artis tractatus* of Conrad von Zabern, a manuscript appendix to his printed treatise *Opusculum de monochodro* (Mainz, *c.* 1470). Though this source is a late one, there can be no doubt that the instrument von Zabern so fully describes had already been in use for at least 300 years. The term *monacorde* occurs in the *Roman de Brut* (1157) in a context which makes it clear that a real musical instrument is intended, not just a piece of demonstration equipment. Similar poetic references occur in *Le Roman de Flamenca* (1235), Guillaume de Machaut's *Prise d'Alexandrie* (1333), and Eberhard Cersne's *Der Minne Regel* (1404). Cersne's poem mentions the *clavicordium* as well as the *monocordium*, and treatises by Georgius Anselmi (1434), Arnault of Zwolle (*c.* 1435), and Ramis de Pareja (1482) make it clear that by the early years of the fifteenth century the clavichord had developed into an instrument having up to ten strings and a chromatic keyboard. Since the notes were no longer all of them obtained from one string, a clavichord of this kind could be used for harmony as well as for melody, and it would thus serve as a practice instrument for organists; it retained its age-old value for teaching music and singing, and it was remarkably cheap to construct.

The several strings of this new and improved kind of

clavichord seem at first to have been equal in length and
thickness, but experience with such contemporary instruments as dulcimers and psalteries (Chapter 9) had shown
how tone could be improved by varying the thicknesses and
lengths of the strings. During the fifteenth century the clavichord followed their lead. Improvements in the art of wire-
drawing led to an increase in the number of strings, the
compass of the instrument was extended to four octaves,
and its sonority was enhanced by the use of pairs of strings
tuned in unison. The clavichord is described and illustrated
by Virdung (1511), and the earliest surviving instrument
was made by Domenico of Pesaro in 1543. It is now in the
Instrument Museum of the University of Leipzig. Virdung's instrument appears to have had thirteen or fourteen
pairs of unison strings at most, the lower ones of brass and
the higher ones of steel. Domenico's has twenty-two pairs
and a compass of four octaves ($C–A$ diatonic, $B\flat–c'''$
chromatic). The eleven lowest pairs of strings serve for one
note each; the next two pairs serve each for two notes a
semitone apart (and therefore never simultaneously needed
in the music of this period); each of the remaining pairs
provides three or four notes in chromatic succession, thus
giving a total compass of four octaves corresponding to the
forty-five keys of the keyboard. Such a clavichord, with
fewer strings than notes, was known as 'fretted' (German
gebunden). By the end of the century its keyboard had become
fully chromatic, with a short octave in the bass (p. 78) and
two extra notes at the top, giving a sounding compass of
four octaves and a half ($G'–d'''$) corresponding to the usual
compass of the other keyboard instruments then in use. It
was about 50 by 12 inches in size.

Clavichords of this kind were in use throughout Europe
by musicians of all classes. This may be illustrated by a few
of the numerous references to the instrument to be found in
British sources:

1477 William Horwood, organist and choirmaster of Lincoln
    Cathedral, paid for teaching selected choirboys to play the
    'clarichord'.

1497 A payment for transporting the 'monicordis' belonging to King James IV of Scotland.

1502 Queen Elizabeth of York, consort to Henry VII, was given 'A payre of clavycordes' (i.e. a single item consisting of two parts: instrument and case – cf. 'a pair of scissors').

1660 The import duty on a pair of 'claricords' was 13s. 4d.

1663 John Hingston paid for tuning the 'claricon'.

1670 The manuscript keyboard book of a Sussex gentleman includes two 'Allemandes fitt for the Manicorde'.

All these are different names and spellings for the same instrument, and other variants may be found, with their definitions, in various dictionaries published in England between 1573 and 1678.

The earliest music written specifically for the clavichord seems to date from the seventeenth century, though it is probable that much of the music in the famous Buxheim manuscript of German keyboard music (*c.* 1470) may have been intended for a clavichord. Various sixteenth-century collections of printed keyboard music list the clavichord with other instruments on their title-pages – for instance, seven books for *Orgues Espinettes et Manicordions* (Paris, 1530–1), or the *Intabulatura nova . . . per Arpichordi, Clavicembali, Spinetti et Monachordi* (Venice, 1551). Manuscripts of the same period may well include clavichord music, even though their compilers did not think it worth specifying the instrument to be used. But the first composer to choose the clavichord in preference to other instruments because of the unique features it possesses appears to have been J. J. Froberger (1616–67). His poetic and individual style is idiomatic only when his music is played on the clavichord, and it is ironic to find so many of his works published posthumously for the harpsichord, an instrument on which they do not sound nearly so well. Other clavichord composers of note include Buxtehude, Kuhnau, Krieger, and J. S. Bach. All these men were organists, and it was in the German-speaking countries alone that the organ and its music rose to unquestioned greatness during the period from 1650 to 1750 or so. It is not surprising, then, to find Germany becoming the centre of clavichord-making and German composers leading the way in its music. For these men the clavichord was more than just a practice instrument for organists, its traditional use. It was also the best instrument other than the lute for expressing personal feelings of an agreeably melancholy kind, a role it retained until the end of the eighteenth century.

Most of the new developments in the instrument were designed primarily to improve its suitability as a practice instrument, and to make it increasingly resemble the organ. Lady (Susi) Jeans has pointed out that 'any improvement of the organ keyboard, whether an increase in compass or the insertion of divided keys, was imitated on the clavichord from earliest times.' A one-manual pedal clavichord had been described earlier by Paulus Paulirinus of Prague in his *Liber XX Artium* (*c*. 1460), and there is a rough sketch of such an instrument in a German manuscript of *c*. 1475. The pedal clavichord of the early eighteenth century consisted of two clavichords placed one on top of the other, with a separate pedalboard lying beneath them, having its own set of strings. Such an instrument could reproduce in miniature the effect of an organ with two manuals, and by the opening years of the eighteenth century it had already developed a literature of its own. Thus, when his wife and son died of the plague in 1683, Pachelbel commemorated them in a book consisting of seven sets of variations on chorale tunes *auf dem Clavier* ('for the clavichord'), and Bach's fine set of six trio-sonatas were probably composed as studies for Wilhelm Friedemann Bach, when he was learning the pedal clavichord, although they are customarily played today on the organ. Another development, traditionally due to Daniel Faber in 1726, was the 'unfretted' (*bundfrei*) clavichord, with a separate pair of strings for every note on the keyboard. Such a step was long overdue, and it was forced on the clavichord by the steady widening of harmonic vocabulary and range of tonality, the increasing use of equal temperament, and the ubiquitous harpsichord. Without such a step, the music of the most idiomatic of all clavichord composers – C. P. E. Bach – would have been impossible. His magnificent sets of sonatas, fantasies, and rondos 'for amateurs and connoisseurs' were published between 1779 and 1787, and they are the instrument's swan song. His earlier *Essay on the True Art of Playing the Keyboard* (1753) is the latest and greatest of clavichord Tutors. By this time the instrument's compass had been increased to five octaves and more, with a corresponding increase in its range of expression and size (63 by 20 inches). Since the lowest strings lacked brilliance, it was customary to add to them an octave string, but in other respects the instrument had not changed. Hass, one of the greatest German clavichord makers, is mentioned in Chapter 5 (p. 91).

The next step was clear. The early pianoforte combined the clavichord's expressiveness with a far wider scale of dynamics, and it could be used in ensemble. Bequeathing its perfected style of composition to its conqueror, the clavichord expired. Though its use lingered on into the early decades of the nineteenth century in some out-of-the-way places, its delicate and beautiful tone was not to be heard again in public until the antiquarian revival that has been so characteristic a feature of the last sixty years of Western music.

# 4. *The Harpsichord, Spinet, and Virginal*

## RAYMOND RUSSELL

THE harpsichord is the largest member of a group of keyboard instruments with strings sounded by a plucking mechanism. Our knowledge of its history covers the three centuries between 1500 and 1800, and, though we know it was in use in a primitive form earlier, we have little factual knowledge of that period. The instrument was the principal keyboard stringed instrument during the sixteenth and seventeenth centuries, attained its fullest development as regards both construction and musical composition in the first half of the eighteenth century, and was gradually replaced by the pianoforte during the last quarter of that century. In the years since 1890 a revival of harpsichord-making has resulted in the appearance of many new instruments, so far used almost entirely for the performance of the works of the early masters, as few modern composers have been seriously interested in the harpsichord.

In England today the members of this group of keyboard instruments are known by three main names: harpsichord, virginal, and spinet. The word 'harpsichord' is reserved for the largest form of the instrument, in shape like an early grand pianoforte; 'virginal' for a smaller oblong model; and 'spinet' for an instrument of similar musical content to the virginal, but polygonal or leg-of-mutton in shape. In earlier times, however, the term 'virginal' or 'pair of virginals' was loosely used in England to cover all domestic keyboard instruments with a plucking action. Thus the title-page of *Parthenia*, a collection of keyboard pieces published about 1612, shows a woman playing an oblong virginal, but the title-page of *Parthenia Inviolata*, published about twelve years later, shows a woman at a harpsichord, though in both cases the compositions are advertised as for the 'virginalls'. Our present system of nomenclature was established by the end of the seventeenth century,*

* In France the large instrument is called *clavecin*, and the small

The specification of the harpsichord has varied considerably in the various countries and periods, ranging from a simple instrument with one keyboard and with one string for each key to an elaborate model with two keyboards and four or five strings to each key controlled by hand stops and pedals, besides various other devices for changing the tone. The virginal and the spinet have always been quite simple, having only one string for each key and no mechanical devices to assist the player. These two instruments bear much the same relationship to the harpsichord as does the modern upright pianoforte to the grand, though tonally they often possess characteristics which are musically attractive in their own right.

In all these instruments the basic unit of mechanism is the 'jack', which incorporates the plucking device. It will be described in the following general outline of a typical mid-eighteenth-century English harpsichord. On opening the lid (Pl. 4a) we are at once struck by the familiar appearance of the interior, which, broadly speaking, reminds us of the modern pianoforte; this is not surprising when it is remembered that the latter instrument developed from the idea of a harpsichord with hammer instead of plucking action. There are two keyboards or manuals, each with a compass of five octaves, and above the upper keyboard there are four stop levers, the purpose of which will be described later.

Beneath the music desk, which has been removed, is the wrest plank (marked 1 in the Plate), and in it are set the wrest pins, or tuning pins, round which are wound the proximal ends of the strings. This harpsichord has three complete sets of strings: two tuned at 'unison' or '8-foot pitch' (i.e. ordinary pianoforte pitch), and one tuned an octave higher at 'octave' or '4-foot' pitch. There are therefore three rows of wrest pins. On the wrest plank are also placed

---

models *virginale* or *épinette*. In Germany the harpsichord is *Cembalo*, occasionally *Flügel* or *Clavier*; here it must be borne in mind that the latter two words often cover our pianoforte, while *Clavier* was also used in Germany for clavichord. In Italy *clavicembalo* has always been used for the harpsichord, and *spinetta* for the smaller instruments.

the 'nuts' or wrest plank bridges, over which the strings pass
and at which point their speaking length begins. The nut
for the 8-foot strings is marked 2 at each end, and that for
the 4-foot, which naturally has much shorter strings, is
marked 3. Beyond the wrest plank are placed the jacks,
arranged in three rows, one row for each set of strings. The
remainder of the instrument contains the soundboard, over
which the strings continue their course, passing over the
4-foot bridge (4) and 8-foot bridge (5), which transmit the
vibrations to the soundboard for amplification. Beyond their
bridges, the 4-foot strings are attached to hitch pins let into
the soundboard, while the 8-foot hitch pins are attached to
the interior of the case. A decorated metal 'rose' or trade-
mark, bearing the initials I.K., identifies the maker of this
harpsichord, which was built by Jacob Kirckman in London
in 1755.

On the end of each key there is placed a wooden jack to
operate each string which that key can play. A jack (Plate
4b) is between 5 and 8 in. high and its upper part is level with
the string that it is to pluck. In a slot cut in its upper part
is placed an upright piece of hard wood, about $1\frac{1}{4}$ in. high,
called the 'tongue', held in place by a horizontal metal pin
on which it can pivot backwards. It is kept upright by a
spring of hog's bristle which presses on it from the back.
A small slot is cut in the upper part of each tongue, and in
this is placed the plectrum, a small wedge of hard leather
or quill, which projects from the front of the tongue about
$\frac{1}{8}$ in. Attached to the side of the jack at the top is a small
piece of felt, the damper. When the key is at rest, the plectrum is beneath the string it serves, and the damper is in
contact with the string. When the key is depressed, the jack
rises, and the plectrum plucks the string as it forces its way
past on its upward journey. When the key is released, the
jack falls back, the plectrum comes in contact with the string
again, and this pressure causes the tongue to turn back on
its pivot so that the plectrum can pass the string without
plucking it again. The jack arrives back at its position of
rest, the hog's bristle spring returns the tongue to the up-

ight position, the plectrum is once more beneath the string
n readiness to attack it again, and finally the damper
ilences the vibrations on coming once more into contact
vith the string.

The jacks in each row are placed in wooden slides or
registers' which keep them upright. These can be moved
ideways by stop levers so that the plectra no longer pluck
he strings when a key is depressed. The four levers which
an be seen in Pl. 4a operate as follows: no. 6 controls an
8-foot playable from the lower manual only. No. 7 is the
other 8-foot stop, and this is playable from both keyboards.
No. 8 controls the jacks of the 4-foot stop, which was always
played from the lower manual. No. 9 is, strictly speaking,
an extra effect called the 'lute' stop: a row of jacks, placed
diagonally in the wrest plank, to attack the strings of the
upper keyboard 8-foot at a point much nearer the nut than
he row of jacks controlled by stop no. 7, and thus providing
a second tone colour from one set of strings. The lute stop
appeared almost exclusively in English harpsichords of the
middle and second half of the eighteenth century.

The harpsichord just examined is typical of the large
eighteenth-century English model, but one stop commonly
in use was not included in this instrument, namely the
harp' stop: a wooden slide, placed against the 8-foot nut
and armed with a small pad of buff leather or felt for each
string of one of the 8-foot stops. On moving the slide, the
pads come in contact with the appropriate strings, muting
them and causing a *pizzicato* effect.

The keyboard compass of the harpsichord family has
varied. The sixteenth-century instruments usually have only
a four-octave compass from $C$, but eighteenth-century
models have commonly five octaves from $F'$, while a few
special instruments were made with five and a half octaves
from $C'$. Within these limits every variation of compass is
found. The earlier instruments very generally had a 'short'
or 'broken' octave in the bass – a practice which continued
fairly commonly until the late seventeenth century, though
in organs it persisted for longer. It took two forms, and was

intended to save the expense and space of providing bass
notes unlikely to be required. A compass from low C with
bass short-octave shows a keyboard ending on key E. In
fact this key was tuned to sound $C$, key F♯ to sound $D$, key
A♭ to sound $E$ (Fig. 19a), while the rest of the instrument
was tuned conventionally. Thus, the bass octave lacked the
lowest C♯, E♭, F♯, A♭ notes, which were little used in early
music. The other common short-octave keyboard is shown
in Fig. 19b. The lowest key appears to be B, but was tuned
to sound $G'$, key C♯ to $A'$, key E♭ to $B'$, and the rest of the
tuning was conventional. Here we have a compass from $G$
without the accidentals $A'♭$, $B'♭$, $C♯$, and $E♭$.

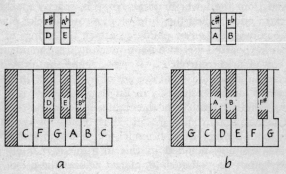

FIG. 19. Short-octave arrangements on harpsichord

Towards the end of the seventeenth century these neglected bass accidentals were more often used in keyboard
music than formerly, and it became necessary to include
them in the instruments. However, in order not to muddle
performers who were used to the short-octave keyboard, the
missing notes were at first often provided, as shown in the
upper diagrams in Fig. 19. Each of the lowest accidental keys
in both the $C$ and $G'$ keyboards was divided into two parts,
a front half and a back half. The front half provided the old
short-octave tuning, while the back half gave the note we
should expect today. Thus the two compasses were enlarged
by the addition of two of their four missing accidentals.

A very rare stop in the classical harpsichord is a 16-foot, the strings of which sound an octave below normal pitch. It appears in so few old harpsichords (the writer knows only six in which it is an original feature) that it may be left without further explanation. It is, however, included in most modern harpsichords. Equally rare are original harpsichords which have a 2-foot stop, harpsichords with three keyboards, upright harpsichords, harpsichords with pedalboards for organists, and harpsichords combined with organs or pianofortes.

An important mechanical feature is the coupler. Harpsichords with two keyboards have always been built with one 8-foot (together with the jacks of the lute stop, if present) on the upper manual, and the other 8-foot, the 4-foot (and in modern instruments the 16-foot) on the lower manual. In England the upper 8-foot jacks were always coupled to the lower manual as described above (stop no. 7), but not the lute jacks. In France and Germany, however, the upper keyboard could be coupled to the lower one by one of two systems: either the upper key frame could be pushed into the instrument for about half an inch; or else the lower key frame could be drawn outward. In either case the movement caused the two keyboards to engage one another, so that the keys and stops of the upper manual could be played from the lower. In modern harpsichords this coupling is effected by a rather complicated mechanism between the keyboards.

It is sometimes thought that the harpsichord is not amenable to touch, and that the player has no more to do than to play the notes of his piece. This is quite untrue. If the keys are first struck violently, and then in contrast are gently pressed down, it will be found that the tones produced are, dynamically, very little different. But the sensitive player feels very acutely his contact with the string through key, jack, and plectrum, and much of the fine art of harpsichord-playing lies in detailed technique in this direction. A resolute and smooth pressure on the key, designed to make the plectrum sweep against the string and displace it to the maximum, rather than a violent attack calculated to force the plectrum past the string as roughly as possible, is the basic touch likely to produce good tone and *cantabile* playing, the latter so fundamental a quality of the harpsichord. In the same way, detailed attention must be paid to the release of each note, to careful articulation, to the layout of a work between the two keyboards with strict attention to its musical structure, to the careful shaping of phrases, and to the inclusion of adequate breathing spaces in the performance. Undue preoccupation with such things as registration – a matter which fades from the mind when the instrument is tonally satisfactory – and details of elaborate ornamentation is a pitfall for the newcomer which tends to obscure the fundamental musical requirements of the instrument. Modern concert players, whether solo or continuo, by no means always respect the careful instructions of the old masters in these matters, and their performances are often far from authentic in letter and spirit.

*

The history of the early keyboard instruments of the harpsichord kind is a history of national schools, originating in Italy, spreading to the Low Countries, and thence to the rest of Europe. It is important to look briefly at these different schools.

Surviving Italian instruments date from the first quarter of the sixteenth century, and Italian work of the following two hundred and fifty years exists in considerable quantity. Most of this consists of harpsichords and polygonal spinets, and they are usually plainly made of cypress wood, though often enclosed in elaborately painted outer cases from which they can be removed. The harpsichords are very simple, and usually have one keyboard and two 8-foot stops only. Italy also produced a great many Octave Spinets, and these too are generally made of cypress wood. Italian harpsichords and spinets have a most characteristic tone in which the twelfth (the third harmonic) is prominent, and the suggestion of clarinet tone which results is often quite marked. These harpsichords and spinets usually blend very well with strings and voices, and they are unsurpassed for *continuo* playing, perhaps their most usual duty when first made.

By the middle of the sixteenth century the influence of the Italian school was strong in the Low Countries, and Flemish instruments of that period usually look like copies of Italian work. The chief artistic life of the Low Countries was centred in Antwerp; there the painters' guild, dedicated to St Luke, recognized the musical instrument makers and guarded the standard of their work. Antwerp was the home of one of the best-known families of instrument makers: Hans Ruckers (*c.* 1550–*c.* 1620) and his sons Jan (1578–1643) and Andries (1579–*c.* 1645). This family produced vast numbers of oblong virginals, besides harpsichords with both one and two keyboards. Ruckers harpsichords and virginals were built to fairly rigid designs, and most of the harpsichords, both single and double manual, had one 8-foot and one 4-foot stop only. There is good reason to think that the double-manual harpsichord originated in this workshop in the late sixteenth century as an instrument built to facilitate transposing. The two manuals both used the same 8-foot and 4-foot sets of strings, thus needing four rows of jacks. The upper keyboard had a four-octave C compass, but the lower keyboard was a fourth away with F as the top note. Thus the top key of the upper manual (*c'''*) played that note, but the top key of the lower manual (an F), sharing the same strings with the upper manual, also produced the note *c'''*. Hence the lower manual transposed a fourth, the approximate interval which separates adjacent voices of instruments in any group. Towards the end of the seventeenth century this type of instrument became obsolete; the lower keyboard was rebuilt as a second C keyboard, and a coupler and second 8-foot were added. The resulting two-manual instrument, with one 8-foot on the upper keyboard and a second 8-foot and a 4-foot on the lower, provided the basic harpsichord for the great classical composers of the early eighteenth century. France, England, and Germany relied early on Italian, and later on Flemish, instruments for much of their supply, and they received many instruments from the Ruckers workshops in the seventeenth century.

France in particular had a large number of Flemish instruments, and in the first half of the eighteenth century French harpsichord makers had a reputation for their skill in altering the old Antwerp harpsichords, rebuilding them to a size and condition suitable for the keyboard music of Couperin and Rameau. These reconstructions usually involved the lengthening and widening of the instruments, to make possible an increase of compass from four to five octaves (from $F'$), an operation known in France as *ravalement*. Particularly associated with this was the Paris family of harpsichord makers founded by Nicolas Blanchet, whose grandson François II (d. 1766) was followed by the foreman Pascal Taskin (1723–93), who made a great name for this distinguished workshop.

Very few Ruckers instruments escaped *ravalement*, and only one transposing harpsichord (Edinburgh University) is known to have survived unaltered. Tonally, Ruckers harpsichords are very satisfying, and those examples which have escaped enlargement have some of the tone quality associated with Italian instruments. Their tone was not always much altered by *ravalement*, though the operation tended to make them less percussive; but their qualities of richness and brilliance place them in a special class as general purpose instruments, suitable for all the literature, which cannot be said of the simple Italian instruments. The large French harpsichords made by the Blanchets and by Taskin are copies of the rebuilt Antwerp instruments. They have two manuals with five-octave compass from $F'$, and the usual three registers, besides the sliding upper keyboard coupler which has already been described. Occasionally a fourth row of jacks was provided to pluck the 8-foot strings of the lower manual by plectra of either quill or leather – a different treatment of the idea which in England resulted in the lute stop on the upper manual.

A large part of the English demand for keyboard instruments was met in early times by the importation of Italian and Flemish harpsichords and virginals, and instrument makers from those countries immigrated from time to time. The first real sign of a national school in England is to be found in the group of oblong virginals, some twenty of which have survived, made between 1641 and 1679 (Pls. 2b and 3). There is no doubt in the writer's mind that these were inspired by Ruckers virginals, many of which are very similar in design. By the last quarter of the seventeenth century these instruments were out of fashion, and their place was taken by spinets, leg-of-mutton in shape, which persisted in popularity as small and convenient instruments for nearly a century (Pl. 5a). A family particularly associated with high-quality spinet-making was the Hitchcocks: Thomas, father and son, and John in the third generation, working c. 1660–1774.

Only one English harpsichord from the sixteenth century has survived, two from the seventeenth century, and two from the first twenty years of the eighteenth century; it is clear that the smaller instruments were more popular during those times. In 1718 a Swiss, Burkat Shudi, came to London, followed about 1730 by the German Jacob Kirckman, already mentioned above. Both were apprenticed in the London workshop of a now obscure maker named Hermann Tabel, on whose death Kirckman married the widow. Subsequently the two firms of Shudi and Kirckman built large numbers of harpsichords of the highest quality, many of which survive today. They are based on one or two manuals with a five-octave compass from $F'$ (occasionally extended down to $C'$ by Shudi and his partner John Broadwood), and two 8-foot stops. To this foundation were variously added 4-foot, lute, harp, 'machine', and 'Venetian swell'.

These latter two devices appeared exclusively in English harpsichords built after 1760. The 'machine' was a composition pedal to change the stops, otherwise always done by hand. The 'Venetian swell' was a set of shutters placed above the strings, and opening upwards under control of a pedal in a manner familiar to organists. These two expressive devices were reflections of the lack of expressive power as seen at that period in terms of crescendo, diminuendo, sforzando, etc., when the harpsichord was unfavourably compared with the rising pianoforte. They are not part of the development or requirements of the classical literature, since they did not appear until that literature was already in existence. These harpsichords, and similar work by other smaller firms, belong to the period when the harpsichord was obsolescent and the pianoforte in the ascendant: all Kirckmans were built after 1750, and so were the great majority of Shudis. It is unlikely that more than a fraction of the classical literature we know today was available or known to their original owners. These instruments were restricted to performance of the many books of harpsichord lessons, flavoured with Handel's influence, which were published in England at that period, the accompaniment of songs, continuo-playing, and the early pianoforte works (published in 1766) by John Burton, and those of his successors. The last surviving Shudi harpsichord is dated 1793, the last remaining Kirckman 1800.

German harpsichord-making came into its own in the early years of the eighteenth century, and Hamburg was the centre of this trade. Far the most distinguished work was that of Hieronymus Hass and his son Johann, whose work covers the approximate years 1710–70. Elaborate harpsichords were a speciality of the elder Hass; three survivors from the Haas workshop contain an original 16-foot stop. In Dresden the Grabner family produced a number of harpsichords with two 8-foots and a 4-foot, and these are dated between 1722 and 1782. There are few German spinets, almost all the survivors coming from the workshop of Johann Silbermann (1727–99) of Strassburg. It must be stated that, despite a common belief to the contrary, and despite many modern German instruments, the 4-foot stop was *never* on the upper manual as an original feature of old German harpsichords.

The construction of these early keyboard instruments died out in the last quarter of the eighteenth century, and little

musical interest was shown in them from that time, though
a number of large collections were formed during the nineteenth century, preserving many instruments which would
otherwise have been destroyed. In the 1880s, however,
Érard, followed by Pleyel, undertook the construction of a
few harpsichords which were based on the old French model,
and these were exhibited at the Paris Exhibition of 1889.
The example of these French pianoforte makers was shortly
followed by Arnold Dolmetsch (1858–1940), whose first
harpsichord is dated 1896. Many workshops both large and
small have taken up this work in the last fifty years, and the
early keyboard instruments are now made in profusion.

It is unfortunate that the type of harpsichord which has
usually attracted modern instrument makers, and from
which they have developed their plans, is the instrument
which – already decadent – was condemned by the composers and overwhelmed by the pianoforte of the late
eighteenth century. The swell, the machine stop, and various
other devices planned to vary tone colour were a last attempt
to display powers of romantic expression comparable with
those of the pianoforte. It is interesting to see this same
phenomenon displayed by many harpsichord makers today,
whose preoccupation with contrasted tone colour and with
expressive powers inherent in the pianoforte but foreign to
the harpsichord betrays both a lack of appreciation of the
sterling musical quality of the classical instrument and also
doubts concerning its popular acceptance.

Modern harpsichords are fitted with pedals instead of
hand stops, and a 16-foot register is almost always included.
Leather is more often used for plectra than quill, and is far
more reliable, though formerly quill was almost invariably
used. Covered strings are usually found in the bass, because
convenience of transport and modern living conditions
demand an instrument as short as possible. The tone of
covered strings is, however, very inferior to that of uncovered. The casework and frame are much heavier than
in the old harpsichords. This is due partly to the influence
of pianoforte-making, and partly to the fact that many

makers use a much heavier stringing than was formerly
thought necessary, which requires a stronger frame to bear
the extra tension. The result of this, inevitably, is that most
modern harpsichords are far less resonant and possess far
less carrying power than their predecessors. Electrical
amplification is therefore sometimes resorted to in concert
performance – though unnecessary when old instruments in
good condition are used.

Individual features in modern harpsichords are good,
but one undeniable fact must be faced: all the greatest
masters of harpsichord-writing and playing – Byrd, Bull,
Gibbons, Frescobaldi, Chambonnières, Louis Couperin,
Purcell, François Couperin, Scarlatti, Rameau, Handel,
and Bach – were content with small or moderate-sized
instruments with one or two manuals, a maximum of
two 8-foots and one 4-foot, and without means of changing
the stops while playing. Large harpsichords equipped with
16-foot and pedals could have been produced as easily as
they can be today, but this tremendous weight of experience and musicianship was perfectly satisfied with
those simple instruments, many of which have survived
to our day. The great masters planned and constructed the
texture of their compositions in terms of these instruments,
whose musical characteristics they knew so well, and it is
impossible to pretend that unrestrained use today of the
resources of the modern harpsichord can fail to detract very
seriously from the authenticity of performances. There is no
evidence that any of these great composers and players had
access to harpsichords with a 16-foot or with pedals for
working the stops.

A few modern composers have been attracted to the
harpsichord, but the response has so far been disappointing. Works for solo harpsichord are few, as most composers
have preferred the concerto. Manuel de Falla scored his
Harpsichord Concerto for violin, violoncello, flute, clarinet,
and oboe, and his treatment of the harpsichord is very effective. Poulenc, however, in his monstrous *Concert champêtre*,
employed a large orchestra including tuba. Frank Martin

has produced a most interesting *Petite Symphonie Concertante* for solo harpsichord, pianoforte, and harp, with double string orchestra. Problems of balance make this valuable contribution difficult to perform in the concert room, but radio and recording, which can resolve many problems of this kind, have proved an excellent medium for it. Vittorio Rieti's Partita for solo harpsichord, with flute, oboe, and string quartet, is also a successful venture in this field.

It is unfortunate that the large modern harpsichord of today should imperil its prospects by elaborate and often unreliable mechanism, its consequent great cost, unresonant tone, and unpopularity with many practical conductors, players, and composers. A return to the simple instruments approved by all masters of the past would rectify these faults, besides bringing prices within the range of many people. There are signs that opinion is moving in this direction.

# 5. *The Pianoforte*

CECIL CLUTTON

THE history of the pianoforte has proceeded by fits and starts. For seventy years it almost stagnated, then followed another seventy years of intensive development, and the last hundred years have been a period of standardization and refinement.

Its early neglect shows that when an instrument maker invents something before the composer is ready for it, his rewards will be slight. Thus, when Bartolommeo Cristofori (b. 1665) devised his *gravicembalo col piano e forte* at Florence in 1709, no one paid very much attention, and it was not until Mozart began to write for and play upon the instrument in the 1770s that it gained any wide recognition. On the other hand, when Beethoven and later Liszt began to make increasingly exacting demands upon the pianoforte, they stimulated its rapid development into very much what we know today.*

In point of fact, Cristofori was probably anticipated in his 'invention' by a full two and a half centuries. The essential difference between the pianoforte and its contemporaries, the harpsichord and the clavichord, lies in the fact that the performer's finger has no point of contact with the string through the key. In the clavichord, his contact is complete and permanent for as long as the note is held. In the harpsichord, it is limited to the moment of plucking. But in the pianoforte the player merely throws a hammer at the string from a distance. If one presses a pianoforte key very gently, nothing will happen; one has to hit it hard enough for the hammer to leave the key and travel in free flight to the string, subsequently falling back on the key. This was probably the action of the *échiquier d'Angleterre* or *dulce melos*,

---

* In England the pianoforte confusingly started life, about the mid eighteenth century, as a *fortepiano*, but was changed to 'pianoforte' a little before 1800. It will be referred to throughout as pianoforte.

one of which Edward III of England gave to the King of France in 1360. The precise action of this instrument is somewhat doubtful, but Galpin interpreted it as free-moving, and actually constructed one in this form which worked reasonably well. In the manuscript of Arnault of Zwolle (*c.* 1435) such an action is described. It consists of an ordinary key upon which rests a strip of wood, much resembling a harpsichord jack but without plectrum, and weighted with lead. The travel of the key is limited by a stop. If the key is struck with sufficient force, it is arrested by the stop, but the jack continues moving upwards until it hits the string, after which it falls back on the key. The instrument was, of course, undamped. The strength of the note depended upon how hard the key was struck. Here were all the essentials of a pianoforte.

But be that as it may, the pianoforte as we know it was invented by Cristofori in about 1709. He made upwards of twenty in all, and by 1726 he had arrived at all the essentials of the modern pianoforte action: that is to say, his final design had double action, a check, an escapement, and an *una corda* mechanism (all of which will be further described later). It was this action which the German organ builder, Gottfried Silbermann, adopted in 1745 after earlier unsuccessful experiments of his own, and which was later used by the English school in the last quarter of the eighteenth century, and finally developed into the modern pianoforte action. Although it reached England only at third-hand, it was exploited so successfully that it became known as the 'English' action. But throughout the first century of its existence, the Cristofori action suffered from a disability: the frame was not sufficiently strong to carry stringing heavy enough to stand up to and give musical effect to the strength of blow which the action was capable of imparting. It was not until metal bracing began to be developed, leading eventually to the full metal frame, that Cristofori's remarkable mechanism of 1726 really came into its own. As it was, his work achieved little recognition in his lifetime, although within a year of his death in 1731 there

appeared probably the first compositions specifically desig-
nated for the pianoforte: twelve Sonatas for *cimbalo di piano
e forte* by Lodovico Giustini di Pistoia.

It is somewhat remarkable that the new instrument was
not taken up by anyone more eminent than this quite un-
memorable composer, since Italy had been the birthplace
of the new 'expressive' music towards the end of the sixteenth century. The truth is probably that Italy had lost
interest in keyboard instruments at that time. It would
certainly be wrong to suppose that Cristofori's instruments,
as finally developed, were too experimental or too crude to
satisfy sensitive performers; the 1720 Cristofori in the
Metropolitan Museum of Art, New York, will stand comparison with anything made up to the end of the century.
Later players complained of the heavy and deep touch of
the Silbermann and English pianofortes, but this criticism
cannot be levelled at the New York instrument. Its touch
is as light as any eighteenth-century pianoforte (only $\frac{3}{16}$ in.
deep) and excellently sensitive. The stringing is bichord
throughout, and while the treble is not as good as, for
example, a 1770 Stein, its relationship to the bass is better
than in the eighteenth-century British grand pianofortes.
Like the Viennese pianofortes, the Cristofori model inclines
to flutiness in quality. It has a surprisingly wide dynamic
range, although the acceptable maximum is probably a little
softer than on a Stein. Moreover, Cristofori clearly realized
that the conventional harpsichord frame would have to be
strengthened; the New York instrument stands in tune
remarkably well, despite the American climate. It can
safely be said that the Cristofori model was not surpassed,
as a balanced instrument, for a century after its introduction.
Scarlatti had access to several Italian pianofortes, one of
which was made by Ferrini, a pupil of Cristofori, in 1731,
and while he never specifically stated whether he was
writing for the harpsichord, organ, or pianoforte, the style of
some of his sonatas suggests the latter; to this extent he may
perhaps be regarded as the first front-rank composer to
write for the new instrument.

But in the end it was neither the Cristofori nor the 'English' pianoforte which brought it popularity, but a fundamentally different mechanism, invented, probably, by Johann Andreas Stein (1728–92) in about 1770 or a little earlier. This became known as the 'Viennese' or sometimes the 'German' action. In it, for the first time, the action was nicely matched to the frame and stringing. Performers had all along complained of the deep and heavy touch of the Silbermann instruments, whereas in the Stein model – of which a modern replica is shown on Pl. 6a – the touch was light and shallow, and almost as sensitive as that of a clavichord. Also, the very light hammers gave a blow which the stringing could sustain, resulting in a singing tone of very great beauty and clarity. Another of the qualities of the Stein model is that the power of the trebles is well matched to the basses. In the English school, the bass is remarkably powerful and sonorous but quite overpowers the treble. Moreover, in an attempt to keep up the trebles, a somewhat hard, wooden tone resulted. In playing on an early English pianoforte widely-spread passages, such as those which occur so frequently in Beethoven, quite a different touch has to be employed in the right and left hands if the bass is not to swamp the treble. The difference almost certainly stems from the fact that the English makers were thinking in terms of an expressive harpsichord, whereas Stein was aiming at a rather more powerful clavichord. The remarkable qualities of the large German clavichords of the second half of the eighteenth century, as exemplified at their best by Hass and, doubtless, Silbermann, are very little known in England today, and this is a great pity, because they have a musical range – both in compass and general capability – far beyond the miniaturist approach to clavichord-making and playing which is now fashionable in England. Even Beethoven sonatas by no means come amiss to a Hass clavichord. This is clearly the sort of tone at which Stein was aiming. The similarity of tone quality between a Hass clavichord and a Stein pianoforte is most striking, and the Stein is perhaps only twice as loud as the Hass. Almost its only corresponding loss is that no vibrato (*Bebung*) is possible upon it. (Here it may be stated that, despite all that has been said about the possibility of producing a *Bebung* on early pianofortes, and its supposed intended use in the recitative of Beethoven's op. 110, the thing is manifestly impossible. The player can, with skill, exploit the uncertain escapement and check action to make the hammer bounce and hit the string twice. But Beethoven notated *Bebung* as a pair of tied notes fingered 4, 3 and probably intended no more than an ordinary repetition.)

Turning back once more to early composers for the pianoforte: of J. S. Bach's sons, Carl Philip Emmanuel continued to prefer the clavichord, but Johann Christian played by choice on the pianoforte and was largely responsible for popularizing it in England, where he first performed in 1768. C. P. E. Bach did, nevertheless, use a pianoforte and wrote as follows on its technique, in his *Essay on the True Art of Playing Keyboard Instruments*:

I leave dexterity to the knights of the keyboard, preferring to sing upon my instrument; music ought principally to move the heart, and in this no performer on the pianoforte will succeed by merely thumping and drumming, or by continuous arpeggio-playing. During the last few years my endeavour has been to play the pianoforte, despite its deficiency in sustaining tone, as much as possible in a singing manner – this is by no means an easy task, if we desire not to leave the ear empty, or to disturb the noble simplicity of the *cantabile* by too much noise.

But both these sons of Bach were unfortunate enough to have lived and worked during a time of transition, and the little sentimentalities which stirred such deep emotions in their day have become sadly tarnished with the passage of nearly two centuries. So it was left for Mozart to launch the pianoforte conclusively, and he rapidly developed a style of keyboard composition quite divorced from anything the harpsichord could express. It has been claimed that Muzio Clementi anticipated Mozart in developing an exclusively pianoforte style – in his Sonata Opus 2 (1773) and his *Gradus ad Parnassum*, which was certainly the first

ianoforte Tutor. In this he showed how to develop equal-
ess of touch and melodic power. But Clementi, like the
Bach sons, is now less often played, and anyway Mozart
ame very quickly after him. Mozart first encountered a
Stein pianoforte in 1777, and described it in a letter to his
ather in the following well-known passage:

This time I must start at once by telling you about Stein's
ianofortes. Before having seen these it was Spath's pianofortes
which I liked best. But now I must give my preference to those of
Stein, for they damp the resonance much better than those in
Ratisbon. When I strike hard I can leave my finger on the key, but
n taking it away the sound dies away almost immediately. I
an do with the keys what I like; the tone is always equal; it does
ot tinkle disagreeably; it has neither the fault of being too loud
or too soft, nor does it fail entirely. In a word, the tone is per-
ectly equal throughout. . . . His instruments, above all, have this
advantage over others, that they are made with escapement
mechanism. Now, not one in a hundred makers bothers with
escapement, and yet without it, it is absolutely impossible for a
ote not to jingle or to continue vibrating after being struck.
Stein's hammers, when the keys have been depressed, fall back at
he instant they strike the strings above, whether one continues
o hold down the key or let it go.

Certainly, for Mozart's music, the Viennese piano was
and remains the ideal instrument, though of course it will
ot stand up to the dynamics of a modern string ensemble in
he pianoforte concertos. The Stein instrument has a depth
of touch of only about $\frac{1}{4}$ in. and hardly heavier than that of
a large clavichord. Like the clavichord, it calls for a light
et firm finger touch, and a perfectly-controlled *cantabile*
tyle, placing no reliance on the sustaining pedal. Stein
ianofortes do have two knee-operated levers for raising the
ass or treble dampers at will, but their artistic uses in
Mozart are rare; John Field (1782–1837) was the first
erson to develop the use of the sustaining pedal as part of
is technique, and, like Chopin, he pedalled after the note.
Even when virtuoso technique had outstripped the capabilities of the Viennese action, some performers continued

to prefer it, notably Backhaus, and it continued to be made
by Bösendorfer, certainly until as late as 1914.

*

Thus far, the artistic history of the pianoforte has been
traced up to the point where it can be said to have established itself as a solo instrument in its own right, and with
special reference to the relationship between the English and
Viennese actions. Before going on to the next stages in its
development, the three basic types of eighteenth-century
instruments must first be examined in further detail: (a) the
single action, mostly found on the British square pianofortes
(b) the double action, as used by Cristofori, Silbermann
and the British builders, notably John Broadwood; (c) the
Viennese action.

(a) *The single action, and the early British square pianoforte*. This
is the simplest form of action, with which Cristofori started
but which he rapidly developed into the double action. It
was, however, almost universally employed in the British
square pianofortes of the third quarter of the eighteenth
century and onwards until about 1785, which gained very
widespread popularity long before the pianoforte had supplanted the harpsichord as a solo instrument. The pianoforte was introduced into England, effectively speaking, by
Johannes Zumpe, one of Silbermann's workmen who came
over about 1760. Nevertheless, as far as is known he never
emulated the double-action grand pianoforte of his master
but concentrated entirely on the simplest sort of square
instrument, resembling a clavichord in shape and size
(Pl. 5b). Zumpe's single action is shown diagrammatically
in Fig. 20.

The key (1) is pivoted at (2). Fixed to it is the jack (3)
popularly known as the 'mop-stick'. On depressing the key
the jack strikes the hammer (4) which rises and hits the
string (5). Almost the sole merit of this action is its simplicity.
The player has remarkably little control over the tone, since
at its loudest it is quite feeble, and if the key is not struck

reasonably sharply the hammer never reaches the string at all. If the key is struck too hard, there is nothing to prevent the hammer from bouncing and hitting the string more than once. Since the power of a Zumpe is not much greater than

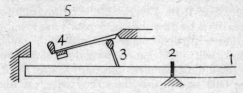

FIG. 20. Pianoforte, single action

that of a large clavichord and its potentialities in every other way are so much less, its popularity can only be explained by the fact that the clavichord was never popular in England. Zumpe did, however, introduce one innovation which was of lasting importance, and this was a mechanism for raising the dampers out of operation. This he did by two hand stops to the left of the keyboard, one for the bass and one for the treble.

(b) *The double action.* The form shown in Fig. 21 is Cristo-

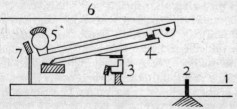

FIG. 21. Pianoforte, Cristofori double action

fori's double action of 1726. Neither Silbermann nor the British makers introduced any important improvement on it, and it is the basis of all modern actions. The key (1) is pivoted at (2). The escapement (3) actuates the intermediate lever (4), which in turn imparts impulse to the hammer (5), hitting the string (6). The check is (7).

This mechanism overcomes most of the shortcomings of the single action, and the most important improvement it embodies is the escapement. The jack on the Zumpe action was rigidly fixed to the key, but in the Cristofori it is hinged to its lever in such a way that as soon as it has given impulse to the hammer it is deflected so that, even if the note is held, the hammer will fall back to its normal position of rest. This in itself is an almost complete safeguard against the hammer bouncing back and hitting the string twice, or 'blocking', but in addition if the note is held, the hammer on falling back is caught and held against the check. The slow acceleration of the hammer is a major defect of the single action – certainly as made by Zumpe and Broadwood – and it is this that accounts for its very limited dynamic range. Interposing a secondary lever between the key and the hammer multiplies the velocity of the jack and thus greatly increases the control of the player. On the one hand he can play more loudly, but without the risk of blocking owing to the escapement and check action; on the other he can play more softly without risk of the note failing to sound at all. If the action is set (as it should be) so that the hammer does not escape until only a tenth of an inch before it reaches the string, the touch is very sensitive.

The hammers are covered with buckskin, and the tone alters substantially as the skin hardens with playing. It is therefore difficult to know just what was regarded as the ideal tone quality. When new, it is round and flute-like almost to the point of dullness; when really worn, the tone becomes brilliant, almost to the point of harshness. But there is a middle range between the two extremes where leather gives an entirely characteristic quality and excellent attack and definition. Experiments were made with a variety of materials, such as cloth over leather, or leather over felt. But all-felt hammers were first introduced by Henri Pape as late as 1826. Many early English pianos have been completely ruined by being fitted with felt hammers, often much heavier than the originals. The worst offenders here are unfortunately those who should know best. It is nonsense to pretend that the right sort of leather is no longer available.

The English grand pianofortes (Pl. 6b) are trichord throughout with brass strings in the bass and steel in the treble. None of the strings is covered, and this is tonally a most important attribute. Thus, the *una corda* produces a uniform change throughout the compass. A distance piece is let into the treble key-check which limits the sideways travel of the keyboard, and can be varied in thickness so as to produce a *due corde* or *una corda* at will. The different

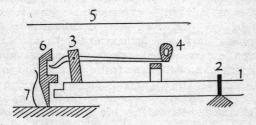

FIG. 22. Pianoforte, Viennese or German action

striking point of the hammers produces a marked change of tone quality, as well as a reduction in power, which is most valuable. The dampers consist of a piece of cloth clipped in a sort of clothes-peg on the end of a jack, resting on the tails of the keys. The jacks are very light, and the cloth quite soft, so that the damping of an early British grand is by no means instantaneous, but this hardly seems a defect in use.

(c) *The Viennese, or German action* (Fig. 22). The key (1) is pivoted at (2). The '*Kaspel*' (3) is rigidly mounted on the key and carries the hammer (4). (5) is the string. (6) is the escapement. (7) is the escapement return spring.

The fundamental difference between this and all the other

T – D

important escapements is that the hammer is mounted on the key itself, and not on the frame, while the escapement is mounted on the frame and not on the key. As the key is depressed, the tail of the hammer is arrested by the notch in the escapement, so that the hammer-head swings upwards and hits the string. Further pressure on the key pushes the escapement aside and allows the hammer to return. The hammer and the key traverse quite different arcs, so that no check action is possible, and the repetition on a Viennese action is not quite as good, or at any rate not as easily achieved, as with the English action. But as made by Stein, Walter, and their better contemporaries, it was not only almost as sensitive as a clavichord, but the instruments are tonally superior to those of the English school. But whereas the Viennese pianoforte had reached perfection by 1780 and if anything deteriorated by further development, the English action was as yet a long way from perfection, and continued to improve substantially throughout the first half of the nineteenth century, and in detail even afterwards. The hammers of an early Viennese pianoforte are even lighter than those of the English, and are sometimes made hollow. They are, of course, covered with leather.

Because it was perfected earlier, the Viennese pianoforte seems artistically superior to its British contemporary up to about 1810, and it certainly throws an entirely new light on Mozart, Haydn, and early Beethoven. It is now gradually becoming recognized that it is not merely the modern pianoforte in a primitive form, but a mature instrument in its own right. There is probably only one original instrument in England, and even on the continent they are rare, but a demand for them is beginning to arise, and they have been reproduced in England by Hugh Gough with great artistic success (Pl. 6a).

The square pianoforte meanwhile kept popularity, with increased size, until about 1860. In its earliest form it was practically limited to five octaves ($F'$ to $f'''$), since any extension either curtailed the sound-board or made the instrument excessively long. But in about 1794 a means of overcoming this was found. A small subsidiary action-frame for the treble notes was placed under the sound-board, and the hammers came up through a small slit cut in it. In this way the compass was enlarged to five and a half octaves $(F'$ to $c'''')$ with no reduction in the size of the sound-board and very little increase in the overall size of the instrument. This compass remained standard for many years, and is sufficient for the performance of all Beethoven's sonatas prior to the *Hammerklavier*.

Square pianofortes are difficult to keep in tune because of the great overlength between bridge and wrest pins. Broadwood somewhat improved this by moving the wrest pins to the back of the frame, opposite the player. The defect was finally overcome in 1820 by Stodart, who made the hitch-pin plank follow the line of the bridge, and thus eliminated the overlength. The early square pianofortes rested in a separate stand with square legs. From about 1800 this was given up, and turned legs were screwed direct into the base of the instrument.

By about 1860 the 'upright' pianoforte had completely replaced the square one for use in small rooms. The early uprights had their strings starting from keyboard level, and thus had to be very tall; many of them were made in elegant shapes, such as the 'Pyramid', 'Giraffe', and 'Lyre'. The first upright with strings going down to floor level was made by a progressive builder, Isaac Hawkins, in 1800.

*

From 1800 onwards the development of the pianoforte centred around increasing string tension and the designing of frames which would stand the heavier loads without collapsing. Since about 1800 the down-tensions on the sound-board of a grand have increased from one hundred-weight to ten, and string tensions have been trebled.

Up to and including Beethoven in early life, all the early virtuosi had brought to the pianoforte a *legato* touch –

something between a harpsichord and a clavichord technique. But with Beethoven's increasingly dramatic demands upon the instrument (and his own increasingly violent style of playing in his later years of deafness, which is said to have played havoc with even the most robust of the early instruments), the pianoforte began a rapid growth towards its modern form, which, for all practical purposes, it reached by 1855. Beethoven wrote his first pianoforte concerto in 1795. His first eight solo sonatas are for pianoforte or harpsichord, and are reasonably effective when played on the latter. His first solo sonatas for pianoforte only, op. 14, nos. 1 and 2, were not composed until 1799. 1800 may therefore be taken as the major turning-point in the history of the instrument.

The players who, after Beethoven, did most to shape the development, were Liszt, Field, and Chopin. Liszt was a hard hitter. His wide, spatulate hands gave him an unrivalled control over the keyboard, which he exploited to the full in his playing and compositions. He also adopted a higher seat level, so that he could bring the whole weight of his arm from the shoulder to bear upon the keys. In this he was even surpassed by some of his pupils, and to such an extent that in the 1870s manufacturers were forced to increase the weight of touch to as much as four ounces, to give their instruments some measure of protection against these onslaughts. This is more than twice the weight of the Viennese action.

Chopin was much opposed to a heavy touch, and for this reason often preferred to play on an old square rather than a more sonorous grand. The grand which Broadwood made for him in 1848, which still exists, has a weight of touch of $2\frac{1}{2}$ ounces. Field and Chopin developed the musical qualities of the pianoforte. The music of both demands an evanescent tone, and a singing quality and sustaining power in the treble which none of the earlier instruments possesses. As we have seen, Field was probably the first to appreciate fully the artistic uses of the sustaining pedal. (The two pedals that we know today had become almost universal by 1790; a debased vogue, *c.* 1800–40, for pedals giving percussion effects, etc., need not detain us.)

The inherent structural weakness of the early pianofortes lies in the gap that has to exist across the full width of the sound-board to allow the hammers room to come up and hit the strings. The full pull of the strings is at right angles to this gap, which accordingly tends to close up. (The problem exists, of course, in the harpsichord, but the string tension is so much less that it is not a serious one.) Even Cristofori was aware of the problem, and placed a number of light wooden braces across the gap. The first maker to tackle it seriously, however, was Stodart, who built metal arches across from the wrest-plank to the soundboard of his grand pianofortes in 1788, or perhaps even earlier. Stodart was very early in the field in Britain, and made his first grand in 1777. Broadwood used metal bracing for his trebles (where the tension is highest) from 1808, but most of the development of the metal frame took place in the 1820s, especially in America, where Alpheus Babcock of Boston evolved a complete cast iron frame for a square as early as 1825. William Allen, a tuner at Stodart's, devised an iron frame for a grand in 1820, but its primary object was to counteract the differing coefficient of expansion under heat of brass and steel strings. Broadwood and Érard both experimented with the increasing use of metal during the twenties, and it was at this time that the covering of bass strings and the use of the heavy, felt-covered hammers introduced by Henri Pape became widespread, although felt hammers were not universal before 1850.

One novel approach to the bridging of the gap was evolved by Robert Wornum, who put his strings and sound-board in the bottom of the case, with a downstriking action placed entirely above them, so that the gap was eliminated. His instruments have an agreeable and sensitive touch, remarkably sonorous tone, and are highly stable in holding their tune.

Broadwood produced his first completely iron-framed grand for the Great Exhibition of 1851, and in 1855 came the Steinway, which has been the model for all successful metal frames ever since. By 1859 Steinway had also perfected their system of overstringing, in which the bass strings cross over the treble ones. This not only permits the use of a relatively long string in a short case, but also spreads the tension better. In the meantime, the compass continued to spread, reaching over six octaves ($C'$ to $e''''$) by 1840, which is really about its musical limit. Further extensions can be achieved, but they can hardly be described as musical sounds. However, in about 1840 appeared the standard seven-octave compass ($A''$ to $a''''$) and by soon after 1880 a further three notes, to $c'''''$, had been added in the treble.

Érard made great developments in action, culminating in his double escapement or 'repetition' action of 1821. This is really only a refined and greatly complicated form of the conventional English double action. If the note, after being struck, is held, the hammer does not fall straight back, but is held against the check in the half-way position, thus making for rapid repetition. From the Érard model, the modern highly complicated but durable and reliable action has developed.

In 1862 C. Montal invented a third pedal, called a *pédale de prolongement*, making it possible to sustain a given chord but not the notes struck subsequently. It had some success, but despite its obvious artistic uses this complication has never been widely adopted.

By 1885 the pianoforte had attained its modern form in all important particulars. The final century of the pianoforte's history has been one of detail development. From the musical standpoint, not much has been said since Liszt on the one hand and Chopin on the other. Indeed, in the hands of Stravinsky and others, it has sometimes been brought to the level of a mere percussion instrument, but there are signs both in playing and composition of a renewed appreciation of its lyrical and orchestral qualities.

# 6. *The Violin Group*

## I: THE VIOLIN

DAVID D. BOYDEN

THE violin is one of the most remarkable of all instruments, being that in which the art of instrument-making has achieved its greatest triumph in terms of simplicity of material, beauty of tone and appearance, and acoustical effect, in which the emotional expressiveness and flexibility of the human voice are combined with a special brilliance and agility quite of its own. To these it owes its wide appeal not only to musicians and music-lovers, but also to scientist, connoisseur, historian, dealer, speculator, aesthete, and snob, all of whom have come under its spell. In the following pages we will examine the violin itself – this unique creation of human ingenuity and inspiration – and, not less important, the bow, 'the soul of the instrument', without which the violin must remain a mute *objet d'art*. It is proposed also to explain the action and nomenclature of the modern instrument and bow, the acoustics of the violin, and its development in the context of composers, players, and makers for the four hundred years of its existence.\*

To the casual eye the violin appears unchanged through the centuries, but it has in fact experienced a considerable evolution to meet the demands of successive generations of composers and players. Its first hundred and fifty years culminated in the magnificent 'classical' model of Antonio Stradivari about 1700. But this was by no means the end. Every Stradivari violin in concert use is now different from the instrument which left the master's bench over two centuries ago. To be sure, the top, back, ribs, scroll, and pegbox have

\* I wish to acknowledge my gratitude to Mr Kenneth Skeaping for extensive help in preparing this chapter, and to the late Dr F. A. Saunders, Professor of Physics (Emeritus) of Harvard University, for information concerning the acoustics of the violin. – D. D. B.

not changed, but other parts that vitally affect the quality and volume of tone have been substantially altered to obtain more powerful and brilliant effects from the instrument and give increased convenience to the performer in displaying them. To withstand the greater tension on the top of the violin, the bass bar has been lengthened and strengthened, and the soundpost somewhat thickened. The bridge has been increased in height and the playing length of string increased. Partly for this reason and partly for ease of playing, the neck and fingerboard have been altered in shape,

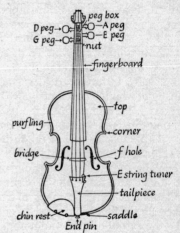

FIG. 23. Violin

lengthened, and tilted back (Pl. 7). In Stradivari's time, gut strings were used, but nowadays the top string is steel and the others are overspun, a variety of materials being employed. A chin rest, unknown to Stradivari, has been clamped to the instrument. These changes in the violin, and also those in the bow, were brought about by new styles of music and playing. Plates 8 and 9 show more vividly than words how players in centuries from the seventeenth onwards held violin and bow: it is obvious from the pictures of Geminiani and Isaac Stern that the eighteenth and twentieth centuries are here worlds apart. All these changes, however, should not automatically be regarded as improvements. It is at least a moot point whether ours is the best of all possible worlds, violinistic or otherwise, and we must keep firmly in mind that the instrument, bow, and technique of a particular era were those which players and makers believed to be best suited to the music of their own time. In any case, these changes over the centuries have been elaborate and fascinating, just as they have been in music, and how and why they took place are among the chief themes of this chapter. Before embarking on them, however, a few points must be clarified concerning the violin and its bow.

The simplicity that the violin presents to the eye is singularly deceptive. In fact, its construction involves some seventy separate parts, which in the best instruments require a master craftsman to cut and assemble; and acoustically the violin is one of the most complex of all instruments. Pl. 12a shows the visible and hidden parts of the modern violin. It is a hollow box, usually 14 in. long. Its four strings are stretched over a carefully fitted bridge of maple, and are made to sound normally by the friction of a horsehaired bow, but sometimes by plucking with the finger (*pizzicato*) or even by striking with the wood of the bow (*col legno*). The top, also called the table or belly, is made of soft wood, usually close-grained European spruce, while the back is of hard wood, usually maple. Both back and top are arched, and both may be made of one piece or two pieces joined. The neck, head, scroll, and ribs (which join top and back) are also made of maple as a rule. The standard modern fingerboard, nut, saddle, and tailpieces are of ebony, and ebony or rosewood pegs are very usually fitted. With metal strings of a particular kind a metal tailpiece is often used. Chin rests are generally made of wood or vulcanite.

Inside the violin, the top, bottom, and corner blocks and the side linings (Fig. 25) give added strength and stability to the structure. Inside, too, are the soundpost and the bass bar, both of which serve as supports. The soundpost, usually of spruce, stands upright just behind the right foot of the bridge, and must be fitted exactly to the inside surface of the back and top. Its height, width, grain, and location are crucial factors in the tone of the instrument. The bass bar, also of spruce, is glued lengthways to the under-surface of the top, and runs under the left foot of the bridge; it helps the top to support the heavy string pressure on the bridge, and also serves an acoustical purpose which will be described later.

The beautiful design and shape of the violin and its parts are not merely ornamental but are determined to a great extent by their function. The arches of back and belly are essential for strength and for acoustical reasons. The whole body is designed to furnish a large surface for amplifying the sound to the maximum, while the narrow waist admits ease of playing on the highest and lowest strings. The scroll is decorative, but the instrument can also be hung up by it. Even the purfling, which so vividly emphasizes the beauty of the outline, justifies its presence by minimizing cracks and by preventing any damage to the overhanging edges from going farther into the body. The sound-holes (f-holes) and the bridge serve an acoustical function, but their actual forms are probably as much decorative as functional*. The composition of the famous Cremona varnish, which adds greatly to the beauty of an Amati, Stradivari, or Guarneri violin, remains largely a mystery, although there could hardly have been anything mysterious about it at the time. Its use was not even confined to Cremona, since Jacob Stainer in the Austrian Tyrol knew all about it, and the Venetian makers used a similar and equally fine varnish. Some of the Dutch and a few early English makers also produced a varnish comparable to that of the Italians. However, easier, cheaper, and quicker methods of varnishing were later applied, and by the 1760s the fine old process had practically disappeared. Nevertheless, excellent var-

---

* Early bridges were very varied in design. Violin bridges of the late eighteenth century generally resemble those of today, though the cuttings are more delicately executed. A peculiar feature in many of them is the stiffly horizontal line of the underside between the feet. The modern bridge usually shows a more graceful and flexible line here.

nishes are being used today. Varnish is indispensable as a preservative, but it cannot improve the tone, although it may affect it. A varnish that is too hard, too soft, badly or too heavily applied may prevent the best tone qualities inherent in the instrument from being fully realized.

Like the violin, the bow was evolved over a long period of time, and its changes, brought about through the same demands of composers and players, are more obvious to the eye than those which were taking place in the violin itself (Pl. 10). When the instrument first came into being, violinists simply adopted the bow already being used by players of other stringed instruments: rebec, lira da braccio, and viol, etc. These bows were quite unstandardized with respect to weight, length, and wood, but they all had certain general features in common which were quite different from the corresponding features of the modern bow. The bow stick curved outwards from the hair, not inwards as it does today, and there was no device to loosen or tighten the hair, which was strung at fixed tension between the pointed head and the horn-shaped nut. Pl. 10c clarifies most of these points, showing the length and shape of various bow sticks and the contrasting appearance and shape of nut and head. In the old bow, the width of the hair was considerably narrower, less firmly held, and less evenly spread out.

The modern bow dates from about 1780, when it was perfected in all important particulars by François Tourte (1747–1835), the Stradivari of bow makers, and generally considered the greatest of them all. From the sixteenth century to the advent of the modern (Tourte) bow late in the eighteenth, the bow stick became longer and for the most part straighter; in a few early eighteenth-century bows it had already become slightly concave. The head began to take a more distinct shape in order to separate the hair from the stick at the point and increase the effective playing length of hair. Various methods of adjusting the hair tension were invented, and the best of these, which became a feature of the Tourte bow, was a screw regulating a movable nut, thus tightening the hair. Some of these changes will be noted in more detail later, but at this point we must return to Tourte and the description of the modern bow. The bow stick is generally round or octagonal, and in bows of any consequence it is invariably of Pernambuco wood, a species of brazil-wood. The hair is fastened to the hatchet-shaped head at one end and to the movable nut (or 'frog') at the other (Fig. 24), where a metal ferrule secured by

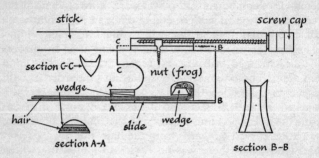

FIG. 24. Modern violin bow, detail of nut (after Heron Allen)

a small wedge serves to spread out the hair and hold it in a firm ribbon. The nut is made of ebony, or sometimes of ivory or tortoiseshell, and the bow is tightened by turning a screw-cap which draws back the nut. The lower extremity of the stick, with which the fingers come into contact, is usually lapped with leather or windings of silver and gold. The overall length of the bow is about $29\frac{1}{4}$ in. The bow hair, about $25\frac{1}{2}$ in. of playing length, comes from carefully selected strands of the tails of white horses, and is given friction by rubbing on a coat of resin; without this no sound would be produced.

When the bow sets the strings of the violin in motion, the bridge transmits some of the vibrations to the belly, while other vibrations, including unpleasant ones, are filtered out. The right foot of the bridge is nearly immobilized by the soundpost (Fig. 25), so that the vibrations are conveyed to the top mainly through the left foot of the bridge. The bass bar transmits the vibrations from the left foot of the bridge to the wide areas of the top, and hence to the rest of the instrument, thus amplifying the sound. The vibrations of the back are less important to tone than those of the top, and they are often reduced further by shoulder pads, chin rests, and contact with the player's clothing. As the name implies, the sound-holes let the sound out, but they also give greater freedom of vibration to the central area of the top. The player can damp or muffle the sound by a mute, a pronged clamp placed on the bridge to cut out some of the vibrations, particularly those of highest pitch.

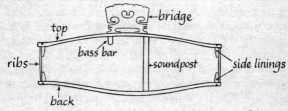

FIG. 25. Violin, cross-section of body at soundpost

The factors that determine the timbre of a single note or all the notes of a particular violin – and distinguish different violins in this respect – have been the subject of numerous experiments. In the last thirty years, electronic scientific instruments have shown that existing theories, including the 'formant' theory, will have to be modified or discarded. But these results, which show the complex interaction of upper partials (sometimes numbering over twenty in an individual note), peaks of loudness, and the 'air tone' (the pitch of the main vibration of the air inside the violin body) can scarcely be discussed here.*

The quality and material of the strings are important factors in the violin tone; early accounts of the instrument stress repeatedly the importance of the selection and use of the best strings. Originally all four strings were of gut, but

* A short report of modern electronic analysis of the acoustical properties of two violins owned by Jascha Heifetz is by F. A. Saunders: 'A Study of Two Famous Violins', *The Strad*, June 1957.

early in the eighteenth century some players began to use a G string wound with silver or copper wire to improve its speaking properties. The aluminium-covered D string and the steel E string were not widely used until the end of the First World War. The steel E string is usually attached to the tailpiece by a 'tuner', a device to permit fine shades of tuning without using the tuning peg (nowadays all four strings are sometimes equipped with tuners). Nylon strings are today used mainly as cores for wound strings. Under conditions of low tension prevailing until the end of the eighteenth century, the gut E string was quite satisfactory, and it had certain advantages of tone and was less liable to the high squeaks of the steel string. But the steel E is more responsive in the highest register, less subject to breakage at modern tension, and more reliable under varying conditions of moisture, to which the modern professional must expose his instrument, particularly when travelling. The same remark applies to the other strings, which today are usually made with cores of gut, nylon, plastics, or ropes of fine steel wire, and wound with silver, aluminium, or stainless steel.

*

The violin probably emerged about 1550, if by 'violin' we mean a four-stringed instrument, played on the arm by a bow, without frets, and tuned in fifths upwards from *g*. A three-stringed instrument of similar characteristics may have preceded the four-stringed instrument by at least a generation. In any case, documentary evidence points to the existence of a true violin about 1550, the approximate date assigned to the oldest violins extant today. For instance, Jambe de Fer in his precious *Épitome musicale*, Lyons, 1556 (a single copy exists in Paris), speaks explicitly of the four-stringed violin, played by supporting with the arm, and tuned in fifths upwards from *g*.

It is fruitless to try to attribute the 'invention' of the violin to any one man or country. France has its claim, the book just mentioned being significant. In the early sixteenth century a three-stringed instrument was called a 'Polish' fiddle by Agricola, who was born in Silesia adjoining Poland, and this phrase was repeated in a description of the violin by Praetorius, also German, and one of the most meticulous writers on instruments. The most impressive contributions, however, were those of northern Italy, where shortly after the middle of the sixteenth century, the Italian school of violin-making dominated all others. The first famous makers came from Brescia and Cremona, and a century later Cremona produced Antonio Stradivari (*c.* 1644–1737), the greatest of them all.

The early violin combines features of several immediate ancestors that flourished about 1500, notably the rebec (Fig. 26), the Renaissance fiddle (Fig. 27), and the *lira da braccio* (Pl. 10a), which may be considered an extension of the principles of the fiddle and is remarkably similar in body outline to the violin, although it is usually considerably larger. Like the violin, it has an arched back and top, over-lapping edges and ribs, and (normally) no frets. Unlike the violin, the typical lira da braccio of about 1500 had seven strings, of which two ran off the fingerboard and were not stopped by fingers, the five stopped strings being tuned *d''*, *a'*, *d'*, *g'*, *g*; also unlike the violin, the tuning pegs were set horizontally in a leaf- or heart-shaped tuning head. Sometimes *f*-holes are seen on these instruments, sometimes *C*-holes.

The viol is not a forebear of the violin in any important respect. For one thing, its construction and stringing are decidedly different. For another, all viols from the largest to the smallest are played on or between the knees, and the bow is held underhand (Pl. 19a), not overhand as in the violin bow. Thus sixteenth-century Italians distinguished the viol family from the violin family by the respective terms *viole da gamba* (violas played at the leg) and *viole da braccio* (violas played on the arm), though this distinction was not factually consistent since only the soprano and alto members of the violin family – violin and viola – were played on the arm, the cello being played between the knees and the double bass standing. By common error the viols have often been regarded as the ancestors of the violin simply because they preceded the violin in time, and became obsolete earlier on

FIG. 26. Rebec, fifteenth century

FIG. 27. Fiddle, fifteenth century

ceasing to fulfil a needed musical role (see Chapter 7). Only when this fact is understood can the relationship of the two families be properly appreciated.

Among the earliest violins to survive were those made by
Gasparo Bertolotti, known as Gasparo da Salò (1540–1609).
Born in Salò, Gasparo moved to Brescia in about 1562, to
become the first famous violin maker of that city. His work
shows the hand of a master, also the variety and vitality of
the sixteenth century. But the somewhat plump, even
massive, appearance lacks the elegance that characterizes
the body outline, f-holes, and scroll in the classical Stradivari (Pl. 11b). Gasparo's work was carried on and improved
on by his pupil Gio. Paolo Maggini (1580–c. 1632), also a
Brescian, most of whose instruments are distinguished by
double purfling and sometimes by elegant ornamentation on
the back (Pl. 10b). In the sixteenth and seventeenth centuries the violin was made in a small and large model (body
lengths varied from about 13½ in. to 14½ in.), and it was not
until the classical model of Stradivari that the present body
pattern of about 14 in. became more or less standardized.

Violin-making must have begun in Cremona and Brescia
at about the same time, but it is extremely hard to trace the
early history of the Amati family, the earliest Cremonese
makers here concerned. We cannot even be sure of the birth
and death dates of Andrea Amati (c. 1505–c. 1580), the
first of the family, and few authentic violins of his still exist.
A small-patterned violin, preserved in the Ashmolean
Museum, Oxford, is dated 1564; one or two of his extant
violins are believed to date from the 1550s, somewhat
earlier than those of Gasparo da Salò, none of whose
violins is dated before 1562. Nicolò Amati (1596–1684),
the grandson of Andrea, was the greatest of the family, and
the reputation of the Cremona school reached its highest
point in Antonio Stradivari, his pupil, and in Giuseppe
Guarneri del Gesù (1698–1744). Moreover if we had any
doubt about the beauty and sometimes perfection of the
early violin from the surviving specimens, we could allay them
by examining certain Italian paintings of about 1600 – those of
Caravaggio, for example – in which the violin is depicted
with the glowing colours of its pristine varnish and in outlines
which sometimes reveal the hand of a master craftsman.

Though a few specimens of the sixteenth-century violin have been preserved, bows of the period are practically non-existent. While the old instruments were repaired and refashioned to the needs of successive generations, the old bows were eventually displaced by a new type of bow that made them obsolete, and with no further use and no commercial value they practically vanished. A few bows have, however, survived from the seventeenth century, and particularly from the early eighteenth.

After 1550 the violin played an increasingly active part in musical life, but there was relatively little music written specifically for it before 1600. For one reason, much instrumental music of the time was composed for 'all kinds of instruments', or for one of specific alternatives, as in Dowland's *Lacrimae or Seven Teares, figured in seven passionate Pavans* (1604), 'for lutes, viols, or violens'. The individual identity of the violin was obscured by such uses, and it is rare to find *violino* specified, as it is for the treble part of Giovanni Gabrieli's *Sonata pian e forte* (1597). The violins, in common with other instruments, were also used to double voice parts, as is suggested by the directions '*per sonar et cantar*' and 'for voyces and viols'. Actually, we know less about the widespread use of the violin and its social function from the music itself than from theoretical and general sources. But by all accounts the violin's main function was playing dance music for all ranks of society from peasants to princes, and its players, as dance musicians, were professionals, relatively low in the social scale, particularly compared with players of the viols, who were more likely to be gentlemen and amateurs. Court weddings were often accompanied by elaborate spectacles that required dance music. An example is Beaujoyeulx's *Circe ou le Ballet comique de la reine*, performed in Paris in 1581 on the occasion of the marriage of the Duc de Joyeuse to Mademoiselle de Vaudemont, the Queen's sister. Born in Italy, as Baltazarini, Beaujoyeulx, 'the best violinist in Christendom', had been sent to France *c.* 1555 to be principal violinist of the violin band of Catherine de' Medici. The music and an account of this lavish production of 1581 are preserved; five-part ensembles of the violin family were used to accompany two of the dances.

Whatever the sixteenth-century violin sounded like, its tone must have differed in some ways from that of the modern instrument. It was strung with gut strings at a lower tension, and consequently the tone was probably comparatively small. Furthermore, there was none of the continuous vibrato inseparable from modern violin-playing, for although vibrato was known in the sixteenth century, it was used largely as an occasional ornament, generally on long notes. Early playing technique must have been derivative; we must allow for the fact that the early violinist came to his instrument as a player of other stringed instruments, and paintings show the violin held on the arm against the breast (as the rebec) or against the neck (as the lira da braccio and sometimes the rebec) but not anchored under the chin. The bow was relatively short, and the bow stroke was usually short, especially where the clear articulation of dance rhythm was required. Contemporary paintings show the bow held near or on the nut, and sometimes grasped in the fist or enclosed in a moderately relaxed hand. But there is practically no specific information regarding violin-playing in the sixteenth century, although certain technical features common to all string-playing are described in treatises for the viols. From Sylvestro Ganassi (*Regola Rubertina*, 1542–3) we learn to draw the viol bow at right angles to the strings and at varying distances from the bridge, depending on the kind of effect desired. Ganassi and others describe the single bow-stroke, the stroke in which several notes are slurred, the use of *pizzicato*, and playing in third and fourth positions. Nuances of expression, characteristic of vocal technique in the late sixteenth century, may also have been common in violin-playing, which took the voice as the model of expression. The simplicity of instrumental music of the time is not a decisive argument against a more advanced technique. From musical practice with the voice and the viols, we know that the printed notes, often simple and with no marks of expression, were frequently a mere starting point for the performer, who improvised quite elaborate ornamental passages or 'divisions'. If the violin was treated idiomatically anywhere, especially as a solo instrument, it was in the realm of these unwritten and improvised *passaggi*.

In the seventeenth century, the advent of the opera and the sonata, and the penchant of the Baroque era for the expressive, the individual, and the soloistic, made the triumph of the violin inevitable. The violin makers, especially in Italy, were kept busy furnishing instruments for consumption at home and abroad, those of Brescia and Cremona in particular fetching prices far above those of other countries or of other towns in Italy. Outside Italy the only maker of really outstanding stature was Jacob Stainer (1621–83), whose reputation in the latter part of the century equalled, and sometimes even surpassed that of Amati. The violin was the subject of considerable experiment in the seventeenth century. The highly arched models of the Amati and of Stainer produced a sweet tone well suited to small rooms and chamber music, whereas the flatter instruments of Maggini had been built for power. Nicolò Amati, doubtless searching for volume of tone, produced his 'grand' pattern, and Stradivari in his 'long' model appears to have been aiming at a combination of Brescian and Cremonese virtues (Plates 10b, 11).

The bow was still unstandardized. Convex, and commonly of snakewood, its playing hair length varied between approximately 18 and 23 in. The nut was a fixed one, often of boxwood fitted into a slot in the stick and held in place by the pressure of the hair (Fig. 28b). The longer bows were preferred for solo and sonata playing and the shorter ones for consort and dance music. The most impressive developments were the gradual straightening of the bow and the devising of ways of regulating the hair tension. One of these was the movable nut adjusted by a wire loop hitched to one of several notches on the top side of the stick (dentated or crémaillère bow; Fig. 28a); another was the nut moved by a screw, probably dating from about 1700 and later standard on all bows.

Such variation and experiment are but reflections of the post-1600 musical innovations with which the violin was closely associated over and above its traditional role in dance music. After Monteverdi's *Orfeo* (1607), written for both viols and violins, the latter became the mainstay of the strings of the opera orchestra, while it is significant that the most famous orchestra in the seventeenth century was the 24 *Violons du Roi* established by Louis XIII in 1626. Technical development was particularly rapid in the accompanied

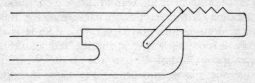

Fig. 28(a). Seventeenth-century crémaillère (after St George)

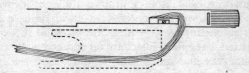

Fig. 28(b). Detail of detachable nut of early bow (after Heron Allen)

solo sonata. The compass was extended upwards by playing in positions as high as the sixth (occasionally even the seventh), while the register of the lowest string was no longer neglected as it had been earlier. Violin figures and arpeggios grateful to the hand and to the instrument developed as composers, most of them also players, sought to understand the violin's true nature. Multiple stops, used discreetly by the Italians, were a hallmark of the German school later in the seventeenth century. A number of different tunings or *scordature* were employed, particularly in Germany, while special effects (*pizzicato*, etc., and *sul ponticello*, i.e. bowing near the bridge to make a brittle, glassy sound) and the mute were all used on occasion, partly for expression, partly for imitative effects ranging from tempests at sea to farmyard noises and bird calls.

Early in the seventeenth century the vital role of bowing was well appreciated, and the basic relation of down-bow on the strong beat understood (mentioned for example by Mersenne). The violin was still held in the old way, and the bow was held either in the 'French' manner – at the extremity of the nut, with the thumb under the hair – or in the Italian manner – with the thumb between hair and stick, and the fingers from one to three inches above the nut, depending on the length and balance of the bow and the kind of music being played. (Pl. 8a). The bow-strokes consisted of a separate non-legato stroke, particularly effective in the upper third of the bow and for dance music, and a legato stroke joining two or more notes as indicated by slurs; slurs embracing as many as thirty-two rapid notes in one stroke occur in J. J. Walther's *Hortulus Chelicus* (1688). Dots and vertical dashes indicated different degrees of separation between the notes, and some quite complex bowings were employed among the virtuosi, though it is not clear to what extent lifted strokes and especially bounding strokes (not impossible with the old bow) were used in practice. In any case, the Italians and Germans had a relatively long bow for the sonata, and had developed a longer and more powerful stroke than the French, whose musical demands were quite different.

Among a host of violinist-composers in Italy, the following may be singled out as representative: Biagio Marini (1597–1665), active in both Italy and Germany; G. B. Vitali (c. 1644–92), associated with the important school of Bologna and later with Modena; and Arcangelo Corelli (1653–1713) in Rome, whose music and pupils played such an important part in the development of the violin and its music in the eighteenth century. In Germany the two most important figures were Heinrich von Biber (1644–1704) and Johann Jakob Walther (1650–?).

England and France were more reluctant to accept the violin and the new sonata associated with it. The French reacted strongly against the abstract sonata of the Italians, partly because it did not mean anything to the French, who cherished an 'imitation of nature', and partly because dance music occupied most of their energies. French violin music of the seventeenth century was practically synonymous with dance music, and as a result it was technically simple and musically unsophisticated compared with the Italian. Nevertheless, the rhythmically precise style, clear articulation, and orchestral discipline required by Lully resulted in a standardization of the French style within the limits of its technique and musical aesthetics. In England the polyphonic tradition, embodied in the Fantasies for a consort of viols, was still strong in the first part of the century and the violin occupied a secondary position, but after the Restoration English tastes were strongly influenced by the French court and the French dance style. Violin technique was moulded by the limited aims of the French, and any advances were inspired by violinists from Germany or Italy, like Nicola Matteis, who settled in England in about 1672. Matteis made a great impression. A contemporary, Roger North, reported of him: 'his manner of bowing, his shakes, divisions, and indeed his whole style of performance was surprising, and every stroke of his bow was a mouthful'. At the end of the century, Purcell wrote his trio sonatas in imitation of the Italians, inveighing in the preface to his *Sonnatas of III Parts* (1683) against the 'levity and balladry of our neighbors' – the French. Yet neither England nor France fully accepted the violin until the eighteenth century, when it was too late to do otherwise.

In certain respects the eighteenth century was the Violin Century. In Italy, the violinist-composers began to exploit the instrument in the solo concerto, and successively Vivaldi, Locatelli, Veracini, Tartini, Viotti, and many others made technical demands which required alterations in violin and bow and greatly expanded the technical scope of playing. Indeed, Locatelli's Caprices, the written out cadenzas for

*L'Arte del violino* (Concertos of op. 3, 1733), demand a
virtuosity hardly exceeded until the time of Paganini.
Germany was little behind. J. S. Bach contributed his three
well-known concertos, and continued the German multiple-
stop tradition in his Sonatas for solo violin – works of
such enigmatic difficulty that they have inspired not only
a 'Bach bow' but also a whole literature concerning questions
of their performance. In France, while the old dance
tradition continued, musicians began to recognize the sonata
and the concerto. After 1725, the more ambitious composers,
among them notably Leclair (1697–1764), modelled their
efforts on the Italians, and by 1750 the French came to the
forefront of technical advances – a position which they have
continued to hold to the present day. Significantly, the
modern bow was perfected by the Frenchman Tourte.
England produced no native violin composers or players of
international importance, but supported many foreign
violinists, notably Italians, the most important of whom
was probably Francesco Geminiani (1687–1762).

Changes in the fittings of the violin and especially in the
bow were aimed to satisfy a refined and expanding technique, a desire for increased *cantabile*, and a need for greater
power to fill larger halls and compete with a larger orchestra. For the first time, too, works seriously devoted to violin
instruction appeared, the first important ones being Geminiani's *The Art of Playing on the Violin* (1751) and Leopold
Mozart's *Violinschule* (1756). A number of changes took
place in the violin. Stradivari abandoned his 'long' model
(1690–1700) and the 'classical' model he made afterwards
has never been surpassed, while the mature work of Guarneri del Gesù harks back to the strength and vitality of
Maggini and Gasparo da Salò. Other Italian cities had
already become important centres of violin-making, especially Venice (Gofriller, Serafin), Milan (Grancino, Testore),
and Naples (Gagliano). Makers in France and the Low
Countries followed Italian models, while in Germany the
numerous Klotz family, and many others, adhered to
that of Stainer; in England Stainer influence became very

strong early in the century and remained so until near its
end.

*

The old bow, brought to a high state of perfection by
1750, showed several distinct types, including the long,
straight sonata bow of the Italians, the relatively short dance
bow of the French, and the outwardly curved German bow.
The greater convexity of the German bows and the polyphonic style common to German violin music (e.g. Bach's
unaccompanied sonatas) have given birth to a plausible but
completely erroneous theory of a 'Bach bow'. According
to this, Bach used a flat bridge, a bow of exaggerated convex
arch, and the old thumb-under-hair bow grip of French
dance music, single notes being played by tightening the
hair with the thumb, and multiple stops by releasing the
thumb pressure. This theory has been disproved time and
again by every serious student of violin-playing on historical
musical, and anatomical grounds. The origin of the theory
may be attributed to insufficient historical knowledge, a
misunderstanding of the meaning of the notation, and
the immense difficulties of playing the chords of the Bach
sonatas as written. The fact is that the 'paper polyphony'
of these works is an idealized version of what the violin could
actually play, and this particular music was not intended to
imitate the organ by sustaining continuous chords, but to
suggest the polyphonic web by arpeggiating the notes of
most triple and all quadruple stops rapidly one after the
other. The irony of the 'Bach bow' is this: in order to put
theory into practice, the Bach-bowers have been obliged to
design and build a modern mechanical monster of a bow
which never existed before.

The change from the old to the modern bow cannot be
traced in detail. The Tourte family had much to do with it;
so, in all likelihood, had the violinist Wilhelm Cramer
(1745–99) and John Dodd (1752–1839), the greatest
English bow maker, believed to have arrived independently
at the same results as Tourte. For this bow of greater weight,

strength, and elasticity Tourte chose Pernambuco wood as
the ideal material, and standardized its length as already
noticed (p. 108). The pronounced inward curve of the new
bow required a higher (and consequently heavier) head to
prevent the hair from touching the stick. Tourte's design
for the head became universally accepted, its additional
weight being counterbalanced by that of the modern nut
(Fig. 24) which replaced the old one with its narrow open
face. The slide covering the face, and the ferrule and wedge
securing the hair on the tongue of the modern nut are said
to have been Tourte's invention, but this is uncertain. (That
Viotti assisted Tourte in perfecting the bow is a legend
which cannot be verified, but it is true that makers have
always been influenced by outstanding players.)

Up to the early eighteenth century the violin was commonly held at the breast or at the collarbone against the
neck. With these rather loose grips, shifting of the left hand,
particularly downwards, required an adroit manipulation
of thumb and wrist on the comparatively thick neck. Leopold
Mozart had this in mind when he remarked that the collarbone position 'looks well but is insecure', advocating
rather a steadying of the violin by holding it under the chin,
slightly to the right of the tailpiece. The old French under-
hair bow grip was still used, largely for dance music, but
gradually became obsolete after 1725 as the French accepted
the Italian sonata which required the Italian grip. As a rule,
the stick was still grasped well above the nut (as by Geminiani, Pl. 8b), but one of Leopold Mozart's plates shows a
bow grip close to the nut.

The solo sonata and concerto brought elaboration of the
left-hand technique. The seventh position was the normal
limit for good players about 1750, and by the end of the
century the fingerboard had been extended to accommodate passages an octave higher. Various solutions to
fingering problems were proposed, including Geminiani's
use of different fingers for successive chromatic notes
(fingered chromatics), a solution so advanced that it had

to be rediscovered in the twentieth century. Especially interesting was the idea of linking fingering to tonal effect. The open strings were more and more avoided in order to preserve uniformity of tone colour, and frequently passages were played entirely on one string to preserve one tone colour throughout, even if this meant playing in higher positions. Passage work became more complex, double-stops of all kinds were prevalent, while composers demanded successive trills – in thirds and even in sixths. The 'Devil's Trill' in Tartini's sonata of the same name is a good example of a complex passage combined with a trill. Among special effects the French used harmonics with particular relish. Mondonville (*c.* 1738) lists all the natural harmonics and L'Abbé le Fils (1761) gives all the natural and artificial harmonics in common use today. An intense interest in bowing is evident in the treatises and in the number of studies devoted to it. Leopold Mozart gives an astonishing variety of strokes, including the slurred *portato* and even a species of 'flying staccato', and these bowings more and more become indicated by specific signs. A favourite device for presenting varied bowings was the theme and variations, such as Tartini's *L'Arte del arco* (fifty variations on a theme of Corelli).

The old bow prevailed until well past the middle of the century. Compared with the modern bow, its basic stroke had less momentum but more 'give', since the hair was more yielding. Consequently, the stroke began with a barely perceptible crescendo as the 'give' was taken up and the bow fully weighted into the string. The result was a stroke clearly articulated. Compare this with the modern bow-stroke, the ideal of which is the 'seamless' legato, continuously welding one stroke to the next without perceptible articulation. The old bow was also very responsive to delicate and varied nuance, rapid detached bowings in the upper half, and complicated bowing patterns across the strings. The modern bow was evolved in response to musical changes which occurred after the death of Bach and Handel. The new style called for a predominant melody with supporting harmonies, and the new bow with its greater momentum and elasticity was well adapted to this *cantabile* style. Also it was more powerful, and its strength and the quicker take-up of the hair permitted *sforzando* effects such as *martelé*, which had been rare previously. Similarly the elasticity of the bow and the tautness of the hair permitted new varieties of bounding and thrown strokes. Moreover, whereas the earlier music – and consequently the earlier bow – made elaborate use of nuances of short duration, the new musical style called for long crescendos sometimes bars in length, such as the 'Mannheim crescendo' in that orchestra after 1750. The new bow could bring more power to bear upon these effects because it was longer, stronger, and wider in hair*. It is a mistake, however, to imagine that the old bow was always played with ladylike delicacy. Leopold Mozart advocated teaching a strong 'manly' stroke, and this stroke, coupled with dynamic 'divisions' – here meaning long strokes on a single note with different combinations of crescendo and diminuendo (in French: *sons filés*) – aimed at achieving purity of tone, to which, with expression in general, technique was subordinated in the best instruction. Vibrato was used still as an ornament to certain notes, though in Geminiani's case, in a continuous manner 'as often as possible'.

\*

About 1800, the violin underwent its last important transformation. With the decline of the old patronage system, instrumental music shifted from the private chambers and ballrooms of the aristocracy to the public hall, and as musicians came to be paid by the middle-class audiences of the commercial concert, both audiences and hall had to be big enough to pay the fees of touring virtuosi like Paganini. The star system became part of concert life – it had flourished in opera long before – and in these circumstances the

* The usual width of hair band in an old bow is $\frac{1}{4}$ in.; in a modern bow, $\frac{7}{16}$ in.

violin needed greater power and brilliance to fill the large
halls and, in a concerto, to compete with the larger orchestra of the nineteenth century. These qualities were made
possible by the greater tensions resulting from slightly
higher playing-pitch, a heightened bridge, and a playing
length of string increased by $\frac{1}{4}$ in. to $\frac{1}{2}$ in. Various changes
then had to be made in the violin. Up till then the neck, seen
in profile, had emerged in a more or less straight line from
the body, and the fingerboard was raised to meet the
strings by a wedge between it and the neck (Pl. 7). Raising
the bridge, *c.* 1800, would have called for a still thicker
wedge and consequently a thicker neck, but this result
would have been contrary to playing demands, which
required a thinner neck for reasons of facility in shifting
and playing in positions, especially on the lower strings.
Therefore the wedge was discarded altogether, the fingerboard being tilted parallel with the strings, and the neck
tilted back to match with it. It also had to be lengthened as
the playing length of the string was lengthened, and it was
made stronger by being mortised into the top block whereas
previously it had been set flush and nailed from the inside.
The greater tension of the strings produced increased
pressure on the bridge and the instrument, and the old
bass bar had to be replaced by a longer and stronger one
to prevent the collapse of the belly. For ease of playing, the
fingerboard was narrowed at the pegbox end, slightly
broadened at the bridge end, and also somewhat more
arched throughout and elongated to its present length for
increased range. Finally, the chin rest was introduced by
Spohr about 1820, coming directly over the tailpiece, not
to the left side as is usual today. It must be understood,
however, that the developments in the fittings of the violin,
like those of the bow, took place through stages of transition
which cannot be detailed exhaustively here.

Few old violins escaped these alterations, which often
affected their fate and value. The flat-model Stradivari,
designed in the first place for power and brilliance, respon-
ded magnificiently; but the somewhat highly-arched models

of the Amatis and especially of Stainer, whose sweet tone of moderate strength was geared to small halls and chamber music, came off relatively badly. As a result the whole hierarchy of values changed, and the Stainers which in 1700 had sometimes brought higher prices than Stradivaris retreated to second place in the public esteem and in the eyes of violinists, who could not use them to advantage in large halls.

In nineteenth-century violin-making, the Italians continued their old traditions (e.g. G. F. Pressenda), but there was no Amati or Stradivari among them. The Stainer model was largely abandoned by the Germans, and a remarkable development took place in France. Its important contributions to violin technique (and bow-making, e.g. François Lupot, Dominique Peccate, N. F. Voirin) were matched by those of important violin makers. For the first time France produced a violin maker of international reputation in Nicolas Lupot (1758–1824), who took Stradivari as his model. After him J. B. Vuillaume (1798–1875) was celebrated both for his violins and his bows. Another important factor in violin-making was the increased output of cheap 'factory fiddles' manufactured in quantity in France at Mirecourt and in Germany at Mittenwald and Markneukirchen.

Another result of the rise of the middle classes was that violin instruction became more systematized in schools and available to a larger number of students. The French revolutionary Government founded the National Conservatoire at Paris in 1795, and Baillot, Rode, and Kreutzer collaborated in writing an official book of violin instruction for it (*Méthode de violon*, 1803). This and Baillot's enlarged *L'Art du violon* (1834) had a profound influence on the technique and aesthetics of whole generations of violinists to come. A similar centre in Germany was the Leipzig Conservatoire, with which the famous violinist-teacher Ferdinand David was associated. In Vienna, Joseph Böhm and Hellmesberger held similar positions. Technical problems were summarized in books of studies such as those of Kreutzer or

Fiorillo, and numerous Methods appeared on the market. Among the most influential were those of Campagnoli, Spohr, Bériot, and that of Joachim and Moser (1902–5). Only a few details of violin-playing can be told here, for they vary considerably from one school to the next. In general, the violin was held horizontal, parallel with the floor, and braced under the chin at the left side of the tail-piece. After 1820, more and more violinists used a chin rest. The bow, held with high wrist and with elbow close to the body, was grasped in various ways – generally with an increasingly firm finger-grip as the century progressed. Sometimes, as in the case of Spohr, the bow was held at the nut; other times recalling the eighteenth century, an inch or even more above the nut, a practice sometimes even used by Paganini. With a heavier bow that had more momentum and was less responsive to the change of direction, the fingers came into more prominent play, and the little finger was more used to counterbalance the stick when playing in the lower part of the bow.

In the eighteenth century there had been two principal schools, the French and the Italian. In the nineteenth their relationship changed, while the number of other prominent centres increased. The connecting link between the schools of the two centuries was G. B. Viotti (1753–1824). A descendant of the eighteenth-century Italian school through his teacher Pugnani (who in turn traced his lineage through Tartini and Somis back to Vivaldi and Corelli), Viotti had a profound effect on the new Paris school represented by Baillot, Rode, and the German émigré Kreutzer. Viotti taught Rode and was the admired model of Baillot and Kreutzer. Through the great influence of the Paris school on all subsequent European playing, Viotti became declared the father of modern violin-playing. Habeneck, the pupil of Baillot, taught Alard and Léonard, Alard being the teacher of Sarasate. Kreutzer taught Massart, whose pupils included Wienawski and Fritz Kreisler, while Joseph Böhm, a pupil of Rode, taught Vieuxtemps, Joachim, and Dont. Vieuxtemps in turn taught Ysaÿe, while Dont taught

Leopold Auer, who numbered so many of the great violinists of the twentieth century among his pupils.

Meanwhile the Italian school was coming to a close. Among the last of the influential Italians was Campagnoli (1751–1827), a pupil of Nardini, himself the student of Tartini. Campagnoli's teaching was spread abroad by his Studies and an important Method (1791, with later editions and translations). The real end of the Italian school, however, was Niccolo Paganini (1782–1840), who burst like a meteor on the musical horizon. Like Berlioz and Liszt, he was a romantic figure *par excellence*: a mysterious, exciting presence on stage and off, and endowed with an unprecedented technique, Paganini was both a true genius and a prototype of the modern showman. He could arouse audiences to hysterical enthusiasm for a kind of violin-playing they did not completely understand and could scarcely believe. From the evidence of trustworthy musicians there is no doubt that Paganini played in a miraculous manner, although he specialized in, and achieved the best results from, his own music. In fact he did not invent any new technique. He improved what he had learned from his predecessors (particularly Locatelli) and added his own variants, combining and heightening the effect with a kind of playing hitherto unknown for technical perfection, verve, and intense projection of a hypnotic personality. In his music, including the Twenty-four Caprices, the two concertos, and numerous other pieces published and unpublished, Paganini used all the technique of his time in a grand, virtuoso manner, including fingered octaves, *glissandi*, harmonics of all sorts and combinations, *pizzicati* of both right and left hand, trills, the solo on one string, multiple stops, extensions and contractions of the hand, and the *scordatura*. Staccato strokes, ricochet bowings, chromatic effects, and mixed bowings of all sorts were among his stock in trade.

After Paganini, the Italian school practically ceased to exist, the public being engrossed in opera, and France and Belgium assumed the leadership. The Belgian school centred on the Brussels Conservatoire, and around the figures of Bériot, Vieuxtemps, his pupil Ysaÿe, one of the greatest of all violinists, and César Thomson, who in 1898 succeeded Ysaÿe at the Conservatoire. Léonard succeeded Bériot and instructed many influential nineteenth-century violinists.

In Germany, Louis Spohr (1784–1859) was the most important violinist early in the century. He was a pupil of Franz Eck (Mannheim school), admired Rode, and imitated him in certain respects, thus linking the German school to the French and to Viotti. Spohr, although impressed with the technique of Paganini, opposed his 'tricks' and the idea of a continuous vibrato. Spohr wrote an influential *Violinschule* (1831) and a number of violin concertos of which the eighth, '*Gesangsszene*', is still occasionally played. Ferdinand David was a pupil of Spohr, and also the friend of Mendelssohn (whose Violin Concerto owed much to his advice) and of Joachim (1831–1907). Joachim, a pupil of Joseph Böhm (the most prominent teacher of the Viennese school), had an immense effect on violinists and on musical life in general. Superbly endowed and trained, he was as great a musician as violinist – a sad but necessary distinction – and in this and with respect to his musical taste and influence he was the antithesis and peer of Paganini. Joachim was responsible for the revival of Bach's unaccompanied sonatas and Beethoven's Concerto, and he also exerted a considerable influence on Brahms. He was also a fine chamber-music player and a composer in his own right (e.g. his splendid cadenzas, while Tovey considered his 'Hungarian' Concerto an unappreciated masterpiece).

It is difficult today to assess the qualities of the great violinists of the past. Written accounts cannot bring back the sound of the violin as it was played by Corelli, Tartini, or Paganini, and it was not until the end of the nineteenth century that gramophone companies began to make records of famous violinists, among them Joachim, Sarasate, and Ysaÿe. From these few and imperfectly recorded discs one realizes vividly some of the differences between their technique and that of today. Most striking are the economical use of *vibrato*, especially in the German school, and the plentiful use of *portamento*.

The present century has continued the trend towards increased power and brilliance. To hold the violin more securely, in addition to the chin rest various kinds of shoulder pad have come to be used by players who wish to relieve the left hand of any responsibility for holding the instrument in order to concentrate freely upon fingering and *vibrato* (Franco-Belgian school). For more secure grip, the bow has become held close to the nut and with greater firmness. Carl Flesch (1873–1944) gives details of the various bow grips in *The Art of Violin-Playing* (1923, with English translation 1930), and Tossy Spivakovsky, intent on yet greater power, has introduced a still more 'advanced' grip. The arm is held freely away from the body, for a more natural and powerful stroke than could be made in the last century with the elbow close to the body (Pl. 9).

By early in the present century the leadership of the French and Belgian schools, as demonstrated by outstanding violinists like Vieuxtemps and Ysaÿe, had yielded somewhat to the 'Russian school' (if such it may be called), the centre of which was the remarkable teacher Leopold Auer. The names of his pupils read like a roll of honour, including among others Elman, Zimbalist, Heifetz, and Milstein. A somewhat more systematic attitude towards instruction, coupled with the highest musical aims, was taken by Carl Flesch. Ottakar Ševčik (1852–1934), the chief teacher of the Prague School and the mentor of Jan Kubelik, based his system of numberless exercises on an exhaustive exploration of all possible permutations and combinations of the semitone system, applied to violin fingering, bowing, and technique in general. In the United States, violin instruction is an amalgam of European systems, while nowadays students everywhere can hear great players through radio and gramophone as well as at first hand. Whether Heifetz and Oistrakh are greater violinists than Paganini or Joachim is an academic question, but there is no doubt that general levels of playing are far higher today than they were a century ago.

Whilst works like the concertos of Sibelius, Glazunov (A minor), and Elgar required no new technique, the chief developments in the early part of this century were Kreisler's introduction of the continuous *vibrato* on *every* note (but cf. Geminiani, p. 124), and the greater emphasis on attaining a 'seamless' legato bow change. But after the First World War, the advent of new violin music including concertos by Stravinsky, Berg, Bartók, Schoenberg, and others created fresh problems of technique and of mental adjustment for the player, for the new tonal systems undermined the security of an intonation founded upon traditional harmony. Besides, some of this music has deliberately avoided the expressive and the emotional, to which especially the nineteenth-century violinists were so addicted. Where the twelve-tone chromatic scale was basic to the music, problems both in intonation and in fingering arose. Flesch, inspired by Joseph Achron, introduced a scheme of fingered chromatic scales (an individual finger for each semitone instead of a slide as previously). Furthermore, the old 'set' positions, which had been worked out in the diatonic scale-system and related to chord structures, was replaced by a more fluid scheme with few if any set positions, but with many more extensions and contractions of the hand. The latter were absolutely essential in fingering multiple stops in such pieces as Schoenberg's Concerto (see Sol Babitz, *Principles of Extensions in Violin Fingering*, New York, 1947).

As one considers the long and exciting story of the violin, one may wonder what the future holds in store for the instrument. It would be a rash prophet who would see the end of progress in sight. But do words like 'progress' and 'development' really convey the proper notion of the future? The facts central to the whole history and existence of the violin are its power to sing and its contrasting brilliance in passage-work. The various stages of the violin's development over the centuries are but extensions or peripheries of these basic potentials. In this sense, the violin will not fundamentally develop; it will only change to meet the needs of another time.

# II: THE VIOLA

### KENNETH SKEAPING

THE viola is the alto member of the family, and is tuned *a'*, *d'*, *g*, *c*, a fifth lower than the violin.* Whether it preceded or followed that instrument has not been conclusively determined, but the question is not a very important one. The development of its bow and fitting followed the same course as that taken by those of the violin, and will need no special comment.

The earliest known violas, as made by Andrea Amati and Gasparo da Salò, were large, with a body length of anything from 17 in. to 18½ in. Andrea's sons, Antonio and Girolamo, occasionally made a viola about 16¼ in. in length, and may have been the earliest makers of this smaller type, of which several beautiful examples by Andrea Guarneri dated between 1676 and 1697 are also known. Most of Stradivari's violas, although he made few, were of these smaller dimensions, but on several occasions when commissioned to supply a complete 'concerto' which included two violas, he made them in two sizes. The smaller one was called *contralto* and the larger *tenore*; this last was a majestic instrument with the exceptional body length of just under 19 in.

In the course of their general remarks on the viola, the authors of Hill's *Antonio Stradivari* observe that the majority of violas made before 1660 were large (many of the surviving examples have been reduced in size by later hands), while between 1660 and 1700 the small viola was superseding the large one, though during this time fewer violas of any kind were being made. In this period of reduced production, the earlier seventeenth-century five-part writing for strings was being replaced by the four-part grouping which has remained as a standard basis for the strings ever

---

* Viola: Fr. *alto*; Ger. *Bratsche* (from Ital. *viola da braccio*). Older names include Engl. *tenor*, and in eighteenth-century Ital. and Ger., sometimes *violetta*.

since, while the three-part layout of two treble instruments
with bass was maintaining and extending its influence on
musical practice everywhere. The viola came off badly in
this situation, and during the first half of the eighteenth
century it seldom got a real part to play save when the
music was written in solid four-part contrapuntal style.
Otherwise its usual fate was to double the bass, or to scrape
the harmonic leavings of other parts. Violas already existed
in sufficient numbers to satisfy the limited demand, and
between 1700 and 1750 the production of new ones came
almost to a standstill in all countries.

Orchestral development after 1750 did very little to improve the lot of the viola; Gluck's appreciation of the
individual character and value of viola tone in the orchestra
stands out as exceptional in his time. But in chamber music
the instrument made real progress, and the string quartets of
Haydn and Mozart, notably those written after 1780, show
a fully developed and finely balanced texture to which the
distinctive qualities of the viola make their proper contribution. By the early years of the nineteenth century this
influence was extending to the orchestra, as can be seen in
Beethoven's symphonies from the Third onwards, where the
viola parts are enlivened with many a touch in true quartet
style.

Before proceeding to deal with the great and rapid developments of the nineteenth century in relation to the viola,
something should be said about the instrument and its
players during the period after 1750, when the influence of
long neglect was inevitably reflected in the low status and
poor quality of regular viola players. It is obvious from the
comments of Quantz in 1752 that many, if not most, of them
were hardly competent to deal with the very modest demands made at this time, and as the century went on it may
be assumed that anything of any importance which came in
the way of the viola would have been handled possibly by
the rare specialist performer like Carl Stamitz, or more
probably by a violinist who 'doubled' as a viola player
where necessary. Mozart, for example, who was a good

violinist and had served as *Konzertmeister* at Salzburg in the 1770s, often played the viola in chamber music during his later years in Vienna. These were the palmy days of the small viola, and instruments with a body length between 14¾ in. and 15½ in. were in very general use. Although they usually lack the tonal richness of the noble old Brescian and Cremonese violas, particularly on the lowest string, they were well enough suited to the conditions of the time, when the violas still played a comparatively insignificant part in the orchestra, and chamber music had not yet begun to emerge from its proper setting into the more exacting environment of the concert hall. The ease with which such instruments can be handled has always been an attraction, especially to the violinist who also plays the viola, and though violas under 15½ in. are seldom taken seriously today, the 15½ in. to 16 in. sizes still do much useful work.

Attention must now be given to some of the nineteenth-century circumstances in which the foundations of modern viola-playing were laid. In the 1830s Berlioz, coming hard on the heels of Beethoven, was developing the modern orchestra; the Müller brothers were making history as the first string quartet to tour Europe giving public performances of a fine repertory which included the quartets of Beethoven; and also there was Paganini. Though his attempt to exploit the viola as a solo instrument was not successful, Paganini did it a real service when, near the end of 1833, he asked Berlioz to write a major work with a solo part in which he could display his extraordinary powers on a recently acquired Stradivari viola. When Berlioz found that his proposed scheme was not going to suit Paganini, he finished the work to please himself, and in *Harold in Italy* he showed once more, as Mozart had done in 1779 with his *Sinfonia Concertante* K.364 for violin and viola (though in very different circumstances), how peculiarly well the latter instrument can carry solo honours when sharing them with others. Although he never played *Harold*, Paganini did make several appearances with the viola, the first being in London in 1834. It was not very well received by the critics, and after two other appearances in England he gave the idea up. The time was not ripe, nor perhaps was Paganini the man to secure acceptance of the viola as a solo instrument. But the time was certainly ripe for an improvement in the professional status and standard of its players in the orchestra. Nevertheless, conditions remained much as they had been in earlier days, with viola-playing still widely regarded as a legitimate field of activity for incompetent violinists, or as a part-time or emergency undertaking for good ones. Berlioz was moved to protest, and in an open letter to Humbert Ferrand in 1846 (*Mémoires*, Chapter 68), while taking the Conservatoire to task for serious gaps in its training organization, he called attention to the need for specialization on the viola, with the establishment of a class for the proper study of the instrument. In his *Instrumentation* Berlioz also denounced the widespread use of undersized violas in the orchestra.

The growing importance of the instrument at this time was revealing something of a problem. The large seventeenth-century viola had offered no special difficulty to a performer in playing the kind of music then written for it, and the small one had given very adequate service under eighteenth-century conditions. By the middle years of the nineteenth century a situation was developing which ideally called for the tone of the larger viola with the technical convenience of the small one. This dilemma has not yet been finally resolved, in spite of numerous experiments and a continuing controversy which has often generated more heat than light. Good tone, particularly good viola tone, is very much a matter of taste, and much depends on finding the instrument to suit the player. It goes without saying that the player must also be fully capable in handling the instrument. The observations of Berlioz on the shortcomings of viola players did not have much effect, and twenty-five years later, when Wagner's gigantic expansion of orchestral resources was setting a new standard for everyone, he was still complaining, as Berlioz had done, of their general incompetence. Throughout the rest of the century composers persisted in writing for the viola players they wanted rather than for those they had, and as has always happened in such circumstances, their requirements were eventually met, though the progress of reform was slow. For instance, in 1894 the London viola players of the Philharmonic Society, faced for the first time with Tchaikovsky's *Symphonie Pathétique*, protested that their part was unplayable. Significantly enough, it was in that same year that the Paris Conservatoire at last adopted the policy advocated by Berlioz fifty years earlier, and established a special class for the viola.

The present century has achieved completion and consolidation of the reforms demanded by Berlioz and Wagner, and has also seen a considerable development of solo playing. Composers of consequence have written concertos and other works for the viola, and in the hands of many eminent performers it is now making a very strong bid for parity with the violin and cello as a solo instrument. Modern makers have given particular attention to the building of violas, sometimes influenced by the investigations of theorists, or the special views and needs of performers. The very large model instruments made by J. B. Vuillaume in 1855, inspired by the scientific observations of Felix Savart, and the 'viola alto' designed in the 1870s by Hermann Ritter, a player of repute, and made by K. A. Horlein of Würzburg, were experimental essays in viola construction which aroused considerable interest in their day, though they proved to be too large for really comfortable handling in the normal manner and failed to hold their ground.

Coming to our own times, the $16\frac{3}{4}$ in. model designed by Lionel Tertis and first made by Arthur Richardson in the 1930s has since found favour with many players, while in the United States recent experiments by F. A. Saunders and Mrs Morton Hutchins have broken fresh ground with their novel approach to the acoustics of the small viola.* But

---

* For further information see Tertis, *Cinderella no more*, 1953, and the articles by Hutchins and by Saunders cited in the present bibliography (VIOLIN).

it does not yet seem likely that the $16\frac{1}{4}$ in. model of the Amati brothers and Andrea Guarneri will be easily dismissed from the position it has so successfully maintained in facing the problems presented by this ambiguous and fascinating instrument.

## III: THE VIOLONCELLO

### CHRISTOPHER BUNTING

A GLANCE at the violoncello immediately reveals its kinship with the violin and viola. On closer inspection, certain important differences become apparent. The proportions of length and breadth are approximately maintained, but the depth is increased in order to provide an enclosed volume sufficient to give the necessary resonance to the lower notes.

The height of the bridge is proportionally greater, and its curvature is different to accord with the different 'tension-spectrum' of the strings. Briefly, the differences follow three rules: volumes increase cubically, areas by squares, and lengths linearly. Requirements related to the size, angles, and movements of the human frame are the least altered; requirements related to the different acoustics of a bass instrument demand greater alteration. Wood is the material favoured for construction, because the alternation of the winter growth, with its enormous tensile and torsional strength and the great speed of sound therein (permitting the minimum delay in all parts taking up the vibrations, and so avoiding a weakening of responses), and the summer growth of greater pliability provides the ideal 'palette' for the enormous variety of tone-colours and frequencies. For a cello, the choice of varnish is crucial, for it must possess many qualities. It must weatherproof the wood, it must be elastic and homogeneous enough to spread the effects of spot and fatigue stresses, and it must penetrate just far enough to act as an acoustic mediator between summer and winter growth without prejudicing their characteristic modes of vibration.

It may be convenient to explain the reason for the distinctive shape of the cello. We know that the sound from a tuning-fork placed on a rectilinear box open at one end is many times greater than that from a fork not so placed. The vibrating cello strings similarly require an acoustic amplifier, but a simple rectilinear box would favour some notes at the expense of others, and internal reflections, by reason of their symmetry, would tend to 'fight' one another. After much experiment, a system of concave and convex curved reflecting surfaces of constantly varying radii was evolved with the idea of reducing acoustic 'coloration' to a minimum. Thus it will be seen that the cello bouts are not related to a need to make room for either bow or knees; guitars have bouts in a rudimentary form, and it was some hundreds of years after cellos took final shape that they were held in a manner that might suggest that the bouts are cut for the player's knees.

The violoncello first appeared in the sixteenth century, and like the other members of the violin group it derived its vaulting from the *viole da braccio* and its *f*-holes from a combination of two of the older *C*-holes back to back, this having been found to give a better solution in view of the new stress and elasticity patterns, a more harmonious appearance, and perhaps, a symbolic suggestion of greater power. However, Gasparo da Salò was still cutting *C*-holes late in the century. The violoncello's size and purpose stemmed from the bass violin or *Bass Geig-da-braccio* described and illustrated by Praetorius. This unwieldy instrument had five strings tuned *a*, *d*, *G*, *C*, *F'*, and was used largely in church music as a support for the bass vocal line. The violoncello, or 'small violone', probably arose from the need for a bass instrument portable enough to go in procession, and on early cellos two small holes may be seen in the back, through which a cord would be passed, this being associated with a simple form of harness around the shoulders. The loss of the lowest string was evidently considered a price worth paying for the increase in mobility. Italian and French sources of the period quote a $g$, $c$, $F$, $B'\flat$ tuning, following the strict succession of fifths below the violin and viola tunings by way of a low tenor violin with lowest string $F$ which is occasionally mentioned but never became established as a regular member of the family.

One of the earliest cellos known was made in 1572 in Cremona by Andrea Amati in his maturity. Presented by Pope Pius V to Charles IX, who only had a few years of life remaining to him in which to enjoy its sounds, it was given the name of the 'King' Amati and carried his armorial bearings proudly through the revolution two hundred years later, and had a blaze of glory as the favoured companion of the great Jean Louis Duport. The instrument makers were constantly experimenting, and various sizes from a body length of 31 in. to 29 in. were favoured. A cello owned by Robert Haven Schauffler, the eminent musical biographer, was made in 1590 in Brescia by Gasparo da Salò on a small pattern; it had not been subsequently 'cut down'. The early makers favoured pearwood or sycamore, later makers (notably Stradivari) preferring maple. The earliest known cello by Stradivari was a 31-in. model made in 1680. After 1700 he seemed to feel that $29\frac{1}{2}$ in. was more ideal. A superb example made in 1720 became the favourite instrument of Piatti. Also in Cremona, Andrea and Pietro Guarneri made cellos, and, in Milan, Nicolò Amati's pupil Paolo Grancino is noteworthy. This lineage continues through Grancino's pupil Carlo Giuseppe Testore to the latter's son, Antonio. Alessandro Gagliano and his son Nicolò were working in Naples, and in Venice Stradivari's pupil Domenico Montagnana produced some of the finest cellos known; that belonging to the late Emanuel Feuermann was an outstanding example. A pupil of Stradivari's later years was Carlo Bergonzi, and a pupil of Bergonzi was the Tyrolean Mateo Gofriller, an example of whose work is in the possession of Pablo Casals.

The beginning of the seventeenth century was also the beginning of a new epoch in music, and as the century unfolds we see emerging the idea of the solo singer and the solo instrumentalist, and with them the *basso continuo*. The style of solo playing was closely modelled upon singing. Corelli, who adapted the vocal practice of *gorgia* to his violin-playing, also developed the animated operatic *accompagnato* into the *concerto grosso*, and it is here that the violoncello begins to emerge from obscurity. He also employed the instrument as a full and sufficient *basso continuo* for the solo performances that took him all over Europe. Tartini also toured Europe with his own symbiotic cellist, and composed a concerto for the instrument. But, as Leopold Mozart tells us, there was a difficulty, in that the violins of that day did not possess a very powerful tone, and the cello unavoidably swamped the sound of the soloist by reason of its resonance. It was in order to tackle this problem, and also to bridge the gulf pitch and produce a more homogeneous sound, that Bach introduced the *viola pomposa*. An instrument called the *Fagottgeige* had a similar origin.

As long as the cello's role was still a supporting one, the bass viol or viola da gamba could offer a successful challenge, and Leopold Mozart was not the first to prefer its tone, though his motives as a violinist are not disinterested in view of the preponderant resonance of the cello; but when an instrument becomes a traitor to its nature, so to speak, its days are numbered. Ganassi's advice as early as 1542 on the abandoning of frets is a presage of the struggle; the gamba, with this expedient, might try to sing the new style in small chambers, but as music came to be made in larger rooms the superiority of the violoncello began to make itself felt, especially with the palm-downwards bow-hold (though this was initially further along the stick than nowadays) and later the concave bow, perfected at the end of the eighteenth century by François Tourte.

The first known works for solo cello are by Domenico Gabrielli of Bologna (b. 1655), not to be confused with the famous Gabrielis of sixteenth-century Venice. Bearing the date of 1689, they include two sonatas with *basso continuo*, and several *ricercars* for celli unaccompanied.

Pietro Locatelli, a pupil of Corelli, wrote virtuoso works for the cello, and Antonio Vivaldi provided sonatas and concertos. A concerto of his for violin, *violoncello all'inglese* and strings, op. 22 no. 3, has given rise to the same sort of fruitless speculation that has attached itself to the name *cor anglais*. Our fantasies about Italy are usually sun-drenched and full of unsullied happiness; contrariwise, Italian fantasies about England, especially at a time when verification by travel was not as simple as nowadays, may well have been at worst of unrelieved gloom, and at best of mellow fruitfulness. Now there was an English instrument called the 'violet' or 'violetta' which was not unlike the *violetta marina* or *viola d'amore* (p. 189), though it had fewer bowed strings and more sympathetic strings, and it was on this pattern that the Italians developed a whole family of instruments for use where a hollow and veiled quality of sound was needed. What more natural, for these two reasons, than that they should be named 'all'inglese'? Certain it is that in Vivaldi's *Concerto funèbre* in B♭ a *viola all'inglese* is the chief protagonist. We may speculate whether an unholy alliance between the violoncello all'inglese and the viola da gamba provided the generation of the *Baryton*, which appears later in the tale.

The first cello soloist of European fame, and a man of extraordinary genius, was Franciscello (d. *c.* 1750). Gemi-niani relates that he was present at a concert in Rome in 1713 in which Franciscello played an *obbligato* part in a cantata by Alessandro Scarlatti, and that Scarlatti remarked 'Only angels in human form can play like that!' The fame of Franciscello was largely responsible for the disappearance of the viola da gamba as a solo instrument in Italy. Quantz, the most helpful of the eighteenth-century commentators, also heard him at a concert in Naples, and was deeply im-pressed with his artistry, noting particularly his palm-down bow-grip. However, one of the greatest reasons for his success, and for his importance in the history of cello tech-nique, was his development of the thumb position – the use of the thumb as a movable 'nut' (like the guitarist's *capotasto*)

in positions above the junction of the neck with the body.
Somewhat earlier there was a revival of interest in the medieval instrument called the *Trumscheit* or *tromba marina*. It
had one long gut string, which was played entirely on harmonics, the bowing taking place *above* the fingering. One
leg of the bridge was free to vibrate against a copper or brass
plate, and this gave it a brassy sound, which explains some
others of its many names: *Nonnentrompete*, *Nonnengeige*,
*Marientrompete* (for symbolic reasons nuns were forbidden
real trumpets). Mersenne describes the use of the thumb in
playing it, and Franciscello evidently adapted the technique
for his own purposes, although one cannot assume he played
above *e″*, owing to the restricted length of his fingerboard.

The thumb position was brought to France by a cellist J.
Baptiste Stück, alias Batistin, who was born in Florence in
1680 of German parents and was employed at the court of
Louis XIV. Martin Berteau incorporated the idea in his
*Méthode, théorique et pratique, pour apprendre en peu de temps le
violoncello* (Paris 1741). His famous pupil Jean Louis Duport
elaborated the theme in his *Essai sur le doigter du violoncelle
et la conduite de l'archet* (Paris 1770). The aesthetic-stylistic
reason for the thumb position is this: the cellists were trying
to transcend their instruments and achieve the eloquence
and directness of the human voice, and the voice is, so to
speak, 'all on one string'; indeed, in French the first string
is called the *chanterelle*. There was felt to be a need to 'carry'
the music (*portamento*) through the intervals without a break
– and it is the interval and not the note which is the
emotional building-brick of music. If the higher note be
taken on a higher string, it has a sound quality unrelated to
the lower note because of the greater effective string length
and the different tension, quite apart from the different
string characteristics, and a loss of emotional continuity
is felt. However, at a time when ideas radiated geographic-
ally more slowly than nowadays, and in a less sunny latitude
it is not surprising to find a land where the older aesthetic
still predominated: where music was more 'instrument-
bound', the aspiration mainly religious, and higher notes

meant higher strings. It is interesting that, to this day, German cellists seem to have a preference for taking intervals across the strings rather than up them. ('Up' here refers of course to the pitch, the actual hand movement being towards the floor.)

Early in the eighteenth century, a combination of events in Germany led to the cello receiving its greatest benediction. In 1713 the frugal Friedrich Wilhelm I of Prussia disbanded his *Hofkapelle* in Berlin, and the best of the outstanding musicians belonging to it were promptly engaged by Prince Leopold of Anhalt-Cöthen, liberal funds for the purchase of fine instruments and the provision of copyists being made available. This enlightened potentate, hearing of the dissatisfaction of a highly gifted court organist at Weimar with his working conditions, invited him to take over his new star-studded *Hofkapelle* as conductor, composer, organist, and viola player. J. S. Bach entered three of the happiest years of his life, only leaving Cöthen on the death of his wife in 1720. Among the instrumentalists of the court were Josephus Speiss, a violinist who inspired the noble concertos and who succeeded Bach as *Kapellmeister*, amd Bernhard Christian Linigke, described as an 'outstanding' cellist – indeed he must have been, to have inspired and played the six suites for cello solo without accompaniment. *Scordatura* is employed in the fifth of these, the first string being lowered by a tone to accord with the dark mood. The *accordatura* of the sixth suite is *e'*, *a*, *d*, *G*, *C*, although nowadays it is usually played with four strings. Various errors about these suites have wide currency. They were not written for the Abels, the court gambists, and they are not sonatas but truly French-style suites. The sixth was not written either for the viola pomposa or for the *violoncello piccolo* (a small cello also tuned *e'*, *a*, *d*, *G*, *C*,) though it may of course have been at some time played on these instruments. Tastes vary with the times, and Schumann even saw it as his duty to provide the suites with pianoforte accompaniments.

The emergence of the cello did not pass without protest. In 1740 Hubert Le Blanc, a French Doctor of Law, published a counterblast entitled *Défense de la Basse de Viole contre les Entreprises du Violon et les Prétensions du Violoncel*. Therein he permits himself:

> The violoncello, that until now has been looked upon as a miserable, hated, and pitiful wretch, whose lot was to starve to death for want of a free meal, now flatters itself that it will receive many caresses. . . . It conjours up a bliss that will make it weep with tenderness. . . . How dreadful are the thick strings demanding an exaggerated pressure of the bow, and a tension that makes them shrill . . . it sets itself up in an immense hall. . . .

(The implied slur is that its coarse sounds will not bear close scrutiny.) Despite these fulminations the cello continued to develop, and C. P. E. Bach wrote a concerto for it.

In the second half of the eighteenth century what might be called the Duport Axis became established, and its influence upon the whole of Northern European cello-playing and literature was incalculable. The elder of the two brothers Duport, Jean Pierre, was born in Paris in 1741. He made a pilgrimage to Genoa for the sole purpose of meeting Franciscello. After at first demanding a demonstration fee, Franciscello relented on hearing that the young cellist had spent all his money on the fare. He played for an hour, and an inspired Jean Pierre returned to Paris with enthusiastic descriptions. Never before or since can one hour have been so portentous for the development of cello-playing. The elder Duport was called to Berlin and was given an appointment in the *Hofkapelle* of Frederick the Great, and was later solo cellist and *Kapellmeister* to Friedrich Wilhelm II. Thus he came to have a great influence on both Mozart and Beethoven. The former's three quartets, K.575, 589, and 590, dedicated to the King, show a knowledge of advanced cello technique, as do also the Two Sonatas for piano and cello, op. 5, with the same dedication, by Beethoven. These were times when composers of the greatest genius did not feel it an indignity to acquaint themselves with the possibilities, limitations, and nature of the instruments for which they wrote.

Duport's younger brother, Jean Louis, born in 1749, was destined to enjoy an even greater and wider fame. He learnt of Franciscello's thumb-position and bow-hold from his brother and also from his master Martin Berteau. Although based on his court appointment at Versailles, his career took him (and his 1572 'King' Amati) all over Europe. Voltaire heard him in Geneva and said: '*Monsieur, vous me faites croire aux miracles: vous savez faire d'un bœuf un rossignol!*', thus echoing Scarlatti's remark to Franciscello; certainly we have all heard ox-like cello-playing, but also the miraculously different variety that can arouse the jealousy of nightingales. In 1789, Jean Louis Duport fled from Paris to Berlin, where he joined his brother in the royal service. It is interesting to speculate whether, if the Duport Axis had been reversed and Jean Louis had had his headquarters in Berlin, we might now possess cello concertos by Mozart and Beethoven.

From Lucca came Luigi Boccherini, who conquered Europe with his virtuosity. He wrote many sonatas, concertos, and quintets with two cellos which are in effect *concertante* works. He writes for, and presumably played, higher notes than are encountered until at least a century later, and must have employed a much longer fingerboard than was common at that time. It is conceivable that he combined the thumb-position technique with the use of a fifth string.

Haydn also wrote cello concertos, the most famous of which has been the subject of a musicological tug-of-war. It has suffered constantly alternating ascriptions of authorship, convulsive editorial remodelling and downright recomposing, and anachronistic re-orchestration and reharmonization. Now Haydn was an expert player on a South German instrument, the *Baryton*, mentioned above. Resembling in many respects a viola da gamba, and in others the violoncello all'inglese, it had six bowed strings and forty sympathetic strings, of which some could be plucked by the thumb of the left hand; tuning it must have been a nightmare. Haydn wrote upwards of 180 pieces for the instrument, since his patron, Prince Nicolaus Esterházy, was also a player; he composed trios for two barytons and cello, which would have been played by the Prince, Haydn, and the court cellist Anton Kraft. A feature of all instrumental music of the time, even that of a deliberately virtuoso character, was that it 'fell under the hand' (Quantz). In this D major Cello Concerto there are many passages that lie uniquely awkwardly, especially passages in thirds. The *accordatura* of the baryton was $f'$, $d'$, $a$, $f$, $d$, $A$; observe the thirds between strings I and II, and between III, IV, and V. Allowing for *scordatura*, we could derive, with only two slight re-tunings, $f'\sharp$, $d$, $a$, $f\sharp$, $d$, $A$ – a D major chord. One might whisper the suggestion that these facts, taken together, would lead to profitable conclusions as to the real origins of Haydn's D major Cello Concerto.

A great cellist of the period, and father of the German school of playing, was Bernhard Romberg (1767–1841). He was held to be the peer of J. L. Duport, and like him wrote a treatise on the instrument. He secured the admiration of Beethoven, but found himself unable to reciprocate. Beethoven was more fortunate in his esteem of Anton Kraft, for it was repaid with adoration. Prince Nicolaus Esterházy had died in 1790, and Kraft went to Vienna, where in 1793 he became the first cellist of the famous Schuppanzigh Quartet. His place was later taken by the deformed Linke, who was also very close to Beethoven and who first performed the two great sonatas op. 102.

In England the most renowned cellist of the time was the Yorkshireman Robert Lindley, but many reports spoke dismally of his coldness and lack of fire, and in general that he was no match for Duport or Romberg. Greatly esteemed was Benjamin Hallett, whose career reached its apogee between the ages of five and nine. In 1745 appeared the first English instructions for the instrument entitled *Gamut for the Violoncello, Printed by Henry Waylett at the Black Lyon in Exeter 'Change*. It is quoted in a survey of cello history published in 1914 purely for the humorous value of the fingering system advocated. The irony is, however, that this system is identical with that developed by Casals as being the soundest physiologically and artistically, while a further twist is that English cello-playing has suffered enormously from faulty fingering systems.

If one can accept the rather sweeping generalization that the seventeenth century saw the development of the instrument and the eighteenth the development of the technique, one might say that the nineteenth century brought an enrichment of the literature and an exploration of the artistic possibilities, with special reference to the new emotional dimension inherent in the Romantic era. Mendelssohn and Chopin both wrote sonatas for cello and piano, and Schumann contributed a concerto and shorter pieces which reveal an aspect of the cello's character hitherto unsuspected. This finds perhaps its noblest fulfilment in the B minor Concerto, op. 104, of Dvořák, a work instinct with intuitive genius. It is a model of the composer's craft, revealing a complete understanding of the 'lay' of the fingers, of the inherent sonorities of the instrument and of the relationship of these sonorities with those of the orchestra, without inhibiting the complete expression of its full-blooded and naturistic romanticism. Brahms, on hearing the work, lamented 'If only I had been told that one could write a cello concerto like that!' Indeed 'if only', for the cello part in his Double Concerto in A minor is glorious to play and sumptuous to hear, and points to the child that was never born. If he could have lived just two more years and could have been present at the Lamoureux concert of 12 November 1899, he might have heard something that would have led him to incarnate the idea.

The nineteenth century saw many renowned players, notable amongst them the Servais, father and son, from Belgium. The elder, Adrien François, introduced the endpin, thus giving greater freedom of movement and making possible the emergence of lady cellists. In the 1860s Fraulein von Katow from Poland was delighting Paris audiences, and in later times Madame Suggia has been immortalized by the brush of Augustus John. Piatti enjoyed great and widespread fame both as a soloist and as a member of the Joachim Quartet.

Among cello works of the twentieth century it is difficult to point with confidence to many as being positive contributions to the unfolding of the instrument's possibilities. Many of the movements in modern music stem from a deep-rooted fear of the emotions; such a negative attitude quickly turns the cello into useless lumber, and in most atonal works the cello is merely a poor substitute for the oscillating valve. Two works from the earlier decades of the century have stood the test of time and enjoy a vigorous life: the fantastic sonata of Debussy, and the noble solo sonata of Kodály in which the two lower strings are tuned to $F\sharp$ and $B'$. It is a great loss that this last composer with his enormous understanding of the instrument has not given us a concerto, and that his great compatriot Bartók only began to think favourably of the cello as a solo instrument towards the end of his life. However, his Viola Concerto is available in an arrangement by Tibor Serly, and his own arrangement of his early Violin Rhapsody is often played.

Outstanding cellists of this century have been Emanuel Feuermann (b. 1902) and Gregor Piatigorsky (b. 1903). Feuermann had already reached great heights when his life was tragically cut short in 1942, but might well have gone on to attain even greater eminence. The century, however, is dominated by the colossal stature of Pablo Casals, who was born in Catalonia in 1876 and who played in October 1958 before the General Assembly of the United Nations in full session, the President of the United States and numerous ambassadors being present. The concert was broadcast to forty-eight countries, and the olympian splendour of his artistry and the eloquent compassion of his appeal were underlined by a speech of irresistible force delivered to the Assembly. The details of his life may be found in the books by Señor Corredor and Dr von Tobel. An exposition of his enormous contribution to cello technique cannot be attempted here, for his ruthless analytical power is only surpassed by his synthesizing vitality. Similarly, in the field of artistic realization his almost demoniac power to see into the living tissue of the music is dominated by an angelic simplicity in the final presentation. Despite his worldwide fame for more than half a century, his significance as a musician, as a cellist, and as a man has yet to be fully acknowledged and understood.

Since the Second World War many fine cellists have appeared before the public. The trend has been, as in all the arts, to eschew expression of the deeper emotions, and elegance, clarity, and virtuosity have been displayed and gratefully enjoyed. The popularity of steel strings is intimately related to this aesthetic, but Dionysos is not a god who can permanently be banished to the unconscious, and it will be interesting to watch his reinstatement alongside Apollo.

## IV: THE DOUBLE BASS

### ERIC HALFPENNY

THE double bass* also dates from the sixteenth century, but it has always differed from its sister instruments in various respects on account of the practical implications of its size; also like most very large instruments, it has never quite settled to a completely standard form. The average bass stands over six feet high, with a 44-in. body, and shares many features of the violin, including the out-turned corners of the body, the *f*-holes, and the scroll head. Most of the extant sixteenth-century Italian basses, many of which are still in orchestral use, even have the arched back, which many later instruments have retained, though generally it has been abandoned for practical reasons that a bass player well understands. In an instrument of this size and pitch the flat

* On the continent, *contrebasse*, *contrabasso*, etc. '*Violone*' (Ital. literally 'large viola'), which describes the double bass in many eighteenth-century scores, could also denote a double bass viol (see p. 153), and when used today has this latter meaning.

back is in all ways advantageous, reducing the instrument's weight, saving an enormous amount of wood in the manufacture, and rendering the tone less 'close'. It also helps the playing position, the more so through being sloped inwards at its upper part, while the sloping shoulders of the bass are equally necessary for playing comfort. A bass made in pure violin form, with swell back and rounded shoulders, is most awkward to handle. The typical construction is shown in Pl. 12b, in which will be noticed the bar glued across the flat back to take the pressure of the sound-post.

The bass also differs from the violin in being tuned not in fifths but in fourths, the modern number of strings being four, tuned *g*, *d*, *A*, *E* (sounding however an octave lower, following the old convention in music by which a sub-bass instrument plays from the part written for a bass voice or instrument, playing the notes as far as it can an octave lower). Since the distance between two adjacent tones is about as far as the fingers of the human hand can comfortably stretch on a string some 42 in. long, the tuning in fourths gives a diatonic fingering that is somewhat easier than it would be if the strings were tuned in fifths, and also brings the characteristic figuration of bass parts of all ages most conveniently under the hand. The strings are normally of gut, the lower two being loaded with fine copper wire to keep their diameter within comfortable bounds. Latterly, all-metal strings, nylon rod, and metal-loaded 'rope core' have been used, but, as always with musical instruments, the natural substance, whatever its other shortcomings, produces the finest sound.

The bow used exclusively for the bass in France and England, and increasingly in America, resembles the violoncello bow, though it is thicker, heavier, and more sharply curved (Pl. 14b). But all players in Austria, Germany, and Central Europe, and some in America, use the 'Simandl' bow, named after the great nineteenth-century professor at the Vienna Academy who introduced it. The difference between these two types of bow is that whereas the 'French' bow is designed to be used with the familiar 'overhand' technique common to the other stringed instruments, the 'Simandl' marks a latter-day adaptation of the older stance, used for example on the viols, where the bow stick rests above the hand, the palm of which faces upwards. Before the introduction of these two modern types of bow late in the nineteenth century, the bass was played everywhere with the wide, outcurved bow still associated in England with the memory of Dragonetti (1763–1846), its greatest exponent in that country (Pl. 14b). It will be seen that the frog is very wide, in fact so wide that it has to be grasped endways, meat-saw fashion. The chief defect of such a bow, with the instrument as it is strung and fitted today, is the deep and heavy head, and the fact that the hair 'gives' too much under playing pressure, yielding a 'gutty' and rather too 'open' tone. However, there is no reason to suppose that a player of Dragonetti's calibre and using more suitable fittings was unable to produce a magnificent sound with such a bow.

The Simandl bow is a rationalized version of Dragonetti's, similar to it only in the wide frog. The stick itself, longer and far more slender, is given a very marked inward curve, terminating in a small 'hatchet' head, like all other modern bows. The mechanical behaviour of this bow is extremely subtle, for contrary to common opinion, at least in England, it actually requires less pressure than does the French bow in order to make the string speak. It will in fact elicit a clear *pianissimo* sound, even from the heavy E string, with no pressure at all. This faculty of the Simandl bow has an extraordinary effect on the timbre produced; the exceptionally free and undamped vibration of the string develops to the full the bass's ringing overtones, giving a tone of quite exceptional definition and telling quality. This clarity in sustained sounds has nothing to do with loudness. Germans, Czechs, Viennese, and Hungarians like to hear their basses, but it is not any overwhelming power that makes their part sound with such distinctness. On balance, the French bow gives a less satisfactory basic sound, though of course this depends largely upon the player. It has a wider ribbon of hair, and the stick does not flex so freely, and these two factors seem to damp the string's movement rather more. It brings, however, a readier control, and perhaps a wider variety of articulation, at least for comparable effort on the part of the player.

No consideration of the bass would be complete without mentioning the special place that *pizzicato* occupies in its use. The plucked sound of the bass is one of its most characteristic and indispensable effects, and, owing to the weight and pitch of the strings, can be invested with a wide variety of tone qualities from a hard *fortissimo* snap to a soft boom almost capable of a singing *legato*.

Musical instruments designed specifically for playing the bass-voice parts of polyphonic music had been introduced during the latter part of the fifteenth century; the bass viol was the stringed representative of these. Larger instruments for exploring the sub-bass register began to follow about the middle of the sixteenth century, among them the first double basses. Already in 1557 a Parisian musician's inventory included a '*double basse contre de viole*'. At the Florentine *intermedii* of 1565, the instrumentation for an eight-part composition by Striggio included a *sotto basso di viola*, 'sub-bass viola', whether '*da gamba*' or '*da braccio*' not being stated, but Veronese's *Marriage at Cana* (1563, Pl. 18a) shows the kind of instrument this might have been: a still experimental double bass, yet curiously modern with its six-foot height, its four strings, and its independence with regard to form and fittings from the other stringed instruments shown. Meanwhile in Germany, Amman's *Turnierbuch* of 1566 shows a similar double bass, also with frets and four strings, and with *C* sound-holes (instead of *f*-holes, which are on the whole equally characteristic of viols of the period as of violins). These pictures also hint at the early use of the bass not to add a lower octave below a bass part played by a smaller instrument, but to cope with the bass on its own (or in support of singers), bringing the benefit of its weightier supporting tone as well as of any low-octave notes which the player might introduce to add to the general harmonic effect.

A rapid development of the bass by Italian makers in the later decades of the sixteenth century is attested by the surviving instruments already mentioned. Naturally, in Italy, the design inclined towards that of the violin, and four strings (the neck blocks show that they could never have carried more) remained characteristic of the bass in Italy ever afterwards – though for their actual tuning we have to wait until *c.* 1770, when a rare pamphlet, *Principi di musica*, published in Venice and Florence, gives the tuning that is used today. In Germany, to judge by the double bass shown in Praetorius, the instrument was basically like the Italian, with the same six-foot stature, normal string-length, body outline, and *f*-holes; but possibly the influence of the viol may be seen in its longer and still fretted neck, and in the five or six strings, which, however, the players usually tuned in fourths throughout (from low *E*, as today), showing how they understood the special nature and peculiar problems of this large instrument evolved for supplying a solid bass to ensembles of any kind, whether on the older consort basis or with the newer *continuo*. The five or six strings and the fretted neck are still mentioned in Germany even in the eighteenth century, though the use of fewer strings, at least for orchestral purposes, was then fast coming in. In France, peculiarly little interest was shown in the double bass until Lully's time; the largest instruments in the king's band of violins were the ordinary cellos of the time. In England, the Great Dooble Bass' written for down to *A'* by Orlando Gibbons was probably a *double-bass viol*, smaller and shallower than a double bass and built to carry six strings. A few of these have survived, notably one by Maggini, now owned by the Dolmetsch Foundation, 38½ in. in both body and string length. Talbot, *c.* 1697, gives for 'Double Bass Viol' a tuning of a fifth below the bass viol (i.e. *g, d, A, F, C, G'*), which seems appropriate for an instrument of the size just mentioned, and for the performance of Gibbons's Fantasies.

It was not in the character of the period of 1580–1620, having seen the creation of an efficient large stringed instrument of all-round utility, to desist from attempts to go one better. The six-footer once established, an eight-footer followed. The second of the two basses shown by Praetorius is built much like the first but stands 90 in. high with a 56-in. body, which would seem incredible were it not that an even larger instrument has actually been preserved. This is the flat-backed giant bass, once attributed to Gasparo da Salò, now in the Victoria and Albert Museum and shown on Pl. 14a. It is over eight feet high and approaches six feet in body length alone (68 in.). Possibly of this huge kind were the two 'Violdegambaes of an extraordinary greatness' which Coryat heard in Venice in 1607, played with cornetts and sackbuts. Praetorius (1619) describes it as a recent introduction, and seems uncertain how to classify it within the framework of his normal consorts, calling it in the illustration *Gross-Contra-Bass Geig* ('great double-bass fiddle') but in the relevant text *gar grosse Viola di Gamba Sub-Basse* ('very big double-bass viol'). It was, he says, intended for playing the bass in a deep choir of viols in which a small bass viol took the treble part, though he himself preferred to hear it playing the bass, an octave lower than a bass viol would do, in an otherwise normal viol consort and giving at a distance an effect of a sub-bass on the organ.

Though by modern requirements an instrument of this size would be unmanageable, its effect in a large auditorium, playing slow-moving parts, may indeed have been impressive. Again the German example has more strings than the Italian, namely five, tuned as the bass today plus a bottom D string. It ought perhaps to be mentioned that in recent years certain authorities have sought to label the six-foot bass a debased derivative of the viol – chiefly on account of its back and shoulders, Praetorius's terms *Violone, gross Viol de Gamba-Bass*, and a viol-tuning that he suggests for it; and at the same time to label the eight-footer the 'true' double-bass violin.

The history of the double bass for the next two centuries is mainly one of abandonment of the German excess of strings. Speer, in 1697, gives three strings (*f, c, G*) or four (as tuned

oday). Quantz recommends four strings, adding that
he 'so-called German Violone with five or six strings is
ightly discarded', though later in the eighteenth century,
Schubart (also Leopold Mozart in his second edition) cites
the continued use of the five-stringer, sometimes fretted, for
solo use and in trios, etc. But Mozart adds, 'I have observed
that in accompanying with any strength for the purpose of
expression, two strings are frequently to be heard simultaneously on account of the strings being thinner and lying
nearer together than those of a Bass strung with but three or
four strings'. It is significant that during these same years,
1785-7, both Schubart in Vienna and Gehot in London give
the three-stringer as the commonest; the bass parts of the
Rococo demanded a different treatment from those of earlier
periods.

The formerly well-known three-string bass (still played in
much folk music) has generally been tuned g, d, G (or g, d,
A). It appears to have been valued for its smartness of speech
and greater sonority at a time when the individual capabilities of different orchestral instruments were being more
precisely exploited. The English school of violin makers
produced many fine three-string basses, incidentally developing certain details of proportion and body size that are
practically ideal. Its great merit, freedom of speech, comes
from the easy clearance of the bow on each string and the
exceptionally light bridge-loading. Richard Strauss himself
praised its noble *cantabile* tone, and recommended its admixture in bass sections to strengthen the bass line. The
Italian four-stringer was only gradually reintroduced – at
first with an enequal tuning g, d, G, D, the fourth string
being regarded as an appendage to the then usual three –
and for a long time both were played together in English
orchestras. The four-stringer, with its heavy E string, is
undoubtedly more 'close' in tone, and calls for greater
finesse in bowing technique. Workable compromises in the
fitting and adjustment have, however, long been evolved
and together with refinement in string manufacture have
brought to the bass a tone quality which at its best is in every

way comparable with that produced by the other stringed instruments.

The more precise requirements of late romantic composers led to a desire for an instrument capable of descending to low C, sounding an octave below the lowest note of the cello, not only for new effects, but to satisfy the literal outline of the many passages in the concert repertory which go below E with the cellos. It is a moot point whether these very low sounds are really necessary, or justify the trouble needed to obtain them. Even if occasionally obliged to double cellos at *unison*, the bass still adds to the ensemble a quality and weight which have nothing to do with the actual pitch of the sounds. The demand has, however, been met, and in two different ways: by the addition of a fifth string tuned a third or fourth below the E; or by a mechanism called the 'C string attachment'. The first, unless carefully adjusted, is inclined to overload the bridge, which must be heavier and wider, and even so the strings stand rather closer together and there is less bow clearance between them. The second has the merit that the instrument is strung exactly as before, save that the E string is carried upwards to the extreme top of the head so that it is proportionally lengthened to give C with its normal tension; a mechanism with touchpieces beside the neck in the normal left-hand position 'fingers' the semitones between C and E, and can be switched off to clamp the string at the nut when the instrument is played as an ordinary four-stringer.

# 7. *The Fretted Instruments*

THIS is a group of instruments with vastly differing fortunes. Some have risen in history to one splendid zenith and thereafter have declined, to be forgotten until the modern period of revival. The classic example here is the lute. How many of the last six or seven generations have heard the sound of this instrument, whose name and appearance poets and painters have made so familiar? Yet four centuries ago the place of the lute in musical life in many ways foreshadowed that of the pianoforte in modern times, both as the chief instrument of the home and as the first instrument for the professional virtuoso of international fame. In importance to the history of music, the lute certainly comes first among the fretted instruments by virtue of the immense and valuable quantity of music of all kinds that was written and published for its wide ranging multitude of devotees. Other instruments tell a different story, never having matched the lute's fame, but having perennially floated upon the waves of lighter fashions and surviving because somebody has always wanted them, the classic example here being the guitar. This instrument has in the long run proved the most successful of the whole tribe, and it is therefore appropriate to devote a large part of this chapter to describing its forms and its musical repertory, although musical chronology as well as its past preeminence demands that we begin with the lute.*

## I: THE LUTE

### MICHAEL W. PRYNNE

THE classic form of the lute may be seen in Pl. 15. The instrument was introduced into Europe from Arab

* Fr. *luth*; Ital. *liuto*; Ger. *Laute*. N.B. also, older Fr., Ital. *mandore*, a small lute. Guitar names are clear, but less so are those of the Cittern (medieval Eng. *citole*), Fr. *cistre* (cf. *cithare*=lyre, zither); Ital. *cetera* (a zither being *cembalo*); Ger. *Sister*, formerly *Zitter* (whence mod. *Zither*). Viols: Fr. *violes*; Ital. *viole da gamba*; Ger. *Violen* or *Gamben*.

civilization towards the end of the thirteenth century, one of the earliest mentions of it being in the *Roman de la Rose*. As depicted in many European works of art in the fourteenth century it is still the 'Arab' instrument with four strings struck with a quill or plectrum. By the middle of the century these strings became four pairs or 'courses'. With the fifteenth century more detailed information becomes available: the tuning of the courses is given as $d'$, $a$, $f$, $c$ – i.e. with an interval of a third between two fourths instead of the Arab tuning in fourths throughout – and a treble $g'$ (usually single) is added. There was no absolute pitch: the old instruction books agree that the treble string should be tuned as high as it will stand and the others tuned from it. The fifteenth century also saw the abandonment of the plectrum (with which lutes had been played since ancient times) in favour of playing with the fingers, and by 1500 the general adoption of a sixth course in the bass $(G)$ completed what came to be known as the 'old tune' of the lute: $g'$, $d'$, $a$, $f$, $c$, $G$ (sometimes given a tone higher). Variations in the number of courses were known, but Virdung (1511) gives the six-course instrument as the most usual.

By this time the lute had attained a perfection of form and construction that has never been improved upon. Despite the great size of its resonance cavity, a good lute is unbelievably light. The ribs that make up its swelling pear-shaped body are often thinner than $\frac{1}{32}$ in. The belly, of the finest pine, with an intricately carved sound-hole or 'rose', is from $\frac{1}{12}$ in. to $\frac{1}{16}$ in. thick, with up to six or more transverse bars glued underneath to strengthen and increase the resonance (Pl. 15b); it is largely on the quality of the belly wood and the skill of the barring that the tone depends. The broad neck is attached to a small light block of wood on which the upper ends of the body ribs are gathered. The bridge is glued to the belly and the strings are tied to it. Gut frets are tied round neck and fingerboard, their correct spacing being one of the lutenist's necessary skills. For balance, the bent-back pegbox has to be as light as possible with very slender pegs or 'lute-pins'. Many museum lutes

re forgeries, reproductions intended for collectors and
heavy and dead in tone. A good lute trembles in the hand in
response to sounds as slight as the speaking voice. Owing to
his fragility, surviving instruments are far from common.
The earliest school of lute-making to have left examples, and
the most famous of all, is that of Bologna, where most of the
makers were of German extraction. Laux Maler directed
an important and prolific establishment there between 1518
and 1552; his son Sigismond Maler, Hans Frei (Pl. 15b),
and Nikola Sconvelt were other makers of repute. These old
Bologna lutes kept an almost legendary reputation for some
200 years. By about 1600, other makers were becoming
famous, Wendelin Tieffenbrucker and Michael Hartung,
for example, in Padua, Magno Dieffopruchar and others in
Venice, and Roman makers such as Buechenberg for theor-
boes and *chitarroni*.

The notation of lute music dates from the second half of
the fifteenth century, and takes the form of 'tablature', in
which the letters of the alphabet or numbers indicate on
which fret of which course each note is to be played. The
older German system, said to have been invented by the
blind organist Paumann (d. 1473), used different letters
throughout, but the systems in other countries use a stave
on which the lines (or the spaces between them) represent
the courses, and letters or numbers specify the fret required,
thus 'a' (or o) for the open string, 'b' (or 1) for the first fret,
and so on. In Italian and Spanish tablatures numbers
specify the frets; in the French, which the English also used
and which came to supersede the others, the top line represents the top string and letters are used for the frets (see
the example on next page, from Thos. Robinson, 1603).
Symbols standing above the stave indicate the rhythm of
the piece rather than the value of each note.

The earliest printed lute-books were Italian. Italy remained the most prolific producer of such books throughout
the sixteenth century. It is clear from the accomplished
liveliness of much of this music in, for example, the dances
of Dalza (Petrucci, Venice 1508), the improvisational

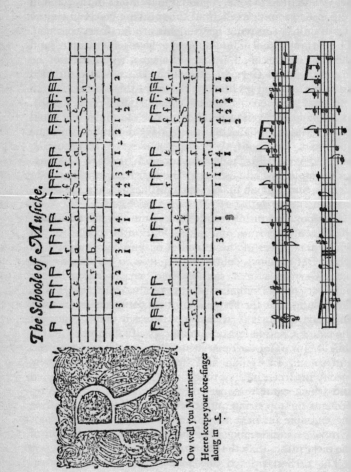

*The Schoole of Musicke.*

Ow well you Marriners.
Heere keepe your fore-finger
along in ♭.

*ricercari* of Spinaccino (1507), and the noble fantasias of Francesco da Milano (various books from 1536 onwards), that the art of lute-playing was already highly developed. The earliest German tablature, that of Schlick (1512), has its own distinctive yet no less well developed character, maintained in the volumes of Judenkünig, Gerle, and Newsidler. Spain's musicians played the vihuela (p. 168), a guitar rather than a lute, although its tuning was that of the lute and its music, from Luis Milan's *El Maestro* of 1536 onwards, has all the easy confidence of the lute tradition.

As the sixteenth century proceeded, the published music developed an international character which reflects the wide reputations and in some cases the consequent travels of many of the greatest lutenists. The works of Francesco da Milano were published in France and the Netherlands as well as Italy, and those of Albert de Ripe (*d.* 1552), a Mantuan who was lutenist to two French kings, were published by a French pupil. The Hungarian Bakfark had works published in Lyon, Cracow, Paris, and Antwerp. This international character is most strongly marked in the music of the lute's golden age from about 1590 to 1630, when great collections were published, such as Besard's *Thesaurus Harmonicus* of 1603, with over 400 pieces from all over Europe. This was also the age when the lute song flourished, beginning with Adrien Le Roy's *Livre d'airs de cour* in 1571 and reaching its greatest heights in the lute Ayres of the English school, those of John Dowland in particular, the greatest lutenist of his day. England saw little solo lute music published, but recent editions give rewarding glimpses of the great riches that survive in manuscript collections.

When in 1600 the French lutenist Francisque published his *Trésor d'Orphée* he marked several pieces '*à cordes avalées*', an indication symptomatic of a dissatisfaction with the old tuning (and found as early as 1553). Even in the golden age there was a tendency to add to the bass; Dowland wrote for a stopped seventh course (*D*), but three bass courses were often added (*C* or *D*; *E♭* or *E*; *F*) and by 1630 as many as six were not unusual. This trend arose from the extensive use of the lute as a *continuo* instrument in instrumental groups where a good strong bass was required. Already in the second half of the sixteenth century a larger form of lute – the *theorbo* – had been invented, with a longer string-length and with still longer bass strings carried on a second peg box and lying off the fingerboard to be struck unstopped (Fig. 29). Unlike the lute the theorbo generally had single strings throughout and no double courses. In its extreme form, the 'Roman theorbo' or *chitarrone* (Fig. 30), the basses were over 5 ft long, while the 'Paduan theorbo' was similar, but with a very large body, awkward to hold. The longer string-length of these 'archlutes', as they are often called, meant wider-spaced frets, which precluded the rapidly fingered passages that formed so large a part of lute technique, and although some solo music exists for the theorbo, the instrument owed its survival almost to the end of the eighteenth century to song accompaniment and *continuo* use.

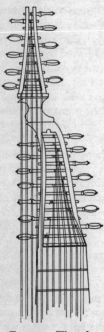

FIG. 29. Theorbo, detail of neck

The double-strung lute survived the coming of the theorbo, but became somewhat modified. A second pegbox was added to carry longer bass strings (as in the theorbo) but the double courses and the closer frets of the earlier lute were retained. This instrument, the 'theorbo-lute', is associated with the French lutenists, including the Gaultier cousins, Jacques and Denis, whose highly brittle ornamental style dominated most seventeenth-century playing and even left its mark on keyboard style. It was for this school, and its followers in England and Germany, that the new tunings were developed.

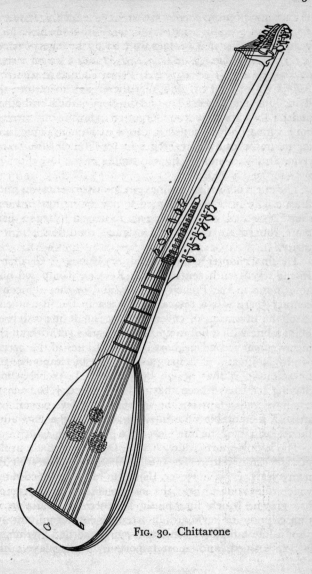

Fig. 30. Chittarone

Francisque's tuning *à cordes avalées* was $g'$, $d'$, $bb$, $f$, $Bb$, $G$, $F$, $Eb$, $B'b$ (i.e. with three extra courses). Within the next thirty years three other new tunings were tried: the 'sharp' ($e'$, $c'$, $a$, $f$, $c$, $G$), the 'flat' ($g'$, $e'$, $c$, $a$, $e$, $B$), and the *accord nouveau ou extraordinaire* ($f'$, $d'$, $a$, $f$, $d$, $A$). When Thomas Mace wrote *Musick's Monument* in 1676, a pathetic plea to restore the dying lute, it is rather sad to find the glory of the Elizabethan and Jacobean lute tradition forgotten in favour of a twelve-course theorbo-lute, tuned in the 'Flat French Tune', and for its music dull dry exercises in the French fashionable style. Strangely enough the old tuning of the lute did persist – in the theorbo itself.

The effect of the new tunings on old instruments was often drastic. Old lutes were adapted to new stringings and tensions, re-necked, re-bridged, even re-barred to make them more robust. An old lute in original condition is now a rarity.

The final chapter in the lute's history belongs to Germany. In the seventeenth century Esias Reussner composed notable music in the French manner, and in the eighteenth century there was a revival of interest in the instrument. Also, the invention of covered strings made it possible to build a lute with a full range of extra basses yet without the inconvenient second pegbox. The finest lutes of the period are by Hoffmann of Leipzig and Schelle of Hamburg; the finest music is that of the Bohemian S. L. Weiss, whose playing may have been that which inspired J. S. Bach to compose and adapt for the instrument a few pieces that strike a memorable note in what seemed for a long time thenceforth to be the lute's last days.

The loving efforts which Arnold Dolmetsch made in the present century to revive the lute bore but little fruit for many years. Now, however, thanks to radio and recordings which allow one to hear the instrument properly, interest has grown. Much lute music has become available in transcription for keyboard, in arrangements for guitar, and also in lute tablature. More and more recorded lute music is being issued, and, most important of all, players like

Julian Bream and Walter Gerwig are bringing the instrument to the notice of thousands for whom the lute had previously been no more than a name out of the past.


## II: THE GUITAR AND OTHER
## FRETTED INSTRUMENTS

### ALBERT BIRCH

ALTHOUGH no other fretted instrument ever rivalled the lute either in reputation or in the favour of composers, it should not be thought that it ever stood alone. Even during the period of its supremacy, other fretted instruments were very much in use, among them the guitar. The explanation of the coexistence of the lute with such other instruments may lie in the very qualities of the lute itself: its readiness of response, its delicacy of tone, and its aptness for intricate expressive playing were products of an extreme fragility of construction and of the use of thin strings of delicate materials. Where conditions demanded greater robustness and greater ease of maintenance or of playing, then other instruments might be preferred, for instance in more popular kinds of music. Sturdier construction, more convenient shape to manage, simpler tunings, fewer courses, metal strings less temperamental than gut or silk, and a less exacting technique of playing – all these advantages were available to a greater or lesser degree in a variety of instruments, some of them medieval survivals, others adaptations, and yet others new inventions. This tendency is apparent throughout the history of the fretted instruments: a stronger, simpler, and more convenient instrument has been available for the less skilled performer in the rougher conditions of popular music.

The Elizabethan age in England offers many examples of the use of various fretted instruments. Thomas Morley's

Consort Lessons (1599) are written for violin, bass viol, flute, for three plucked instruments: lute, cittern, and pandora. The *cittern* (Pl. 17a) was much in vogue; its flat back made it easy to hold and convenient to hang on the wall of the barber's shop with which it is so often associated in literature. Its tunings ('French': *e′, d′, g, a;* 'Italian': *e′, d′, g, b,* or sometimes with five courses *e′, d′, g, a, d*) were re-entrant, with the fourth course higher in pitch than the third, as on the modern ukelele and similarly giving a wide range of easy chords. The bright tone of its wire strings stood out well in consort with other instruments or when accompanying the less expert voice. It could be played with the fingers or with the easier plectrum. The Mulliner Book contains music for solo cittern, not to be compared with the best lute music, yet indicative of the instrument's popularity.

Several other instruments may be grouped with the cittern as one family, all having the same flat back and wire strings. The belly varies in shape: rounded in the cittern itself, of wavy outline or with three bulbous swellings or 'bouts' in the *orpharion* and the *pandora* or *bandora*. This last was used either as bass in the consort or in accompaniment. The orpharion (Pl. 17b), tuned like a lute, and thus able to replace it, had its frets (of metal as on all the citterns) set on a slant to give a greater sounding length to the bass strings. There were other instruments too, for accompanying the voice or for solo playing, 'stump', 'poliphant', and 'penorcon', but little more than their names have survived. Most of these substitutes for the lute fell out of favour during the course of the seventeenth century, despite additions of strings and alterations of tunings to try and keep pace with the changing requirements of the new music. Only the cittern lasted. Playford published music for it as late as 1666 and with different tuning it had a period of popularity towards the middle of the next century, known as the 'English Guitar' (Fig. 31) and pushed by enterprising makers such as Preston. In this form it survives still as the Portuguese *guitarra*, a folk-instrument said to derive from citterns introduced into Portugal in the eighteenth century.

The Mulliner Book also contains pieces for the *gittern*. This is an early form of guitar, also mentioned for one of the first times in the *Roman de la Rose*, while its medieval four-cornered body, extended to form the neck, is well known in sculpture and illustration; the beautifully carved instrument of *c.* 1330 from Warwick Castle and now in the British Museum, shows this well, though in other respects it has been restored as a grotesque fiddle. The gittern, with four pairs of gut strings

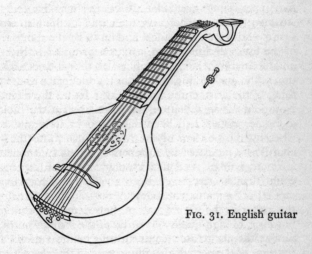

FIG. 31. English guitar

tuned *e'*, *b*, *g*, *d*, and played with a plectrum, was still popular in France and England during the sixteenth century, a sturdy rival to the lute and the citterns, and maintained much of this popularity until ousted by the larger five-course guitar. In Spain, where the lute had little hold, the serious musician played the guitar-shaped *vihuela* (often called *de mano*, as distinct from its bowed version, p. 184) reserving the smaller guitar for more popular occasions. The six courses of the vihuela were usually as the lute's (*g′*, *d′*, *a*, *f*, *c*, *G*), while the guitar was simply a vihuela without the two outer courses. (Bermudo declared that the one instrument could be converted to the other by omitting or adding the two outer courses.) Sixteenth-century composers like Mudarra and Fuenllana wrote for both instruments, elaborately for the vihuela and more simply for the guitar. At some point during the sixteenth century a fifth course became standard for guitar in Spain, and the pitch was raised a tone to give *e′*, *b*, *g*, *d*, *A*, which has remained the tuning for the five upper strings ever since. It was this new five-course instrument which was to carry the name of 'Spanish Guitar' first to Italy, then to France, and on to England in the days of the lute's decline. Then, as virtuosi turned to the violin and the keyboard composers inherited the subtle ornamentation of the lute's music, the guitar found a place as the plaything of the aristocratic amateur, the toy of the dilettante. Notation was in tablature similar to that of the lute, but a simpler system had been developed in Italy and Spain whereby the position of the fingers in forming the usual chords was indicated by numbers or letters (not unlike the harmony symbols used in jazz today). The chords themselves could then be strummed by the right hand to provide a modest accompaniment. Some of the solo music written for the guitar in the second half of the seventeenth century is, however, of high quality. Written in the form of suites with similar themes treated consecutively in the various dance rhythms of the period, this music has a light, elegant touch, now and again with a hint of lute tradition in chromatically treated passacaglias. Roncalli in Italy, and Corbetta, a virtuoso whose travels took him from his native Italy to Spain, Germany, France, and England, are both available in modern editions. But the best includes the delicately contrived work of Robert de Visée, court lutenist and guitarist to Louis XIV; and that of Gaspar Sanz in Spain, whose pieces echo some of the sturdy rhythms of Spanish folk music.

Though fashions change, the guitar continued to be played outside Spain, especially in France. It was there a favourite instrument of the Italian comedians so prominent in French theatrical life during the reign of Louis XIV. Watteau, their friend, painted and drew the instrument with loving care. Two extant guitars built by Stradivari are of much the same pattern as that shown by Watteau, with the sides incurved gently – instead of in the pronounced figure-of-eight of the modern instrument – and the five pairs of strings tied to the bridge glued to the belly (Pl. 16a). The fingerboard is level with the belly, on to which are glued the frets higher than the twelfth. Tuning is by pegs. Many guitars of this period are ornately finished with inlays of mother-of-pearl and ivory; the sound-hole is elaborately worked, and at each end of the bridge is an intricate scroll. Some were adapted to make hurdy-gurdies as a new craze swept the fashionable world, but many were preserved for their decorative value.

The second half of the eighteenth century was for the guitar in France and England a period of decline. Other fretted instruments had their moment of success, like the cittern in its guise of 'English Guitar' and a relative from Italy, the *chitarra battente*, a wire-strung plectrum instrument with the belly and sides of the Spanish guitar but a partly rounded back. Another Italian instrument, that has since remained distinctively national, became known throughout Europe at this time: the *mandoline* (derived from a small-sized lute, *mandora*), which we know best in its Neapolitan form (Fig. 32). This has four courses of wire strings tuned like the violin's and played with a plectrum, but there were other forms, notably the earlier Milanese, which was gut-strung and played with the fingers (Fig. 32). Vivaldi wrote a concerto for two mandolines; Handel and Mozart used the instrument; Beethoven wrote several pieces for the mandoline and piano, and ever since composers have now and then made use of the distinctive, evocative tone-colour produced by its sustained singing tremolo (e.g. Mahler in *Das Lied von der Erde*, and works by Schoenberg and latterly Stravinsky).

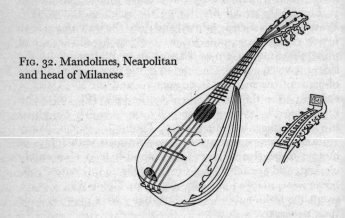

FIG. 32. Mandolines, Neapolitan and head of Milanese

Meanwhile, in Spain the guitar had been established as the national instrument since the sixteenth century; we hear its insistent strumming behind many of the nimble rhythms of D. Scarlatti's Sonatas. Beckford recounts with pleasure how much he enjoyed taking part in the frenzied dancing of the Spaniards, and how much Boccherini deplored the wild, tasteless, and un-Italian music of the guitars which accompanied it; in the hands of Goya's blind singer the guitar is no stage-property but a symbol of eternal Spain. From this background came the next development in the guitar's history, in the form of a series of improvements which extended the tonal range. A sixth course (*E*) was added in the bass; single strings replaced the double courses; and the sound-box was increased in volume by the swelling out of the sides to form the figure-of-eight shape thenceforth typical of the guitar. It was not quite the modern instrument, but there is no basic difference (Pl. 16b). This is the guitar associated with many well-known names, including Schubert, Weber, Berlioz, and Paganini. Germany has so far played no part in the story of the guitar. For one thing, the lute maintained its sway so very much longer there than elsewhere. Yet there was a tradition of guitar-making in South Germany; guitars of Tyrolean craftsmanship dating from the second half of the seventeenth century are in existence, and it seems likely that in some regions at least the guitar played a part in the life of the people, though not until towards the end of the eighteenth century was the instrument well established in the German towns. (The addition of the sixth string has been claimed for the Weimar maker Otto shortly after 1788, but it is likely that this was already in use in Spain.)

By the end of the eighteenth century the six-string instrument was dominant everywhere, while the reappearance of virtuoso players, with their constant search for the perfect instrument, made continual demands on the skill of luthiers in all the principal cities of Europe. Joseph Panormo of London made his best guitars after 1809, when Fernando Sor (1778–1839), the greatest of the virtuosi, had shown him his Spanish-made guitar and made suggestions for further improvement. Experiments by Stauffer of Vienna did not lead to any startling changes in design; improvements of tone were the main object, the basic pattern remaining unaltered. Many beautiful examples from this period are still in use. The shape of the belly varies slightly from a gently curving figure-of-eight to a wider pattern with a more accentuated waist. The woods commonly used are rosewood, walnut, or bird's eye maple for the back (sometimes veneered on to pine); the same woods for the sides; pine for the belly (which is occasionally left unvarnished). The bridge is a small rectangular block glued to the belly, holding the strings by means of six ebony pins inserted downwards through holes in bridge and belly. In Spain, however, the strings continued to be passed and tied through holes in the bridge parallel with the belly. The

fingerboard, of ebony or rosewood, is glued on to a solid
hardwood neck and then on to the belly, continuing to the
edge of the sound-hole (as in the citterns). In Stauffer's
'Legnani' model, this continuation of the fingerboard floats
above the belly (an arrangement often seen in guitars of
Russian make). Heads are of three types: a beautifully
curved solid head with six ebony pegs; a form with geared
machines winding the strings over bone rollers; and an
enclosed type of machine head with all tuning buttons on
one side. Decoration is largely confined to purfling round
the edge of the belly and simple circular patterns of inlay
round the sound-hole.

The furthest departures from this normal type were
adventurous approaches to those shapes of classical antiquity so dear to the interior decorator of Napoleonic
France and Regency England. Guitars shaped like lyres
were very much in the trend of fashionable furniture design
(Schubert's friend, the singer Vogl, used such a lyre-guitar
made by Verdelot of Paris). 'Harp-guitars', 'harp-lute-
guitars', 'Regency-harp-lutes' were among many attempts
to produce decorative and easily played instruments for
the drawing-room, but none had more than the initial
success accorded to novelty; they belong, if anywhere, to
the history of the harp (p. 194–5).

The history of the guitar in the first half of the nineteenth
century was dominated by virtuosi who not only encouraged
the further development of the instrument, but also produced a vast amount of music and did much teaching,
settling where their success was greatest. Paris became the
home of the Italian virtuosi Ferdinand Carulli (b. Naples
1770), Matteo Carcassi (b. Florence 1792), and the French-
born Napoléon Coste (b. Daubs 1806); Vienna claimed for
many years Mauro Giuliani (b. Bologna 1780), Luigi
Legnani (b. Milan 1790), and the finest of the German
composer-players, Johann Kaspar Mertz (b. Pressburg
1806). Of the Spaniards, Fernando Sor (or Sors, b. Barcelona 1780) became a famous figure in English musical
life, while Dionisio Aguado lived for some time in Paris.

Almost all wrote Methods for the guitar, some of which are
still in use. Aguado's and Sor's contain wonderfully constructive material; that of Carcassi, although the most
popular by far, is not so good. Amongst the studies, those of
Sor deserve first mention (they are still essential for acquir-
ing basic technical skill), but there is much lightly pleasant
music in the pieces of Giuliani, Coste, and Carcassi.

In extended forms of music the guitar could, of course, in
no way rival the keyboard. Haydn had used it in an accompanying role in a trio with violin and cello, but there is
nothing from Mozart, and although Beethoven on hearing
Giuliani pronounced that 'the guitar is a miniature orchestra in itself', he wrote nothing for it. Schubert used the
guitar for trying out his songs, but the published guitar
accompaniments are thought not to be authentic. Weber
was a skilled guitarist and wrote a good deal for the instrument, including ninety songs with guitar accompaniment.
On the whole, however, it was the minor composers who
made use of the instrument and the music they wrote,
delightful as some of it is to play, does not rise above the
second-rate; yet the happy Viennese spirit is well expressed
in the sonatinas, bagatelles, serenades, and *Ländler* of Dia-
belli, Hummel, Marschner, and von Call. Berlioz, who
played no keyboard instrument, was fond of the guitar, but
seldom wrote for it. An important name in guitar history is
Paganini, no less a virtuoso on this instrument than on the
violin, but, although he wrote a considerable amount for
guitar, its quality disappoints; in the twelve Sonatas for
Violin and Guitar, in which Legnani accompanied him,
the guitar part is left in a rudimentary form, and even where
he wrote it out in greater detail and with more prominence
it shows little more than superficial brilliance. The best
guitar music of the first half of the century is undoubtedly
that of the guitarists themselves. Sor's more elaborate pieces
contain movements of great merit. Their themes are attractive and competently developed; rhythmically they use the
full resources of the instrument, and the harmony has some
subtlety. Giuliani's concertos and other music for combined

playing were much played for many years, though nowadays it is his smaller pieces that give most pleasure. When in 1856 the Russian nobleman Makaroff offered prizes for original compositions for the guitar, the winners were Mertz and Coste, both composers of real talent whose works are still played.

From this survey the truth must emerge that in the nineteenth century the guitar had not yet won the place it holds in the world of music today. On the concert platform the virtuoso could dazzle the public with the brilliance of his technique, but the musical content of what he played was mediocre, tied to the same few keys and without development of themes in other keys, and thus hardly calculated to interest the fine composer. Nor was the instrument powerful enough to be well heard in the concert hall, except perhaps in the hands of the gifted few. In the drawing-room it was ideal, and this is where it thrived for most of the century: a young lady's romantic accompaniment for ballads; a decorative item rather than a serious instrument. The typical figure of the Victorian guitar world was the dignified Madame Sidney Pratten (Catherina Pelzer), a child prodigy whose public career seems to have established the guitar as that instrument of well-bred domesticity which it remained until Segovia came.

The modern history of the guitar begins also in Spain. A single-minded enthusiast, Francisco Tárrega (1854–1909), forsook the piano to devote his life to the cause of the guitar. Not only did he renew and invigorate the whole technique of playing, but he also extended the repertory with transcriptions of classical keyboard works and of the colourful new pianoforte music of his contemporary Spanish composers. In guitar design, Antonio Torres had begun in 1854 to produce a model which offered far greater tonal qualities than any before, and this has remained the standard to our own day. The body is larger (the maximum width of the belly is $14\frac{1}{2}$ in., about 2 in. greater than in the model described above) and gives deeper response. Special care is given to the making of the belly, which Torres considered all-important, the barring underneath being arranged fan-wise to transmit the maximum vibration. (Fan-barring (Pl. 16c) was not new, having been used in Spain fairly early in the century and a feature of Louis Panormo's 'guitars in the Spanish style'; nowadays it is universal except in cheap models and the guitars of some German and Austrian makers.) The technical innovations of Tárrega are concerned with the holding of the instrument, the correct placing of the hands, and the cultivation of right-hand technique – particularly the striking of the string downwards towards the belly (*apoyando*) instead of plucking, the use of the third finger, and use of nails, not fingertips, to produce the greatest variety of tone. Tárrega's enthusiasm spread to a group of disciples and pupils, amongst whom Miguel Llobet, Emilio Pujol, Daniel Fortea, and Pascual Roch have done much by their teaching and writing to give the 'Tárrega method' universal acceptance. In only one point is there difference of opinion: a few players have followed Pujol's preference for fingertip playing. In his reorganization of the repertory, Tárrega's work is of prime importance, and in transcribing works by Bach, Haydn, Mozart, and Beethoven, such was the evocative power of the guitar in the hands of an accomplished player that the music might even gain by the transcription. Not that Tárrega was always successful in this field; but he pointed the way for the greater Segovia. Of his Albéniz transcriptions it is sufficient defence that the composer himself should have declared that the pieces sounded better on the guitar.

It is of course to Andrés Segovia (b. 1890) that the guitar owes its greatest debt. Tárrega was too shy to give recitals abroad and his influence remained one of personal contact. Not until Segovia began his successful tours abroad did the concert-goers of Europe and America realize what wonderful powers of expression the once-despised guitar had now gained. Virtuosity of the highest order served a musicianship never before devoted to this instrument, while a serious choice of music made a big impression on players and listeners alike. A glance at Segovia's programmes will reveal the wealth of good music available to the guitar player of today: music by *vihuelistas* like Luis Milan and Mudarra, lutenists like Galilei and Dowland, seventeenth-century guitarists like Sanz and de Visée; eighteenth-century music of great variety from the lute pieces of Bach and Weiss to the keyboard works of Haydn and Domenico Scarlatti, not forgetting Bach's sonatas and suites for unaccompanied violin and cello, which fall gratefully under the guitarist's fingers. Of the nineteenth-century composers only Sor is now regularly played. It is, however, more recent music that provides greatest scope for the tonal resources of the guitar, such as the transcriptions of Granados and Albéniz, and the many pieces inspired by, dedicated to, edited, fingered, and played by the master. Segovia has said that he found the greatest obstacle to the development of the guitar in the lack of music composed specially for it and employing its new resources. Torroba and Turina were the first to endeavour to fill the gap, and then in 1920 Falla composed his beautiful *Homenaje* for guitar as a tribute to Debussy, who had himself approached so closely the spirit of Spain. Roussel, Tansman, and Castelnuovo-Tedesco have written intelligently for the instrument, and in the Americas two composers well versed in the European tradition have devoted much attention to it: in Mexico, Manuel Ponce brought great feeling and a thorough consciousness of the instrument's traditions; in Brazil, Villa-Lobos has pursued its capabilities with ingenuity and effectiveness. A few composers have essayed a concerto for guitar and orchestra, and some of their success has no doubt been due to the ability of recording and broadcasting engineers to establish the necessary balance. In England as elsewhere the last few years have seen considerable use made of the guitar as a solo instrument, in songs, and in chamber works, by composers fully aware of its resources and difficulties, and confident that in young players like Julian Bream and John Williams there are the needed interpreters of high competence. The seed sown by Tárrega and nurtured by Segovia is now a richly blossoming plant.

The genius which Torres brought to the making of the concert guitar produced a succession of Spanish luthiers to pass on the traditions of the art: Enrique Garcia, Ramirez, Santos Hernandez, Hauser (Segovia plays a Hauser), Esteso – the list is long and could be made longer. The use of nylon instead of gut and of nylon floss for the wound strings has solved the problem of maintaining and tuning strings. Increased interest and facilities for hearing the guitar have produced many fine players, Sainz de la Maza and Narciso Yepes in Spain; Alirio Diaz in Venezuela; Ida Presti in France; Luise Walker in Austria; Maria Luisa Anido in Argentina; Bream and Williams in Britain, and many other excellent players in both Europe and the Americas.

During the last few years the guitar has once more become a craze. Never before has the classic guitar, as it is now called, attracted so much attention, while there is also a peak interest in the guitar as accompaniment to song and in dance music; in the latest popular outbreak the guitar seems to be a *sine qua non*. Fretted instruments have always played an important role in folk music and the present interest in the guitar owes a good deal to the popular side. In Spain, for instance, the traditions of *flamenco* singing and dancing are inseparable from the guitar. The instrument used in this is not quite the same as the standard concert guitar, being built of woods of lighter weight to give a shallower, more brilliant tone. Pegs are often preferred to machines since the normal hold of the instrument, on the right knee and fairly upright, is made easier with the lighter head. Apart from *flamenco*, in which it is indispensable, the guitar is a regular stand-by in Spain and the Mediterranean and Latin American countries generally for all kinds of accompaniment and concerted playing.

In these warm countries where much music is outdoors, suitable bands of mixed fretted instruments are typical. Instruments like the five-stringed *guitarillo*, the *requinte*, the *tenore*, which are smaller guitars pitched higher than the normal 'bass', are heard in Spain accompanying expressive derivatives of the cittern family like the *bandurria*

(Fig. 33) and the *laud*; of these last, the first is the more important, with six double strings tuned in fourths (*a''*, *e''*, *b'*, *f'♯*, *c'♯*, *g'♯*). In Portugal the *guitarra*, which we have already noticed, still has the 'English Guitar' tuning of *g''*, *e''*, *c''*, *g'*, *e'*, *c'*, and is usually played to the accompaniment

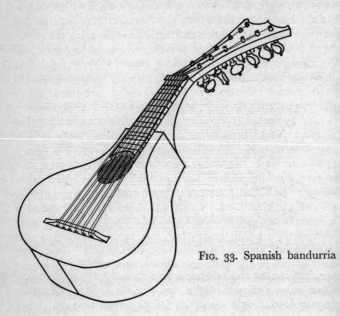

Fig. 33. Spanish bandurria

of the guitar (in Portugal called *viola*). In Italy it is the mandoline that sings the melody to the guitar's accompaniment. In Germany and Austria too there is a long tradition of singing to the guitar; the Christmas hymn *Stille Nacht* was composed and first sung to the guitar in a village church.

The most characteristic folk-instrument of South Germany and Austria is, of course, the *Zither*. This interesting survival of the ancient *Scheitholt* derived its name and some of its characteristics from the cittern during the eighteenth century. It is a shallow box with both sides rounded in the

Mittenwald type but with one straight side in the more usual Salzburg pattern (Fig. 34). There is no neck, the melody strings being carried over a fretted fingerboard on the left (i.e. the straight) side of the instrument as it lies flat in front of the player. These strings, of metal, and tuned either $a'$, $a'$, $d'$, $g$, $c$ ('Munich') or $a'$, $d'$, $g'$, $g$, $c$ ('Vienna'),

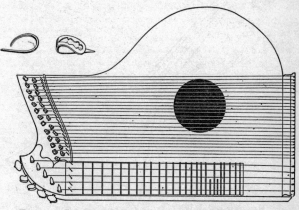

Fig. 34. Salzburg zither with two types of plectrum

are fingered by the left hand and struck with a plectrum worn on the thumb of the right hand. Under the other fingers of the right hand lie from twenty-seven to forty accompaniment strings of gut or nylon, making it possible to play middle harmonies as well as bass. The tuning of these varies according to individual preferences and the effect aimed at.

In Russia the gipsies had long favoured the traditional guitar, particularly with an added bass string to give a rich harmonic bass to song and chorus. Present national feeling seems to prefer a simplified tuning $d'$, $b$, $g$, $d$, $B$, $G$, $D$, to provide easier support for the folk-songs that form the correct repertory. Of the many other fretted instruments of Eastern Europe the *balalaika* is the best known (Fig. 35).

This is made in a variety of sizes, with triangular body-shape and with three strings (tuned *e'*, *e,' a'* in the usual solo model). Balalaika orchestras using a full range down to bass size were heard in Europe and America after the

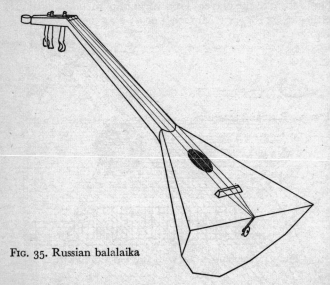

FIG. 35. Russian balalaika

Revolution of 1917. Of other instruments, the *domra*, somewhat reminiscent of the cittern, and the multi-stringed *bandoura* (Fig. 36) have recently appeared in Britain.

The Spaniards and the Portuguese naturally carried their fretted instruments with them to the Americas, and the guitar deals happily with the native rhythms of Brazil, Argentina, and Mexico. In North America the guitar has been the natural accompanying instrument for folk music of all kinds; folk singers such as Josh White, and blues singers like Blind-Lemon Jefferson, have used a rather substantially built guitar, sometimes with its strings doubled, wire-strung for durability but played as often as not with the fingers. The *banjo* is referred to as early as the eighteenth century as an instrument of the Negroes, but there seems to be little doubt that its development and later popularity were the concern of the white man. Beginning as a folk-instrument for playing the nimble rhythms of the fiddle, it developed into an instrument for the amateur (Pl. 17c). Professionally it was heard

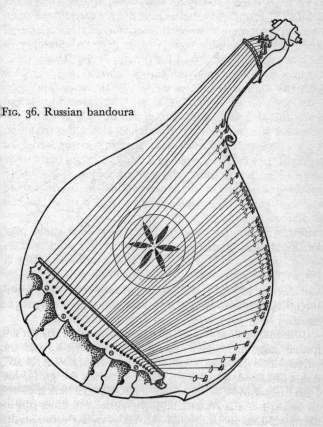

FIG. 36. Russian bandoura

on the music-hall stage and with Nigger Minstrel troupes, but its strength lay in its appeal to the home player. Its music has the bright, four-square rhythms of its original, quick, catchy, unpretentious and limited.

Basically the banjo differs from all fretted instruments hitherto discussed in having a belly not of wood but of vellum stretched over a wooden hoop. Many modifications of what was obviously at first an easily-produced home instrument have been made, the neck now being fretted, while the volume of sound may be increased by covering the open back with a metal or wooden resonator. Many varieties of stringing are available, a sign of its great adaptability to various uses. The standard instrument is the 'finger-style' banjo with five gut or nylon strings tuned $d'$, $b$, $g$, $c$, $g'$, i.e. with the highest string on the left of the bass (and with its peg part-way along the neck). The 'plectrum banjo' omits this shorter string. The 'zither banjo', in which the resonator has been further developed to enclose the sides, is the instrument of the virtuoso, though the standard solos of Joe Morley can be played on either this or the finger-style banjo. For the violinist who wished to play some more suitable instrument in the dance-band of the twenties there was the 'tenor-banjo' tuned in fifths (and if in the thirties he wished to change to the guitar, there was a 'tenor-guitar' with similar tuning). The mandolinist could play the double-strung 'banjo-mandoline' or the single strings of the 'banjoline'. One of the most interesting features of this fretted instrument world is the orchestra of banjos, mandolines, and guitars made up of amateur players and trained to compete in festivals, very much on the lines of the brass band movement.

In the early days of jazz, the banjo was replaced by the '*plectrum guitar*', though it has found its way back to give a period flavour to revived 'traditional jazz'. The plectrum guitar has metal strings fastened not usually to the bridge (which the greater tension would tend to pull away, or cause the neck to warp as has happened to many lighter-built Spanish guitars fitted through ignorance with metal strings) but to a tail-piece screwed to the end of the instrument. A frequent modification is to build the guitar with an arched cello-style belly, and occasionally the body is cut away on the treble side above the twelfth fret to give greater range.

With electrical amplification the guitar loses the disadvantage of quietness and can compete melodically with the loudest. This amplification is done in two ways: by straightforward amplification of sounds already made audible by the resonating chamber of a normally-built guitar; or by the provision of a skeleton instrument in which the vibrations of the strings are converted directly into electrical impulses. All appearance – one might even say all sound – of the guitar seems in this machine to have been lost, but at least it can be said to have frets while it has proved itself as able to deal with the fluent intricacies of modern jazz as to give the inexorable backing of the beat groups – among whom the four-stringed bass guitar has usurped the role of the double bass. In the 'Hawaiian guitar' the frets begin to lose their function. This instrument is played flat on the knees of the performer. Its metal strings are raised higher above the fingerboard than in the normal guitar, and are stopped, not by being pressed down into contact with the frets, but by a steel bar which the player's left hand glides along the string; the frets thus serve only as a guide. The right-hand fingers wear metal or composition tips (as for the Austrian zither). The gliding of the left hand makes possible the *glissando* and *vibrato* effects which are to many people the distinctive sound of this guitar; it is the Spanish guitar introduced by American sailors into Hawaii, where this style of playing was evolved. The *ukelele*, a diminutive member of the guitar family, is presumed to have been similarly evolved from the Portuguese *machete*, and was brought to America and Britain about thirty years ago, when it had some vogue, being easily strummed by the novice and having a convenient tablature of chord shapes. Its tuning (*e.g.* $g'$, $c'$, $e'$, $a'$) is re-entrant and gives close harmony chords. The 'ukelele banjo', and 'banjulele', were simplified banjos with ukelele tuning. The recent skiffle craze brought the ukelele briefly out of retirement, to make one realize how often fretted instruments have felt the ups and downs of fashion, and have suffered from the fickleness of a fond public.

# III: THE VIOLS

## THURSTON DART

THE instruments discussed so far in this chapter have one thing in common: their strings are held against the frets with one hand and are plucked with the other (sometimes with a plectrum). This playing technique is world-wide; it is as normal to fretted instruments as blowing is to reed instruments, and examples can be found in the Indian *sitar*, the Arab lute, the Japanese moon-lute, and such other instruments as the guitar, gittern, cittern, pandora, European lute, banjo, and ukelele described above.

But the development of many instruments may be traced back to a cross-fertilization between one established type of instrument and another established type of playing technique, introduced either as an experiment or through calamity or forgetfulness. Such hybrid instruments are by their nature even more artificial than the basic instruments themselves, and many are hardly more than freaks. One hybrid, however, made a great contribution to the development of European music. Its origins lie in fifteenth-century Spain, home of the flat-backed *vihuela de mano*, the five- or later six-stringed guitar. This instrument was held and played much like the plectrum guitar of the present day; the cross-fertilization consisted of applying to it a playing technique which had always been associated with an entirely different family of instruments, the fiddles, in which there had never been any frets round the neck and the strings were always sounded with a bow. The result was the *vihuela de arco* ('bowed vihuela'), which was to become known throughout Europe during the next three centuries as the *viol* (Pl. 19).

For some time the viol retained unmistakable signs of its parentage. Its standard size was that of the vihuela de mano (tuned $g'$, $d'$, $a$, $f$, $c$, with – later – a sixth string tuned to

5); its playing position was identical with that of the vihuela, the instrument being held across the body, slantingly, and the bow being manipulated rather awkwardly from below, or, more conveniently, from above (see Veronese's painting reproduced in Pl. 18a). By the end of the fifteenth century this soft-voiced newcomer had established itself as a useful and fashionable addition to the world of instruments. It had acquired its standard set of six strings tuned in fourths around a central third; it had bred treble and bass offspring, tuned about a fifth higher and a fourth lower than their progenitor; it had been endowed with the first elements of a repertory of its own, linked with the more solemn kinds of contrapuntal music and with the well-established style of variations on a theme; and it had begun to spread outside its homeland. With the increasing use of the larger-sized bass, Italian players had discovered for themselves that the slanting position and somewhat back-to-front bowing would not do; they therefore adopted a more convenient method of holding it vertically between the legs or knees, whence its new name, *viola da gamba*. This method soon became uniformly used for all the members of the family, including the treble (which was never played under the chin or against the breast like its great rival, the *violino da braccio* or violin).

In 1500 or so the viol still retained the hour-glass shape, with a flat back and belly, characteristic of the vihuela, and preserved in a rather exaggerated manner by the present-day guitar. It retained, too, its 'underhand' bow-grip, a considerable use of double-stops, and its frets; all these, indeed, were to be invariably associated with it throughout its career of nearly another three centuries of useful life, though the outline of its body slowly began to assimilate itself to the features of its younger rival, which by now had developed into the violin family. Influences from this family were probably also responsible for the scroll of the viol's pegbox, the arching of its belly, the introduction of a sound-post, and the ultimate disappearance of the ornamental rose in the belly, which some of the earlier viols of the sixteenth century had kept.

By the latter part of the century, the viol had risen to a
position of unquestioned eminence for the playing of
'serious' contrapuntal music. There are few records of the
violins ever having been admitted at this time to such fields
of musical activity in any country in Europe, though they
retained a virtual monopoly in the supplying of 'light'
music for dancing and merry-making. The viol's homeland
was now Italy, into which it had penetrated both from the
northern ports and courts and from the Spanish-dominated
zones of Naples and the south. Elaborate treatises covering
every aspect of its playing techniques had been published
by Ganassi, a Venetian, and Ortiz, a Spaniard; and the
very fact of publication implies that there was already in
existence a market among amateurs for books of such a kind.
Its repertory had been enriched by at least two Flemings,
Buus and Willaert, and such Italian composers as Tibur-
tino, Lupacchino, and Conforto. It was by no means unknown in France, Germany, Austria, the Low Countries
and the Spanish New World; if you could play a lute you
could, without too much difficulty, learn to play the
viol in consort. Its introduction into England was due
almost inevitably, to Henry VIII's taste for musical
novelties; in the later 1520s he seems to have invited to
his court viol players from Spanish Flanders and from
Venice.

During the second half of the sixteenth century and the
first forty years of the seventeenth, England led the way in
developing the repertory of the viol. This grew along two
principal lines, both of them treated in some detail in
Ortiz's treatise of 1553: consort music woven about a
plainsong (In Nomines) or, later, freely composed (Fantasies); and divisions on a ground – that is to say, extem-
porized variations for a solo instrument over an *ostinato*
ground-bass. As in Ortiz's book, the solo instrument for
divisions was usually a (small) bass viol, tuned $d'$, $a$, $e$, $c$, $G$
$D$. Modelled on the Italian *viola bastarda*, a new instrument – the *lyra viol* – made its appearance in England around
1600. Its size was that of a large tenor viol, and its music

was set down in tablature, partly because it was so similar
in size and general range to the lute, partly to allow for
varied tunings (a contagion that spread from the lute and
led ultimately to the decay both of the instrument and of its
music), and partly because of the polyphonic complexity
of its style. The lyra viol stayed in fashion in England until
about 1680, but made little impression elsewhere. By 1600
the Italian playing position had become standard throughout Europe for 'whole' consorts (i.e. groups drawn from
only one family of instruments), though when the viol was
used in such 'broken' consorts of soft instruments as that
used by Thomas Morley in his Consort Lessons (p. 166) the
older position across the knees was retained, since it gave
a far softer tone. Viols were made in only one form, but in
a large variety of sizes (treble; countertenor; tenor; lyra;
division (Pl. 19); consort bass; 'great dooble bass' (p. 153);
violone), and various experiments were made in their
outlines, though few of these lasted for long. Experiments
were also made, above all in England, with the use of sympathetic strings; these ultimately led to the development of
such instruments as the viola d'amore (mentioned below)
and the baryton, but these have nothing to do with the
history of the true viol or of its repertory.

By 1620 the rich but reedy sound of English viols playing
in consort was often sweetened by the use of a small chamber
organ as an accompaniment. Such composers as Orlando
Gibbons, Lupo, and Coperario had opened a new era with
their fantasies and suites for one or two violins, one or two
bass viols, and organ *continuo*. Much of the vast output of
chamber music composed by Jenkins, Lawes, and others was
for similar combinations, in which the (treble) violin and
the (bass) viol conversed on equal terms. The trio-sonatas
of Young, Blow, and, above all, Purcell lie only two or three
steps down such a path. The more severe style of the fantasy
and the In Nomine culminated in Purcell's music of this
type; the grave and emotional pavan – the only one of the
dance-forms ever firmly adopted by the viols – also found
its way into his music. But from 1680 onwards only the bass

viol remained in use in England and Italy, and all the other
sizes were set aside as outworn rubbish, or drastically converted into violins and violas.

The development of the viol in seventeenth-century
France or Germany is in many respects no more than a
reflection of its development in England, for English viol
players were universally recognized as the best in Europe
and many of them chose to live and work in foreign countries. The consort music of the early seventeenth-century
French composers du Caurroy and Lejeune is a direct
child of the In Nomine and fantasy; the trio-sonatas of
Krieger and Buxtehude follow lines laid down by Gibbons
and Coperario, though introducing new Italian elements;
the solemn allemandes and fantasies of Dumont and Louis
Couperin accurately reflect the styles of Jenkins and Lawes;
the rich and little-known repertory of music for one, two or
three bass viols and *continuo* by their successors, Forqueray,
Marais, François Couperin, and others, has its roots set
deep into the earlier English repertory for lyra and division
viols. Even Bach's sonatas, partitas, and suites for unaccompanied violin and unaccompanied cello may be attempts to
adapt to these instruments the varieties in tuning, multiple
stopping, and polyphonic texture that for a century and
more had been characteristic of the viols; *partita*, indeed, is
the Italian word for 'division'.

In the later years of the seventeenth century the French
bass viol acquired a seventh string tuned to low $A'$; this was
the kind of instrument for which Bach wrote his gamba
sonatas and Rameau his *Pièces en concert*. Although the louder
and more brilliant family of violins was coming more and
more to the fore, the thick-toned bass violin, soon to be
improved as the violoncello, was for long kept out of French
orchestras by the clearer-toned bass viol; see, for instance,
the music of Lalande and Rameau. But the overwhelming
passion of early eighteenth-century Europe for all things
Italian, and more especially for operas, sonatas, cantatas,
and concertos, added new impetus to the formation of the
modern four-part string orchestra; the obscure tenor violin

(p. 139) and the gamba quitted the scene almost simultaneously.

As a solo instrument the bass viol held out longer than any of its relations, its last great player being C. F. Abel, grandson of one of the two viol players for whom Bach's Sixth Brandenburg Concerto was composed at Cöthen. Abel was for many years associated with J. C. Bach in his London concerts, and he made his last appearance as a gamba player in 1787, barely a month before his death. During the eighteenth century certain hybrids between the two families of viols and violins made a brief appearance on the musical scene – for instance, the quinton, the baryton, and the arpeggione – but few musicians regretted their equally abrupt departure. None of these instruments developed a repertory of any consequence, despite the attention devoted by Haydn to the baryton or by Schubert to the arpeggione. A tiny viol – the *pardessus de viole* – found an admirer or two among the court ladies of France, but soon they grew bored with it, and it took its place by the side of their other musical toys, such as the musette, the hurdy-gurdy, and the dulcimer. The *viola d'amore* (Pl. 18b), played mainly in Germany, may be added to this list of hybrids, having been played at the shoulder, without frets, but with six or seven strings (tuned, e.g., $d''$, $a'$ $f'$, $d'$, $a'$ $d'$ $A$). A number of metal sympathetic strings ran below the fingerboard, and 'flame' sound-holes were characteristic. Vivaldi noticed it, and Bach (in the *John Passion*); and its active preservation by a few connoisseurs has been occasionally rewarded by composers from Berlioz to Hindemith, who wrote a concerto for it in 1928 and played it himself. (A folk instrument resembling it, also having sympathetic strings, though the body is violin-shaped, is the popular 'Harding fiddle' of Norway.)

Like other obsolete instruments, the viols have been revived in our own time, partly as the result of the work of Dolmetsch and his family. But a true appreciation of their individual sounds and styles has been handicapped by a lack of modern editions of viol music, and by the persistent activities of well-meaning though ill-advised cellists, who insist upon playing them cello-wise, without frets, bowed overhand, and heavily strung. They have thus introduced a new hybrid into the world of organology: by violoncello out of gamba. It is an instrument that has never been seen or heard before, and it should be called by a new name: cellamba. Its sound, like its playing technique, is wholly unlike that of the true viol; but some gifted players have demonstrated that there may well be room for it in the world of music. A misguided love for quaintness has led some musicians, and many audiences, into sampling viol consorts played on a bric-à-brac miscellany of cellambas, quintons, and viola d'amores. Viol consorts sound far better on an ordinary string quartet than on these. But they sound best of all if you play them yourself, for the pleasure of the performers, on the instruments for which they were written – the ancient and honourable family of bowed guitars, known in England as viols.

# 8. *The Modern Development of the Harp*

## ALBERT BIRCH

THE harp is perhaps the most easily recognized of all musical instruments, even through all the variety of forms which it presents in graphic art from the beginning of history and in the ancient forms in which it is still played in Africa and Asia, already described in Chapter 1. In this chapter, however, we are concerned only with the European species, differing from the others in its bold triangular or three-membered construction, as it is seen in pictures from the twelfth century (though certain of the instruments discernible on the now much eroded tenth-century Irish high crosses are believed by some authorities to represent harps of this kind). The three members include the following (a) the body or sound-chest, leaning back to the player's shoulder and covered by a tapering sound-board, down the centre-line of which the strings are knotted and pegged into their respective holes; (b) the neck, holding the tuning pins and undulating in the 'harmonic curve' by which the strings for each given note of the scale can show a length ratio approaching $1:2:4:8$ through the different octaves of the diatonic compass; with a straight neck the middle strings would come too long and make even tension over the compass very difficult to secure (Pl. 2b, at first glance a harp lying in its coffin, shows the harmonic curve embodied in a keyboard instrument for the same purpose); (c) the fore-pillar with its gentle outward curve which only the Irish harp has kept, supporting the neck against the pull of the strings. Medieval harps varied in size according to the degree of portability required, some having been very small, barely two feet high. Few reached four feet in height before the Renaissance. Nevertheless, the harper played a leading role in medieval entertainment ('Harper' remains in consequence far the commonest of our 'musical' surnames), chanting traditional epics and Breton lays, beginning his performance with a 'tuning prelude' or *tempradura*, to which poets refer sometimes in ecstatic terms as in the *Chanson de Horn*. Where the old forms of society lingered and the traditional songs and tunes were still called for, the harp maintained its position as a solo and accompanying instrument – notably in the Celtic lands, as will be described later on. But where the new music of the Renaissance was beginning to demand greater resources that the harp's single diatonic row of strings could provide, the readily chromatic lute and keyboard were at an advantage. If the harp were to survive, the problem of adding accidentals to its compass had to be solved, and without the instrument becoming either too cumbersome or too difficult to play.

The first attempted solution was the invention of the 'double harp', which Galilei towards the end of the sixteenth century ascribed to the Irish. This is the *arpa doppia* of Monteverdi's *Orfeo* (1607). The single row of strings was doubled, the extra row providing the required accidentals. Praetorius illustrates a rather unwieldy *Gross Doppel-Harp*, and gives a tuning which gives a complete chromatic compass in the middle octaves with diatonic extensions in bass and treble. A yet more complicated solution was the triple harp, first Italian, later Welsh, in which a middle row supplied accidentals while the outer rows gave the usual diatonic range. But the difficulty of playing such an instrument, with some strings barely accessible, especially at speed, made this an unsatisfactory solution.

A new approach to the problem came from the Tyrol, where towards the end of the seventeenth century hooks were fixed in the harmonic curve, to be brought against the string by turning, shortening the string to sound a semitone higher. In a way this recalls an improvised manner of making semitones, recorded in eighteenth-century accounts of Welsh harp traditions and also in certain Asiatic instruments, namely, by pressing a string with the thumb close to the tuning end. The hook idea was elaborated in 1720 by Hochbrucker, a Bavarian, who mechanized it with

The organ in Carshalton Parish Church, Surrey. The organ is by
Henry Willis & Sons, built in 1893 and rebuilt in its present position
in 1932. The case is by Sir Ninian Comper, 1932.

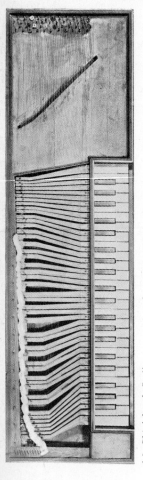

(a) Clavichord, Italian, seventeenth century. Fretted, except for the lowest octave, with some strings shared by two keys and some by three.

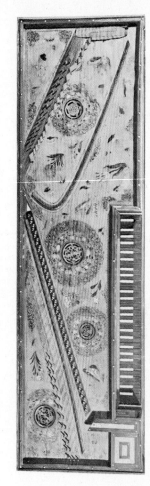

(b) Virginal by Stephen Keene, London, 1668; from above with lid removed.

2

Virginal, 1668; full view of the instrument shown above (Pl. 2*b*).

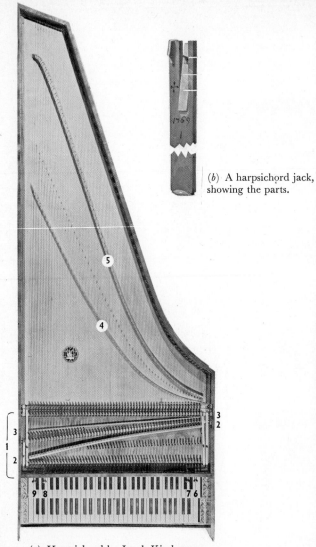

(b) A harpsichord jack, showing the parts.

(a) Harpsichord by Jacob Kirckman, London, 1755.

4

(*a*) Spinet by John Harrison, London, 1757.

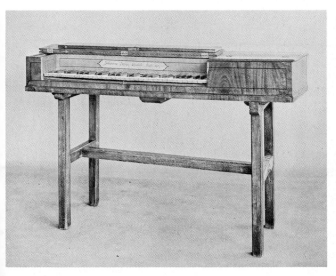

(*b*) Square fortepiano by Johannes Zumpe, 1767.

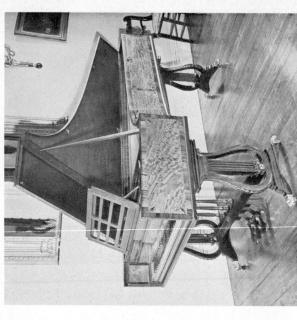

(a) Modern replica of a Viennese pianoforte, c. 1780, by Hugh Gough, London.

(b) Grand pianoforte by John Broadwood, 1807.

(a) Violin by Jacob Stainer, 1668. Original condition, except for pegs and bridge, which have been reproduced in appropriate style. Note original short fingerboard with wedge and the straight neck, which is slightly shorter and thicker than the modern one. Note also the rapid rise of the arching of the top and the clear view through the sound holes.

(b) Modern violin by J. B. Vuillaume, Paris, 1867 (Stradivari model). Modern elongated fingerboard, no wedge, tilted and narrowed neck, which is mortised into upper block. Compare the flatter top and back of the Vuillaume with the Stainer.

(b) Frontispiece to Francesco Geminiani's *L'Art du violon* (1752). Note the position of the violin held at player's neck, scroll of violin lower than tailpiece. Player uses loose arm somewhat away from the body. Note the long sonata bow, Italian grip well above nut, straight stick, and form of head of bow.

(a) Violinist painted by Gérard Dou (1665) showing typical breast position and French thumb-under-hair bow grip. Note also old neck, short fingerboard, and type of bridge.

(b) Isaac Stern (b. 1920), eminent American violinist. Compare bow arm and bow grip with Joachim's.

(a) The young Joseph Joachim playing in a Berlin concert (1854). From a sketch by Adolf von Menzel. Violin horizontal to the floor, presumably held to right of tailpiece. Bow now held at lowest extremity, upper arm close to body, high wrist.

9

(a) Lira da braccio, Giovanni Maria da Brescia, 1540. Note five playing strings and two bourdons lying off the fingerboard; leaf-shaped head with vertical pegs; indentation at base of string-holder; and primitive form of f-holes. (b) The 'Doria' violin by Maggini (early seventeenth-century Brescian). Note the double purfling. (c) Violin bows: (left to right) seventeenth century; early eighteenth century, ascribed to Nathaniel Cross; transitional type, possibly from the 1760s; and modern Nürnberger.

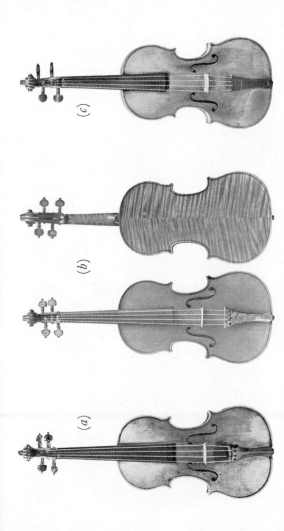

(a) Violin by Nicola Amati. (b) The 'Messie' Stradivari (1716), one of the most famous of all violins. Varnish and instrument in mint condition. (c) Jacob Stainer (1668) in its original condition (see Pl. 7a).

(a) Violin with belly removed, view of inside. *Left*, belly from below. *Right*, back and ribs from above. 1. bass bar, 2. top block, 3. bottom block, 4. corner block, 5. side linings.

(b) Double bass by Charles Theress, 1853. Interior of body.

Dirk Hals (1591–1656): *Cello player*.

(*a*) Giant double bass, attributed to Gasparo da Salò.

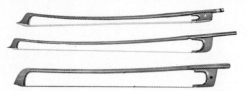

(*b*) Double bass bows: (*top to bottom*) Modern French,
Simandl, Dragonetti.

(a) Lute, Michielle Harton, Padua, 1598.

(b) Lute, Hans Frei, Bologna, c. 1550. Body and belly from inside.

(a) Guitar, Stradivari, 1680.  (b) Guitar, Lacote, presented to
Zani di Ferranti by
Rossini in 1864.

(c) Guitar, Clifford Essex, 1959. Under construction, showing the
barring, including fan-barring of belly. The soundhole (black) is not
yet cut out. Pencil line round both edges marks final size of instrument.

(a) Cittern, Gasparo da Salò.

(b) Orpharion, John Rose, London, 1580.

(c) Banjo, early pattern, c. 1860, with seven strings.

(*a*) Detail from Paolo Veronese's *Marriage at Cana* (1563) showing a consort of the artist and other famous painters with early forms of violin, tenor viol, and double bass: Veronese (tenor viol), Tintoretto (violin), Titian (double bass), and J. Bassano (cornett).

(*b*) Viola d'amore, J. Eberle, Prague, 1737. Note the seven metal sympathetic strings passing below the seven gut playing strings; also the 'flame' soundholes.

(a) Bass viol (division
viol) player, 1670.

(b) A consort set of viols by Arnold Dolmetsch Ltd, Haslemere.
*Left to right:* bass, tenor, treble.

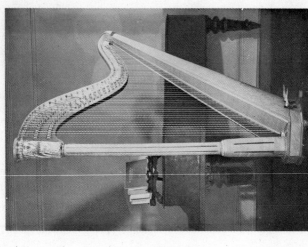

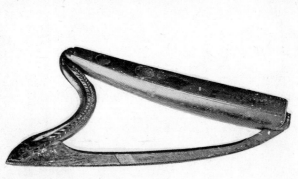

(a) Irish harp, once owned by the famous harper Arthur O'Neill (d. 1818).

(b) Harp by Wilfred Smith, Hampton Hill, 1958.

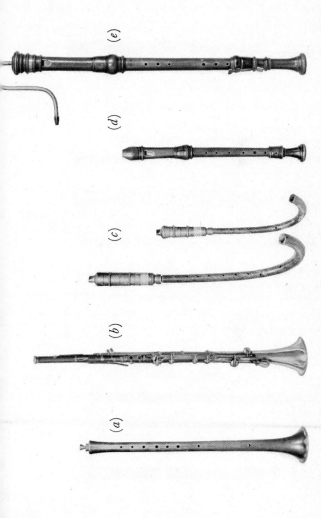

(a) Treble shawm, c. 1600. (b) Tenor shawm (*tenora*), Fabra, Gerona, 1951. (c) Tenor and treble crumhorn, reconstruction, c. 1600. (d) Treble recorder, T. Stanesby, c. 1700. (e) Bass recorder, T. Stanesby.

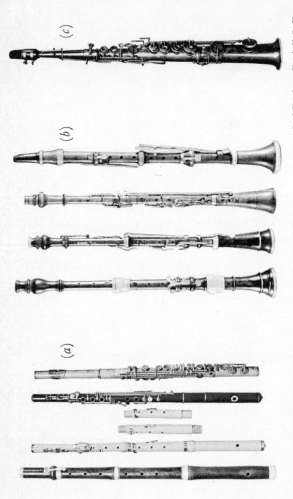

(a) Flutes: (*left to right*) one-keyed Cahusac, c. 1780; eight-keyed Cahusac, c. 1845; cylindrical flute, Rudall Carte 1867 model, in boxwood. (b) *Left to right*: Three-keyed oboe, T. Stanesby, early eighteenth century; oboe, Triébert, Paris, eight keys on blocks and saddles, c. 1825; oboe, Brod, Paris, c. 1840, keywork on pillars on footplates; six-keyed C clarinet, Astor, c. 1790. (c) Soprano saxophone, Adolphe Sax, 1851.

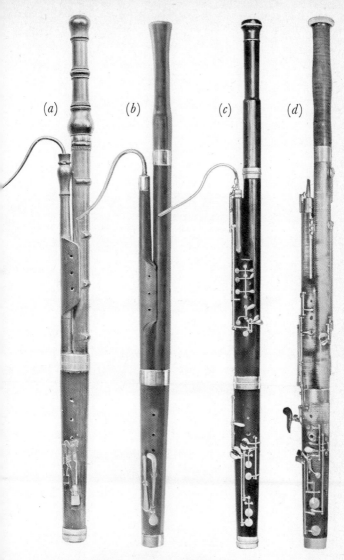

(a) Four-keyed bassoon, c. 1690. (b) Six-keyed bassoon, Wrede, London, c. 1795. (c) Buffet-Crampon bassoon, Paris (modern). (d) Heckel bassoon, Biebrich (modern).

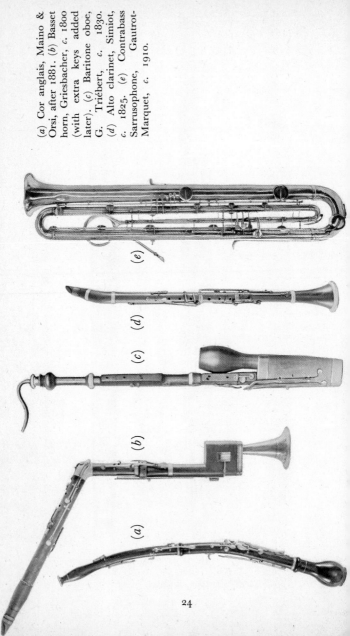

(a) Cor anglais, Maino & Orsi, after 1881. (b) Basset horn, Griesbacher, c. 1800 (with extra keys added later). (c) Baritone oboe, G. Triébert, c. 1830. (d) Alto clarinet, Simiot, c. 1825. (e) Contrabass Sarrusophone, Gautrot-Marquet, c. 1910.

24

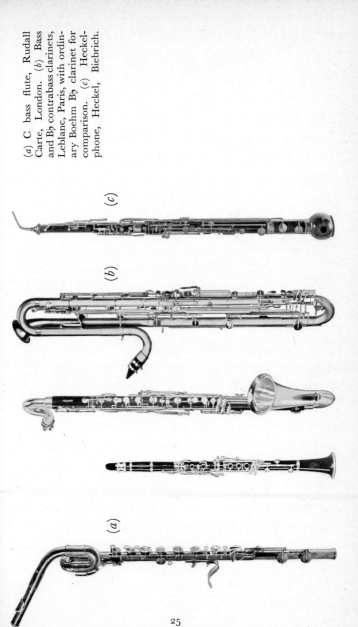

(a) C bass flute, Rudall Carte, London. (b) Bass and B♭ contrabass clarinets, and B♭ contrabass clarinets, Leblanc, Paris, with ordinary Boehm B♭ clarinet for comparison. (c) Heckelphone, Heckel, Biebrich.

(a) Treble cornett, Amsterdam.

(b) Treble cornett, 1605, Oxford.

(c) Bass trombone, Ehe, Nuremberg, 1732.

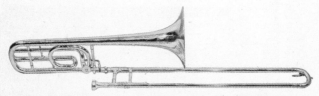

(d) Tenor trombone, Neuschel, Nuremberg, 1557.

(e) Trombone, modern, with F attachment, Conn, Elkhart, U.S.A.

(a) Trumpeters and kettledrummer, from an anonymous
eighteenth-century German engraving.

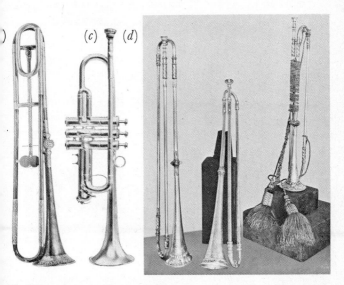

(b) Slide trumpet, Harris, London, c. 1720 (slide added later).
(c) Modern valve trumpet (Besson, London). (d) Three silver natural
trumpets: (left to right) Michael Nagel (Nuremberg, 1657); Anton
Schnitzer (Nuremberg, 1581); Johannes Leichamschneider
(Vienna, 1725).

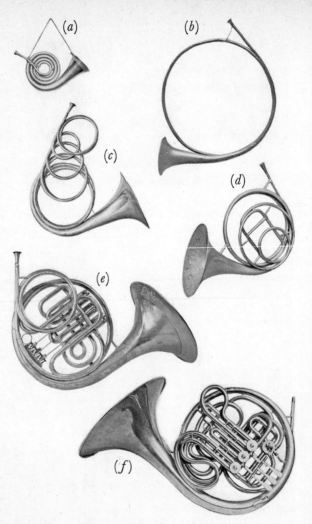

(*a*) Helical horn, Dresden, late sixteenth century. (*b*) Single-coil trompe in C, probably French, *c.* 1685. (*c*) Orchestral horn with crooks of early type, probably English, late eighteenth century. (*d*) Cor solo, with E♭ crook, by Courtois Frère, Paris, 1816. (*e*) Horn with Vienna valves, Uhlmann, Vienna, *c.* 1855. (*f*) Double horn, F/B♭, Paxman Bros., London, modern.

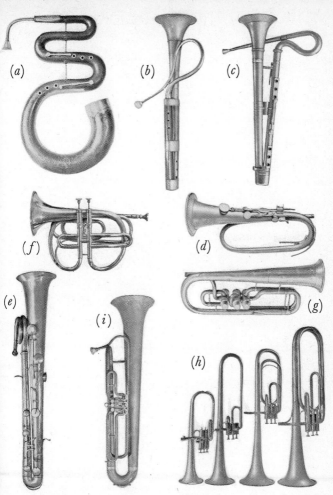

(a) Serpent, Milhouse, London, c. 1800. (b) Upright serpent or *Serpent basson*, very early type. (c) Bass horn, English, c. 1800. (d) Key bugle, Ellard, Dublin, c. 1820. (e) Ophicleide, C. Sax, Brussels, c. 1830. (f) Cornet, two-valve, Collin, Paris, c. 1830. (g) Flugel horn, Zetsche, Berlin, c. 1840. (h) Four Saxhorns – soprano in E♭, contralto in B♭, alto in E♭, baritone in B♭. All by Adolphe Sax, Paris, except the alto, which is by Bartsch, Paris. (i) F tuba, Leibelt, Innsbruck, c. 1860.

(a) Timpani – a modern set comprising two hand-turned and two machine drums.

(b) Side drum, 1600.

(c) Long drum, eighteenth century.

(d) Lapping side drum heads.

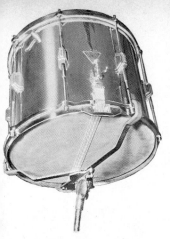

(b) Glockenspiel.

(a) Side drum (modern)
    showing snares.

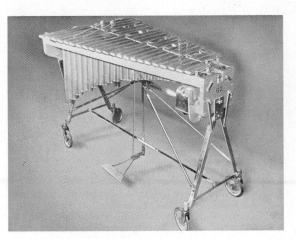

(c) Vibraphone.

(a) Rumba instruments.

(b) A group of musicians photographed near Lake Kioga in Uganda. The xylophones are mounted on banana stems and have five players, each with two beaters. In this instance the two players on the right play one tune in octave parallels, the two men at the ends on the left play a counterpoint, also in octave parallels, and the middle man on the left plays a third melody, not in octaves. The drums underline the xylophone parts. The standing drummers have cup-shaped drums and the seated drummers play kettledrums. Of the latter, one is being played with bare hands, one with one stick and the third with two sticks. In this area, xylophone music is always accompanied by drums in this way.

seven pedals to turn the hooks by a system of levers concealed in the fore-pillar, thus making it possible to modulate while playing. The strings were tuned to the scale of E♭, and the pedal for each note raised its pitch a semitone in every octave. Thirty years later, in Paris, the harp maker Cousineau and his son replaced the hook by two metal plates which the pedals caused to grip the string without displacing it. A further invention of theirs was to double the number of pedals, the extra pedal giving a further semitone on each note. This harp was tuned to the scale of C♭, as the modern harp is still, to give three notes on each string (e.g. C♭, C♮, C♯) and a range of keys again increased. The period saw a considerable revival of interest in the harp; many other improvements were tried and many beautifully finished instruments were made for patrons of wealth and taste by makers like Nadermann of Paris.

It was another Parisian, Sebastien Érard (1752–1831), who took the final step towards creating the modern harp. Érard, whose mechanical genius also furthered the development of the pianoforte, opened a workshop in London during the Revolutionary troubles and took out several English patents for mechanical improvements in the harp. The first

of these was for a fork mechanism to replace the hooks or the metal plates of the Cousineau model. This was the now familiar brass disc bearing two studs which, when turned a quarter of a circle, gripped the string and gave a firm, clear note for the semitone. This was his 'improved single-action harp' of 1792. Next came a series of patents which culminated in 1810 in the 'Grecian' model (Fig. 37) of double-action harp, with a second disc added for each string to give a further

FIG. 37. Grecian harp

semitone, operated not by an additional set of pedals, but
by depressing the existing seven pedals a further notch.
This made the greater range of keys available without
overcomplicating the player's task, and together with various improvements in design – the fore-pillar had by now
become straight to house the mechanism, and Erard
abandoned the old method of building the sound-chest of
staves and generally increased the size and tension of
the strings – the new harp was a great deal more powerful in tone than the old. A further development was made
in 1836 by Erard's nephew and successor Pierre, who
patented the slightly larger 'Gothic' model, with Gothic
architectural style decoration. It was given two extra
strings in the bass and one in the treble. The mechanism
did not operate on these extra strings, but the string spacing
was increased a little. With these inventions, the harp had
become a heavier instrument, less suited to the salons, the
feminine fingers, and the classical pose. Spohr relates how
his wife, brought up to play the single-action harp of the
Nadermann pattern, found the Érard double-action instrument beyond her physical powers, and had to abandon it.
Nevertheless it could be supplied in an elegant drawing-
room size as well as in the full concert size with which
Bochsa, Parish-Alvars, Dizi, and others dazzled their
Paris and London audiences. It was also left to the French
to develop the harp's orchestral role – as by Meyerbeer and
especially Berlioz, since whose day no orchestra has been
without the instrument.

Towards the end of the eighteenth century, just as Érard
was beginning to increase still further the size of the pedal
harp, there was an attempt to introduce instruments which
would have the portability then being lost, together with
some of the qualities of the harp, particularly in accompaniment. These were the various inventions which Edward
Light and his imitators produced in a steady stream in the
first decade or two of the nineteenth century (Fig. 38).
Though they derive their tuning from the English Guitar
and have a fretted fingerboard, their would-be rivalry with

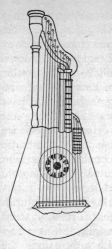

FIG. 38.
Harp-Lute

the harp is clear from their addition of free strings and from the recurrence of the word 'harp' in all their names, some of which are mentioned on p. 172. One, the 'Harp-Lyre', was advertised as giving 'the same sound and effect as the real harp although not more than one quarter of the size or a tenth part of the expense'. They were meant for the drawing-room, an elegant, graceful, yet 'incredibly easy' accomplishment.

Although the improvements of Érard successfully fixed the form of the modern pedal harp, they did not put an end to attempts to further the scope of the instrument, and mention should be made of the 'chromatic harp' developed about the end of the nineteenth century by Pleyel of Paris. This dispensed with pedals and achieved full chromatic compass from two rows of strings which slanted across each other to make each row available to either hand. Debussy wrote his *Danse sacrée et danse profane* expressly for it in 1904. By way of riposte, Érard then commissioned Ravel to compose a show-piece for the pedal harp: the *Introduction et allegro* for Flute, Clarinet, Harp, and Strings was the outcome, and in its cadenza every pedal is used in all positions to demonstrate the instrument's powers in quick modulations. Debussy's pieces are now commonly played on the pedal harp, and are in fact easier on this than on the chromatic harp for which they were conceived.

The pursuit of perfection in the pedal harp has continued to occupy the minds of a few master craftsmen since Érard's time in other countries besides France. Notable work has been that of the firm of Lyon and Healy, of Chicago, who set out to design a stronger and more reliable harp suited to the extremes of American climate. In this they have undoubtedly succeeded, and have made many fine harps since they started in 1889. Their mechanism, a copy of the Érard in principle, is sturdily made and neatly housed between brass plates at the top of the pillar – an innovation foreshadowed by several mid-Victorian harp makers, notably Stumpf, Schweiso, and Dodd, all of whom must have realized the mechanical disadvantages of repeating the action for each note in the lowest three octaves as the Érard harp does. Other improvements have been made by Wurlitzer, New York, from 1909. In England the recent improvements by Wilfred Smith of Hampton Hill, London, embody new features, including a mechanism that is fully compensating, i.e. the strain upon the strings in the 'natural' position (with the pedal in the first notch) is relieved when the 'sharp' position (second notch) is engaged, thus reducing the effort needed to move the pedal, whether up by the return spring or down by the foot. The system also enables the two lowest notes, $C'$ and $D'$, to be altered by the pedals for the first time in the instrument's history, while the layout of the strings in the highest two octaves permits a much wider space for the player's hands, especially for the right (Pl. 20b).

A few technical particulars of modern harp-playing may be noted. The harp is rested against the right shoulder and is played with the thumb and three largest fingers of each hand, the right hand playing mainly on higher strings than does the left hand. For visual recognition the C and F strings are usually coloured, e.g. red for C and purple for F, while on the lower strings, in which the gut is overspun with metal, copper may be used for the C and F strings for the same reason. Many special tonal effects have been devised by soloists. The effects most used in the orchestra are octave harmonics, made by pressing a string at its centre and indicated in the part by a circle above the note; and the sound made by plucking a string close to the soundboard.

\*

To confine this story of the harp to an account of its development into a large and expensive orchestral machine would be to omit an important side-issue: the part that has been played up to recent times (and still today) by the Celtic harps. In both Wales and Ireland tenacious musical traditions were handed down from a highly organized medieval art with a most thorough training for the professional harper. The 'Robert ap Huw' manuscript in the British Museum preserves, though in a somewhat mystifying notation, harp exercises and accompaniments of allegedly fourteenth-century origin. But after the accession of the Welsh Tudors had taken the more influential gentry away from Wales, and seventeenth-century Protestantism had caused the loss of dance tunes and rhythms, the old styles of playing and accompanying were forgotten, even when the melodies were not. Nevertheless, the Welsh harp survived to play its part in the preservation of Welsh culture. (It was, too, for a Welsh harper that Handel wrote the part in *Esther*.) In Ireland the art of the harper continued to thrive long after it had begun to wane in Wales. Barnaby Rich wrote in 1610 that 'the Irish have harpers and these are so reverenced among them that in the time of rebellion they will forbear to hurt either their persons or their goods . . . and every great man in the country hath his rhymer and his harper'. Queen Elizabeth I had kept an Irish harper; Bacon wrote 'No harp hath the sound so melting and prolonged as the Irish harp.' The shape of the Irish instrument is distinctive (Pl. 20a). Several early examples have survived, including the so-called 'Brian Boru' harp preserved at Trinity College, Dublin, and now thought to date from late in the fourteenth century. It shows the typical shape, with sound-box cut from a solid piece of 'sally' (willow), the fore-pillar roundly curved, and the harmonic curve equally robust to take the tension of the brass strings with which the Irish harp, unlike the Welsh and others, was fitted. It is just over two feet in height, its appearance powerful rather than elegant as compared for example with the Welsh harp (Fig. 39) with its tall, slender pillar to

accommodate the long gut or horsehair bass strings. Later
Irish harps are considerably larger (Pl. 20a). The strings
vary from thirty to over fifty, and, being of brass and by
tradition struck with fingernails grown long for the purpose,
were extremely resonant as well as requiring a skilled technique of striking and damping. The training was therefore
a long one, and the famous eighteenth-century harper
Carolan was reckoned to have begun his studies too late to

FIG. 39. Welsh harp

achieve absolute mastery, though he was admitted peerless
as a composer of new airs. The traditional technique was
largely lost during that century, yet the budding romantic
interest in folk music tried hard to preserve it. At a great
gathering of the old harpers – most of them blind – held in
Belfast in 1792, Edward Bunting was given the task of taking
down the old airs, which he did, later to publish them with
piano accompaniments of conventional form but neverthe-

less to tell us something of the old harpers' tradition. The most venerable of the artists who attended, Denis Hempson, was observed particularly by Bunting.

In playing, he caught the string between the flesh and the nail; not like the other harpers of his day, who pulled it by the fleshy part of the finger alone. He had an admirable method of playing *staccato* and *legato*, in which he could run through rapid divisions in an astonishing style. His fingers lay over the strings in such a manner, that when he struck them with one finger, the other was instantly ready to stop the vibration, so that the *staccato* passages were heard in full perfection.

With the passing of Hempson's generation the continuous tradition became broken. Nevertheless, attempts were at once made to revive it, and by 1820 the maker Egan of Dublin had patented a portable gut-strung harp, three feet high, in which some of the new mechanism (but manually operated by levers or 'ditals' mounted on the pillar) was added to the well-loved shape of the old Irish harp. Today, while in Wales the modern pedal harp is accepted in place of the old instrument, Irish and also some Scottish enthusiasts have generally preferred a simplified version of the Egan design, with hooks instead of mechanism and commonly described as a 'Celtic' or 'Gaelic' harp. It is chiefly in this form that the Irish harp survives, under the powerful stimulus of the beauty of Gaelic folksong, and as the only accompaniment acceptable to those who feel the ruinous inadequacy of piano-inspired harmonies.

# 9. *Ancient and Folk Backgrounds*

ANTHONY BAINES

IT will be appropriate at this point, before proceeding to the major wind instruments, to interpose a short account of historical forerunners of our leading musical instruments, including medieval forms which long ago slipped from the mainstream of Western music to undergo their evolution at the slower pace of peasant culture. This is done with the twofold purpose of drawing attention to various points of historical and technical interest, and of providing a guide, though much compressed, to some of the instruments which may now be heard, often so brilliantly played, in actual or recorded performances of music other than our own concert and popular music.

## STRINGED INSTRUMENTS

These may be divided, technically rather than typologically, (a) instruments with open strings only, including harps, lyres, and psalteries; (b) those upon which the melody is made by stopping a string with the left hand, and including lutes and fretted zithers; (c) instruments which are in general similar to those of the preceding group but are sounded with a horsehair bow, generically 'fiddles'.

The harp is as far as we know the oldest: the first in the long sequence of stringed instruments which have shared with the voice absolute supremacy in Old World musical fine art. In the systematized music of both occidental and oriental civilizations, strings have proved the musician's best servants, partly through their perfect and immediate tunability by hand and ear, and partly through their aptness for the accompaniment of song. For more than thirty centuries the harp in its various ancient forms dominated the music of Mesopotamia and Egypt, played by Egyptian queens and by blind virtuosi whose names are commemor-

ated in the hieroglyphs. Though no longer played in its
homelands, it was borne in the centuries preceding and
following the beginning of the Christian era far across Asia,
where a few species have lingered on in the remoter parts,
as the skin-bellied Burmese harp (Fig. 40), with spun silk

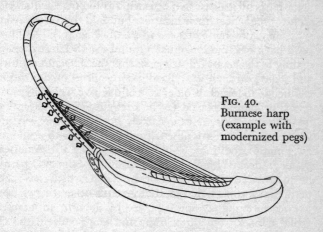

FIG. 40.
Burmese harp
(example with
modernized pegs)

strings tuned pentatonically (as were also, according to a
theory of Curt Sachs, harp strings in Assyria and Egypt).
The Burmese harp illustrates one of the earlier Sumerian
forms. Others, which lasted up to modern times in the
Caucasus and in Western Siberia, differ in the angle at
which neck meets sound-box, or in the position in which the
instrument is held. Unfortunately there are no survivors
of the classic Persian harp, celebrated in the *Shah Nama*
and still heard locally in the last century; it was a diatonic
harp, its tall, graceful sound-box rested vertically against
the kneeling player with the neck jutting forwards from the
lower end just above the floor. The virtual disappearance
of the old harps in Asia followed their replacement during
the early Middle Ages by other stringed instruments,
especially psalteries.

Meanwhile a structurally more solid and weatherproof

harp – the three-membered kind described in the last chapter – was being developed somewhere in Europe, possibly in Ireland, the land to which European tradition has long credited it. (The midget harp of the Sutton Hoo burial ship, of the seventh century A.D. and antedating the true European harp by at least two centuries, is too fragmentary for secure typological identification but may be of an Asian type, an acute-angled cousin to that in Fig. 40.) The European harp has also lost much ground to other instruments, mainly to the keyboard strings during the sixteenth century, and today, through its stylized use in concert orchestration, we incline to forget its older role of a festive melodic instrument, brilliantly played in the diatonic idioms natural to its physique. This we can scarcely hope to rediscover save where pianofortes are absent or scarce owing to economic or climatic conditions, as in many parts of Latin America; many readers will have heard recordings of the old Spanish harp, a large diatonic European harp which has been perpetually copied by the Indians and other rustics from Mexico to Paraguay and is played by them in an intensely virile manner, sometimes using the fingernails in the old way, especially on the higher strings.

The Ancient Greeks heard harp music now and then, mainly as a popular exoticism. Their national instruments were lyres, though they were not the first to use them, since they first appear in Sumeria in the third millennium B.C., shortly after the first harps; indeed, in appearance some Sumerian lyres suggest that a harp had for some reason been rigged with a kind of oblique gantry for carrying strings of nearer to equal length than was otherwise possible on a harp. Subsequently, lyres became neater: either oblique, as in the Egyptian scene in Fig. 41, or symmetrical, as the Greek *cithara* (Fig. 42) and tortoiseshell bodied *lyra*, these being supported against the player's body by a sling worn round the left wrist, leaving the fingers more or less free. With these fingers the citharode accompanied his song as best he could on the few strings provided, decorating the tune in ways that are alluded to in Plato's *Laws*. His right hand

FIG. 41. Egyptian musicians, *c.* 1000 B.C.
Harp, lute, double-pipe, lyre

FIG. 42.
Greek cithara player

grasped an enormous plectrum which, as far as one may imagine the performance in the light of surviving plectrum lyre techniques in East Africa, he swept across the strings during pauses of the voice, meanwhile damping with the left-hand fingers those strings which were required to remain silent in the chord that rang on. Skill on the lyre was assiduously cultivated by the professionals, yet its contribution seems to have been mainly a histrionic background to declamatory song. So, too, no doubt, it was with the simplified, plectrum-less lyres, called 'harps', with which the Germans and Anglo-Saxons regaled themselves until the Middle Ages showed them better instruments (Fig. 43);

relics of these reduced lyres were found still in use in the present century among those Siberian tribes who also exhibited ancient kinds of harp. Other European lyres which reached the Middle Ages came to be bowed like fiddles, like the crwth mentioned later. Nevertheless, strumming techniques recalling that of the classical lyres, if not in some cases directly derived from it, are still found among zithers.

The term 'zither' can well be employed in our present context generically for instruments with strings stretched over a flat or flattish sound-box without a neck.

FIG. 43. Anglo-Saxon lyre

This simple and obvious idea is one that might have occurred independently to many and have manifested itself with differing detail in this place and that, which indeed it has done. *Psalteries*, for example, are zitherized harps; they might be described as harps in which the frame structure has been replaced by a flat sound-box with the strings passing over two long bridges and hitched to pins down one side and to tuning pegs down the other. Typical shapes for the sound-box are basically trapezoidal, as if through truncation of harp corners now devoid of function. Both hands must now play on the same side of the instrument, but retain their equal roles in the technique. The psaltery seems to have been evolved in the Near East about the tenth century A.D., and most of its names are of Greek extraction: 'psaltery' itself preserves the old Greek harp name *psalterion*. It is seen in the West from the twelfth century, held either flat against the chest (Fig. 44) or across

FIG. 44. Psaltery, fourteenth century

the knees, and played with a pair of quill plectra; but from the Renaissance the 'gay sautrie' of Chaucer's Clerk began to be superseded in turn by its keyboard version, the harpsichord, and in folk music by the dulcimers described below. The technical scope of the psaltery is fully demonstrated today on the *qanun* – again a Greek name (*kanon*) – which is the leader's instrument in a normal Egyptian orchestra. It has gut strings and is played with great vivacity using finger plectra akin to the Austrian 'zither rings' (Fig. 34 inset), one worn on each forefinger and probably derived from an earlier harper's practice of playing with long-grown

fingernails. Meanwhile a true psaltery of medieval vintage
survives in Russia in certain forms of *gusli*, much used by
ballad singers formerly; some of the earlier published collections of Russian folksongs included accompaniments for
the gusli, and the instrument has latterly been revived,
notably in the Mari province by the Volga.

Whereas harps have but one string per note, psalteries
usually have two or more, i.e. 'multiple courses', the instrument otherwise sounding rather puny. A further increase in sonority is obtained by fitting metal strings, and

Fig. 45.
Swiss Hackbrett (dulcimer)

then by striking them with a pair of light wooden or cane
beaters. The strings can now be arranged in quadruple,
even quintuple courses. The idea of this beaten psaltery,
or dulcimer, may have come from Persia. Today it is by far
the most important of European non-keyboard psalteries,
played from the Greek regions (*santouri*) to Rumania,
Hungary, and Czechoslovakia (it is known throughout East
Europe as '*cimbal*'). Its shimmering, undamped sound, with
much *tremolando* and quick figuration, backs the music of
violin and double bass in villages to which the pianoforte
has not penetrated. The strings are sloped alternately to
the left and the right to give freer play to the beaters, and
the bridges are placed to divide certain strings into two or
more tuned lengths, to provide a partially chromatic com-

pass with great economy of space (Fig. 45). The most highly developed form, the Hungarian concert *cimbalom*, built on legs and provided with a damper pedal, is a telling instrument that merits exploitation in orchestration as the harp is used, for the sake of sonorities and effects obtainable on no other instrument. Hungarian composers have made a small start, as for example in the cimbalom part in Kodály's Háry János Suite.

In contrast to these harp-like techniques with un-differentiated functions of the two hands, a small north-eastern group of psalteries exhibits a technique of voice accompaniment in which the two hands have different functions as with the lyre. The group includes the Finnish *kantele* (Fig. 46), the 'national' instrument in the *Kalevala*, its name also from the Greek kanon. The

FIG. 46. Finnish kantele player

kantele player can punctuate his song by sweeping the metal strings with a plectrum held in the right hand while the left hand damps the strings which are not to ring on.

FIG. 47. Lithuanian kantele

Thus psalteries appear not to be very old – principally modified harps, which they certainly replaced, and hence remote descendants of the archaic musical bow from which the first harps may have been developed. China, however, already used zithers in 1100 B.C., with their evident archetype not a musical bow, but a long, broad slat cut from wide-stemmed bamboo, with 'strings' cut in the bark itself (see p. 40) – 'half-tube zither' in Sachs's terminology. The natural material gave place to long wooden sound boxes, still round-topped, and to silk strings, still immovably tied at each end and tuned by individual movable bridges (instead of having tuning pegs or knobs in the occidental manner). Many varieties have endured as classical instruments of the Far East. The most played and most fully studied by Western writers is the *koto*, the national instrument of pre-Westernized Japan. Its six-foot-long soundbox (Fig. 48) is placed on the floor, the player sitting near one end. Along it run thirteen waxed silk strings of equal length and played open, each tuned by its own movable bridge to contribute to a pentatonic scale of the 'major third' type (e.g. A, F, E, C, B) over two and a half octaves. Playing is with three ivory finger plectra worn in fingerstalls on the right hand, the left hand keeping busy near the bridges, correcting their setting, preparing the 'missing' notes of the scale, should the piece require them, by pressing a string near its bridge (just as a Burmese harper may press a string close to the tuning end), and making subtle *portamenti* and ornaments, codified in seventeenth-century manuscripts to which only a few leading performers have access, the pieces being taught entirely by ear – formerly much to blind children, as elsewhere in music – yet learnt with the exactness sought in our own performances of classical keyboard works. But unlike these, the koto music has no ancestry of song, dance, and fanfare. Its strongly esoteric character at first startles with its vast leaps, sharp percussions, and abrupt silences, and clusters of contiguous notes struck together as one sound.

Some of the most individual music of European folk stringed instruments is that made on the 'fretted zithers', which include the Austrian Zither described in the previous chapter. On these instruments the tunes are made by stop-

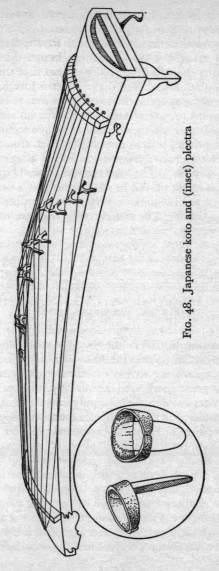

FIG. 48. Japanese koto and (inset) plectra

ping one or more strings against a fretted fingerboard, the
rest of the strings being struck in various ways in accompaniment. One of the classic Chinese zithers, the *chyn*, includes
a stopped string, but the age of the European instruments
is unknown; there is little if any evidence of them before
the sixteenth century. Yet they range in folk music from
Rumania as far as Iceland. It remains a matter for speculation whether they are related to the chyn on some remote
ethnic horizon or whether certain chyn-like features noticeable among them, such as movable bridges, arose independently, perhaps derived from the medieval monochord. The
simplest forms, as Alpine *Scheitholt*, *épinette des Vosges*, and the
Dutch *hummel* last played in the Frisian Isles a century ago,
have a long narrow hollowed-out sound-box, placed on the
knees or on a table. The melody string, nearest the player, is

FIG. 49. Norwegian langeleik

stopped against the frets either by the left thumb-nail or by
a short metal bar held in the hand. The right hand, with a
plectrum, strikes the strings mainly altogether, to and fro
according to the rhythm, so that the open strings, which are
tuned to octaves, fifths, etc., supply a resounding rhythmic
drone, adding much force to the dance music which the
little instrument often has to provide entirely on its own. A
tuning given by Panum for the slightly more advanced
Norwegian *langeleik* (Fig. 49) runs: *a, a* (double melody-
string); *a, a, e', e', e''* or *c''♯* (drones, the three higher notes
being secured by individual bridges). Through their
harmonic relation, these drone strings give the effect of a
rich drone on low *A* with a sound reminiscent of a Highland
bagpipe. The Alpine zithers and the Swedish Hummel (Fig.
50) incorporate features derived from later fashions – cittern-

or guitar-like curves to the sound-box, and a technique of playing in thirds with chordal accompaniment (p. 179). Also of this group is the 'Appalachian dulcimer' or 'Mountain zither' of America, now coming into vogue again.

The lute, despite the fact that its oldest known form appeared in Mesopotamia *c.* 2000 B.C., took a surprisingly long time to win the leading position it has held in Old World music from medieval times. The ancient lute, named in Greek *pandoura*, had usually two strings, knotted

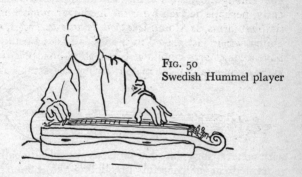

FIG. 50
Swedish Hummel player

round the neck pole without pegs, and the neck was necessarily tied with gut frets in order to give clear stops; but the ancients may well have experienced some difficulty in rationalizing the intervals to tie them, which possibly contributed to the instrument's relegation to minor and ensemble roles despite the new technical facilities which it obviously offered. It is seen in the Egyptian orchestra in Fig. 41, whose sound is hard to imagine. With their various limitations of compass, scale, and technique, these instruments could scarcely have been played in strict unison, or in the clean heterophony of a modern Egyptian orchestra comprising qanun, lute, violin, and nay (rim-blown flute) – a basic unison woven into an elaborate sound-texture through the different figurations upon the various instruments. The ancient court music of Japan might, as one oriental scholar has suggested, in some respects reflect ancient practice more closely; the instruments here do quite different things from one another, each one's part having been evolved in terms of that instrument's peculiar nature.

The pandoura, or 'long-necked' lute, remains a popular instrument from Persia (Fig. 51) to the Balkans (*tamboritsa*),

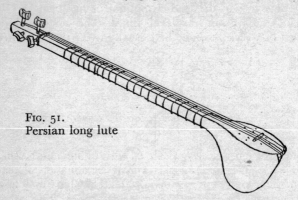

Fig. 51.
Persian long lute

with metal strings played as much as possible altogether and reiterated in a cheerful mandoline-like manner. The balalaika and the Greek *buzuki* are related to it. West Europe never cared for it, but in Asia, disseminated by Islamic influences, it has flowered into important and distinctive regional forms. The large-bodied Indian *sitar* has a broad neck and seven metal strings of which two are struck with a thumb plectrum for the softly reiterated 'drone' on the tonic required by most Indian music; the *tambura* is similar, but without frets and with four strings intended solely for providing this drone background. The Japanese *samisen* (Fig. 52) illustrates the Far Eastern type, fretless, with the small body covered with catskin on both sides; its three strings, tuned to a fourth and a fifth, are struck rather percussively with the huge, axe-like plectrum. By contrast the older Chinese lute *pyipar* (Fig. 53), in Japan *biwa*, is an instrument of obviously different proportions which is seen in some Hellenistic statuettes of the second century B.C. but

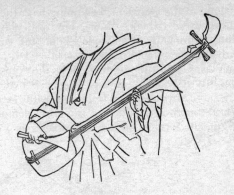

FIG. 52. Japanese samisen player

seem to be more closely associated with Indian and Kushan (*Scythian*) cultures. Dr Picken's close examination of texts from the second century A.D. indicates that China may have become acquainted with this 'short-necked' lute as an instrument which Central Asian nomads found convenient for playing on horseback. Indeed, the sum of the evidence suggested to Sachs that the whole lute family originated not in the Fertile Crescent, but to the north-east of it. With its

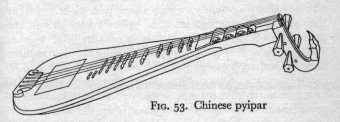

FIG. 53. Chinese pyipar

four strings tuned in fourths – the melodies played mainly on the highest string – and its reverberating deep-pitched tone, the pyipar, or rather its West Asiatic parent, heralds the great lutes of the Occident, beginning with the Arabo-Persian lute, *al 'ud* (whence 'lute', Fig. 54), played with a plectrum traditionally of an eagle's talon and constantly and charmingly mentioned in the *Arabian Nights*; an essential accomplishment for the singing girl as the samisen is for the geisha. Its European progeny has been described in Chapter 7, but if anyone should feel that the lute lacks force, its elemental sonorous qualities are superbly demonstrated by the *cobza*, the form in which it flourishes as a popular

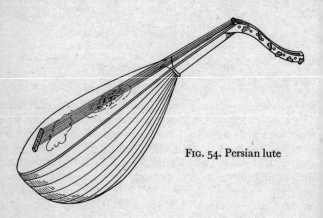

FIG. 54. Persian lute

instrument in Rumania, where there is a class for it at the National Conservatoire. The cobza's four strings are arranged in double courses mainly in octaves (as *d' d, a' a, d' d, g' g*, though as usual with folk instruments players have their individual preferences), and are sounded with a quill plectrum in a robustly rhythmical way in which harmonious and percussive elements are combined in chordal accompaniment to other instruments, most often the violin.

A word should be said about 'hybrids'. Considerations of physical technique have on the whole ensured the perpetuation of distinct classes of stringed instruments like the harps, psalteries, fretted zithers, and lutes so far described, and have correspondingly reduced the likelihood of prolonged success for instruments of mixed character which musicians have now and then created. Some, however, have lasted. Historically, two great areas for stringed hybrids have been India and Central Europe. Even in the last few years a small firm in Calcutta has produced its 'O.K.-phone', a kind of zitherized re-creation of the ancestor of the clavichord. Among leading classic instruments, the North Indian *vina* (Fig. 55), which replaced the

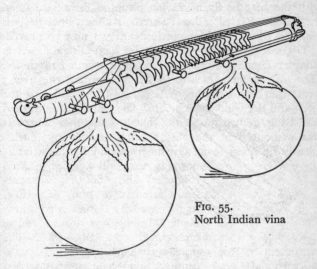

FIG. 55.
North Indian vina

old Asian harp at the time when psalteries did the same in the Middle East, is a zither, presumably of native origin, and has engendered hybrids with the lute. The northern vina shown has two large gourd resonators secured to the bamboo pole with bolts. Four of the seven metal strings are stopped against high brass frets and are struck with two finger plectra worn on the right hand, while the other three strings are struck open with the right little finger and thumb for a softly tinkling drone background. Medieval Central Europe shows some curious half-way forms between harp and psaltery, along with zitherized lutes like the '*ala bohemica*' (for the want of a precise native name), a precursor of the present Russian bandoura (p. 181) with its fan of open accompanying strings for the smaller fingers of the right hand. In other cases, hybridization is related to playing method, with only minor changes to structure. We have seen that the viols may have originated as bowed guitars. A Shetland tradition of playing the guitar across the knees in 'Hawaiian' fashion, considered in conjunction with the islands' Scandinavian affinities, brings to mind the Nordic fretted zithers described above, though it is doubtful whether this connexion can ever now be proved.

The origin of the fiddle is, as we have already seen in Chapter I, one of organology's most intriguing mysteries. 'The instruments which most closely approach the voice', wrote the Baghdad scholar Al Farabi (d. *c.* 950), 'are the *rabab* and the wind instruments.' The rabab, he adds, had one string, or two tuned to a fourth, sometimes paired. It was without frets, the fingers being 'guided by touch'. Clearly he refers to an instrument sounded with a fiddle

FIG. 56.
Chinese fiddle

bow (as *rabab* still signifies in Arab countries) and one that was perfectly familiar to him, as well it might have been, for a bowed instrument is mentioned in a Chinese orchestra *c.* 900 and bowed lute-like instruments are shown in tenth-century Spanish manuscripts. Yet before the ninth century there are no traces of bowing; by the tenth it was practised from the Atlantic to the Pacific.

Though in the West early fiddles were 'bowed lutes', most Asian fiddles show curiously rudimentary yet specialized forms, such as that of the Chinese fiddle (Fig. 56), with two silk strings tuned to a fifth. Its name, *hwuchyn*, indicates Central Asian provenance, confirmed by other occurrences of this form in Tibet, tribal India, etc., and in more advanced forms in Western Asia. It is played with a peculiar stopping technique which is shared by all early and Asiatic fiddles and is quite impracticable on a lute: there is neither nut nor fingerboard; the strings pass well above the neck of the instrument and are stopped by pressing with the fingers or nails, even from the side or below, the fiddle being held downwards like a miniature cello. The sound is thin and veiled, though the playing, as heard for example in the Chinese theatre, can be most sensitive. Another primitive type is represented by the Indian *sarangi* (Fig. 57) and the boat-shaped Moroccan rabab, both now largely superseded by the European violin. These, too, are played without a fingerboard, giving on the rabab 'a purring sound of most pregnant melancholy.' But veiled or melancholy, all these are *sustained* sounds, and it may be a pointer to their original intention that rudimentary one- or two-stringed fiddles are or have been employed in Central Asia, India, Egypt, Macedonia, etc., by professional storytellers to supply a continuous background like a soundtrack to the narration. Tinctoris (*c.* 1487) mentions that 'over the greater part of the world the viola with a bow [i.e. as he explains it, a fiddle] is used . . . in the recitation of epics'.

FIG. 57.
Indian
fiddle,
sarangi

In Western Europe, one early fiddle, though it acquired an Arab name in the thirteenth century (*rubebe* or *rebec*, from *rabab*), was a Greek type, brought west in the eleventh century. Inheriting the name *lyra* from the forgotten lyre of Hellas, it is still popular in Greece, Anatolia, and the Aegean islands (Fig. 58): a short bowed lute carved in almond-shape in one piece with pine belly added, and fingered just as the previous examples. Of the three gut strings, tuned e.g. $d''$, $g'$, $c''$, one is often sounded as a

FIG. 58. Aegean fiddle,
lyra, and bow

drone while the next is fingered
for the melody. But in Western
Europe, almost from the first,
the rebec was generally held up
against the shoulder, reversing
the twists of both forearms (for
all the preceding fiddles are
bowed palm-upwards as well as
being held downwards). This
posture, which best suits a standing player, may have encouraged
the development of fingerboards
on fiddles; but still in 1545 (Agricola's second edition) players of
the 'Polish' fiddles 'only touch
between the strings and stop
with the fingernails'. Unlike the
violin, these rebecs have no
sound-post, except for the Bul-
garian variety, *gadulka*, still
played at weddings and dances. In this, the bridge may
extend to one side where its foot bears directly against a
sound-post which protrudes through the right sound-hole;
or the bridge may have a long foot which itself reaches to
the back, like the bridge of the old Welsh crwth.

The rest of the story up to the Renaissance is mainly a
matter of shapes and sizes, leading to the thirteenth-
century gittern and fiddle, and thence onwards to guitar
and violin, with their box-like bodies with incurved sides.
The built-up construction of top, back, and sides has not
been detected before *c.* 1300, when certain sculptures
indicate it; earlier bodies, with a wide range of contours,
some oval, some with incurved sides, were presumably
hollowed out. But the incurved sides even appear on some
Egyptian and Anatolian lutes of *c.* 1000 B.C. Evidently the
search for the best design of sound-box had been going on
for a long time. Some authorities trace the medieval box-
like sound-boxes to the Greek cithara, whose name is

preserved in 'guitar' and 'cittern'. But the vast admixture
of types during the Middle Ages makes it well-nigh impossible to reach specific conclusions. Plectrum versions are
shown from the tenth century, bowed from the twelfth, the
latter producing the famous 'troubadour fiddle' (Provençal
*viola*, French *vièle*) which held a place in thirteenth-century
France and Germany equal to that of the minstrel's harp in
the British Isles. Its body-shape was waisted or oval (Fig. 59),
and in its use a tradition of
drone or bourdon accompaniment had by no means been
dropped. Jerome of Moravia,
a Dominican, tells something
of its use in a Latin treatise of
*c.* 1250. The *viella*, he says, has
five strings, and the first
tuning for them is: *d* (bourdon), *G, g, d', d'* (these last a
unison top course); but for
secular music, in which one
has to rush about over the
whole musical compass, all
five strings must lie over the

FIG. 59. Thirteenth-
century fiddles

fingerboard, and follow order of pitch: *G, d, g, d', g'* (these
pitches not necessarily meant as absolute). For the bourdon
in general, Jerome adds that 'it is usual and better to make
answer to any desired note of the melody with the *borduni*
at the principal consonances [i.e. octave, fifth, etc.] . . .
which is easily managed with a practised bowing hand,
though only by advanced players'. To this an early an-
notator adds a reference to touching the bourdon 'by thumb
or bow'. Clearly medieval fiddling was an art of some
intricacy, even if the build of the instrument itself left much
room for acoustical improvement, which commenced in the
Renaissance and was no doubt helped ahead by that
period's scientific interest in the mathematics of form.

Much bourdon-fiddling continues today, as in Bulgaria,
and in Scottish reels. In the West, however, a closer survival

to medieval technique was in the Welsh crwth (Middle English 'crowd'), a lyre that was bowed since the thirteenth century and in due course gained a fingerboard. Held up like a fiddle, it had six strings: two octave courses, and a pair of bourdons also tuned to an octave and struck with thumb or bow 'to serve as a kind of bass accompaniment', Bingley wrote in 1798, adding: 'When accompanied by the harp its tone was much mellowed, but still it had an unconquerable harshness.' He

may have heard an unusually rough player, for in the present century, Otto Andersson has studied the bowed lyres (Fig. 60) surviving in Estonia, Karelia, and the Dalecarlia: simple hollowed-out lyres with pine belly and three or four gut or horsehair strings tuned, for example, $a'$, $d'$, $g$ and stopped from behind in the old lyre manner. The instrument is held across the thighs and sounded in Estonia 'soft

FIG. 60. Estonian bowed-lyre player

and gentle, recalling a muted violin'. With its flat bridge, unstopped strings sounded as bourdons. In Iceland, however, it is a three-stringed zither that is bowed, the *fidla*, with its melody string stopped from beneath in the old lyre or fiddle manner. Further applications of the bow have been to a long pyramidal monochord, the *tromba marina* (p. 142), still occasionally played in Central Europe. A photograph taken in Bohemia in 1898 shows a village band consisting of the '*trumerina*', a triangle, and a hurdy-gurdy. The last, whose early appearance was mentioned in p. 69, was widely played in the Middle Ages (in French, *simphonie*, *chifonie*), had its last period of fashion in French society of the bergère period, and has survived as a folk instrument, especially in France and Central Europe (Fig. 61). It usually has one or a pair of melody strings, and up to four bourdons, all of them sounded together by the resined rim of a wooden wheel rotated by a crank at the tail of the instrument. The melody strings are stopped by keys that press against them from the side, and the tunes, especially dance tunes, are articulated by interrupting the crank's rotation, e.g. separate quarter-turns for detached quavers. Mozart scores for the hurdy-gurdy, under its German name *Leier*, in one set of his German Dances.

It will be seen how these folk 'survivals' and their oriental relatives indicate ways of making music that have been of considerable importance in the past and with special reference to the European Middle Ages, when so much of

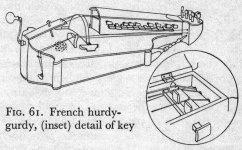

Fig. 61. French hurdy-gurdy, (inset) detail of key

even the best secular music was made by musicians performing alone, or alone in turn. When projecting a practical reconstruction of medieval monody, a modern instrumentalist is constantly faced with the problem of making the tunes sound more lifelike than they appear on paper, only to find that trained artistry and added ornament cannot alone solve it. A necessary science, to be blended with musical intuition, is one of auxiliary noises – broken octaves, swept strings, drones, as well as added ornament – utilizing the data of folk and oriental techniques of the medieval stratum to supplement hints of similar things in early literary and pictorial sources. It is an exciting branch of musical research, only recently begun, and, by resuscitating sounds of the very old in music, may even suggest some fresh ideas for the very new.

## FLUTES AND PIPES BEFORE THE WOODWIND AGE

Jubal, says the Book of Genesis, was the father of all those who play 'the harp and the pipe'. Whether Jubal is correctly equated with Apollo hardly concerns us here, but the Hebrew terms for the instruments, both in this passage and throughout the Old Testament, have been much fought over in the organological world. The prevailing interpretations of the leading terms are now these: our 'harp' translates Hebrew *kinnor*, a lyre; 'psaltery', *nevel*, a harp; 'timbrel', *tof*, a frame drum, ancestral to the tambourine; and 'pipe', *halil*, a reedpipe – except in Genesis and Job, where 'pipe' (or in the A.V. 'organ') translates *ugab*, denoting the archaic rim-blown flute of cane. This flute is traced by Dr Hans Hickmann in Upper Egypt to the period preceding the historic dynasties. Thereafter it was played in Egypt beside harps and singers, while in Sumeria, though in the first place a shepherd's pipe, it was also employed in temple rituals. Like the rattles and jingles, whistles and bull-roarers with which it was associated in the prehistoric period, this long flute was essentially primitive, akin to certain 'harmonic flutes' of primitive cultures in which the melodic compass depends first upon blowing the higher natural harmonics of the tube (roughly those of a bugle call) and second upon filling in the small gaps between them by providing a minimum number of fingerholes; the earlier Egyptian flutes, of which a few specimens have been found in tombs, usually had three. The modern arrangement of six or more holes dates from about the Hellenistic era, and modern rim-blown flutes like the Arab *nay* and the Balkan *kaval* possess these. Curiously, rim-blown flutes (blown across the open top end) have never entered Western Europe.

By the end of the third millennium B.C., this flute was being abandoned to the countrysides and villages, its place

in the cities being taken by a strange series of reedpipes
which thenceforth virtually monopolized the wind music
of Antiquity, culminated in the Greek *aulos* and Roman
*tibia*, and lasted even into the early Middle Ages. They were
short, slender pipes of cane or wood, sounded by reeds (the
Greeks, we know, using double reeds of cane), and they were
almost invariably played in pairs, the piper holding one
pipe in each hand and sounding them both simultaneously
(Fig. 62). There is nothing physically difficult in this; but

FIG. 62. Etruscan aulos

what was its musical intention? We simply do not know.
A great deal of double-piping still goes on today, especially
around the Mediterranean and Black Sea regions. Except
for a Sardinian species, the pipes are all of the equally
ancient 'parallel' kind (Fig. 63) on which the fingers can

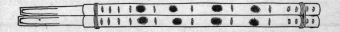

FIG. 63. Balearic (Ibiza) parallel doublepipe

span both pipes if desired, and all are sounded with primitive single reeds made by slitting a tongue in the cane (Fig.
70 h, i). Many are hornpipes, to be mentioned below. Their

diversity of playing techniques appears astonishing to the Western musician brought up to play on his single wood-wind instrument; frequently one of the two pipes has fewer holes than the other, to provide for all kinds of accompaniment from a plain drone to ingenious harmonic and rhythmic counterpoints. These pipers, often shepherds, from across the areas of ancient Greek colonization, provide our only clues to what Greek professional auletes might have done to win their immense popular successes.

While the aulos dominated the picture of town wind music, it is perfectly certain that a musical folklorist traversing the ancient Occident could have collected three or four different pastoral and folk pipes from each region just as he may today. A herdsman, of course, *needed* his pipe, as in many areas he still does, when for example a mist envelopes the grazing animals. In Sicily, one of Theocritus's herdsmen boasts to play four pipes: *syrinx* (panpipe); *aulos*; *plagiaulos* (here a transverse flute); and *donax* (literally 'cane', but possibly the parallel double-pipe mentioned above). Julius Pollux, in his *Onomasticon* (Athens, second century A.D.) gives a most interesting list of regional and national pipes attributed to various peoples from Scythian tribes to the Celts and the 'islanders of the Ocean' – presumably Britons, described as panpipers. After the Dark Ages, similar pipes reappear with a fairly general European distribution. No Western wind instrument of the early Middle Ages need have been unknown to Pollux and his world: panpipes, and the various double-pipes including the hornpipe, which had been associated in the second century B.C. with the Phrygian cult of Cybele. Hornpipes are reedpipes mounted with cowhorn bells possibly derived from religious symbolism. Commoner than is generally realized, they are played today from Spain across to Arabia and East Russia, usually developed into bagpipes (Fig. 64) and always sounded with the primitive single reeds. In Britain they were last played by Welsh and Scottish shepherds in the eighteenth century; they have no known connexion with the dance of the same name, for which the airs are typical fiddle tunes.

Our early medieval list continues with the plain cow horn bored with fingerholes for playing tunes, as shepherds sometimes still do in Scandinavia and Spain (Fig. 78); also the flageolet, of which, curiously, there are no certain traces in the old Graeco-Roman world, though the Alexandrian organ must surely have utilized its principle and there is no Mediterranean region today where pastoral or toy flageolets will not be found.

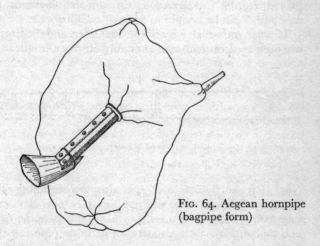

FIG. 64. Aegean hornpipe
(bagpipe form)

From the middle of the twelfth century we notice the onset of a change: the countries of Western Europe begin to establish and to share a wind music of a new formal character – a 'Gothic' wind music, based very largely upon fresh instruments, pipe and tabor for dancing, shawm and trumpet for ceremony, and bagpipe for anything. The pipe and tabor is a one-man band in which the piper beats his own drum. The drum, a small snare drum beaten with the right hand, may stem from the popular double-skin tambourine of the Mediterranean. The pipe (Fig. 65), however, is not essentially different from the Malham pipe mentioned on p. 48, though made of wood. It is a flageolet with three

T–H

holes – two in front and one behind for the thumb – and is played with the left hand only, a complete scale being obtained by utilizing harmonics only from the second upwards, e.g. C to F in second harmonics, G to high C in third, etc. In England the pipe and tabor later became associated especially with the Morris Dance, for which it was last played in Oxfordshire at the beginning of the present century. In Provence and northern Spain it is still much played, e.g. for the farandoles through the vineyards, and new outfits can be bought in Marseilles, Bilbao, etc.

The shawm, which we will consider later, and the bagpipe are both reed instruments, probably of urban origin in the

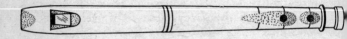

FIG. 65. Basque tabor pipe

Near East shortly before or soon after the beginning of the Christian era. An Alexandrian figurine, now at Berlin, depicts a Syrian street musician playing a panpipe to the accompaniment, as it appears, of a drone pipe somehow arranged to be fed with wind from a bag held under his left arm. Here may be the mode of the bagpipe's origin; but apart from three or four references to 'bagpiper', as in Suetonius's mention of Nero as *utricularius*, nothing further is known about the instrument in Antiquity, despite what is often claimed, and indeed it may for all we know have been re-invented in the Middle Ages. Briefly to describe it, the chanter (melody pipe) is held in a sheep or goatskin bag. So, too, usually, is a drone, normally a 'bass drone' tuned two octaves below the chanter's keynote, while several species, e.g. the Scottish, have additional drones. The pipes are fed by arm pressure on the bag, which is inflated and replenished as necessary, either by the mouth or by bellows strapped to the body, through an inlet pipe fitted with a leather non-return valve. Much of the vigour and charm of bagpiping depends upon the gracing techniques, to which the piper, having no physical contact with the reeds, is obliged to resort in order to articulate a melody, repeat notes, and so on. Thus on many peasant bagpipes the chanter's lowest note may be either struck rapidly between other notes to detach them, or, for a sharp *staccato*, be sustained between them, its sound being swallowed by the drone or its overtones to give an effect of momentary silence in the melody.

Bagpipe design in Europe is zoned in accordance with regional traditions. To the east, from Poland to Bulgaria, much hornpipe ancestry is evident, and their narrow, cylindrically-bored chanters with single reeds sound smooth and clear through the virtual absence of even-numbered overtones that arises when such a bore is sounded by a reed. In the Western pipes, from Scotland to Spain, chanters are conical, giving the wilder, more reedy sound, charged with all overtones, familiar to all in the Highland bagpipe, today played across the entire world. Refined and very beautiful bagpipes played in the British Isles since about 1700 – the Northumbrian small-pipe, and the Irish union pipe with its two-octave compass enabling fiddle tunes to be played – are too complex to be described here, but mention should be made of the bagpipe of Italy, *zampogna*, with two separate chanters, one for each hand and arranged for harmonizing in thirds, often in accompaniment to a small rustic oboe played by a second player. The character of *zampognari* music, associated especially with Christmas, is familiar through its imitations by Handel in *Messiah* (the first eight bars of the 'Pastoral Symphony') and Bach in the *Christmas Oratorio* (appropriately on four oboes in the Sinfonia to Part Two).

The prevalence of pipe and tabor and of bagpipe in the period preceding that of regular ensemble-playing is explained if we consider their sounds. The one with its drum, the other with its drone, enabled a solo musician to hold the attention and sustain the spirits of the listeners or dancers to a degree far exceeding that which is possible with a simple pipe without accompaniment: it may be relevant to recall the emphasis on *double* pipes in Antiquity. The troubadour De Calanson's list (*c.* 1210) of a court minstrel's expected accomplishments refers mainly to stringed instruments, but also to two wind: *tabourer*, to play pipe and tabor; and *estives*, believed by most authorities to denote bagpipes. But the growth of formal and composed concerted music in the fourteenth century began to put an end to this bagpiping and tabouring interlude in the history of our cultivated wind music, and encouraged the use of simple flutes and other pipes, to lead by degrees to the consorts of the sixteenth century.

The transverse flute, keyless prototype of the modern flute, belonged mainly to the east of the Rhine: the fife is still a leading folk instrument in the Alps and Carpathians – though like other ancient European things, such as the lynx, it belongs also to Spain. French and Italian traditions favoured the flageolet kind, which the fourteenth-century instrument makers moulded to its classic European model, the *recorder*. The earliest trace of this name was recently discovered by Brian Trowell in the household accounts for 1388 of the Earl of Derby, later Henry IV: *i fistula nomine Ricordo* – 'a flute called a keepsake', evidently from some Italian nobleman. An essential characteristic of a recorder *vis-à-vis* other flageolets is the width of the bore, allowing ample breadth at the voicing for full tone-production, controlled and mellowed by a contraction towards the lower end – though in the earlier recorders, before 1650, this contraction is less than later and today. This, and the finest professional workmanship, endowed the instrument with the organ-pipe quality and artistic flexibility that have endeared it to so many in past and present.

The recorder may have played a leading part in establishing the Western system of cross-fingering, by which semitones were accurately sounded before the days of woodwind mechanism. The starting point here is the natural row of six or seven fingerholes, spaced equally to suit the spread of the fingers. The acoustic result is a 'natural pipe scale' which one hears in much folk music. There is an absence of distinction of tone and semitone in parts of the scale; the note given by covering four holes, especially, sounds midway between its neighbours (say G and E), whereas ordered musical system requires it to sound at a semitone from one and a whole tone from the other (i.e. as either F or F♯). Juggling with the placing and relative sizes of the holes can correct this one way or the other; but by leaving the holes approximately as they were and by employing cross-fingerings as the rule, one can command both corrected pitches, which is what we

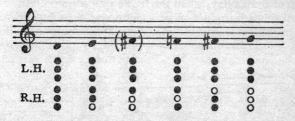

require (see musical example). For the F natural, the 'neutral' fingering is flattened by closing the lowest hole; for F♯ the G is flattened by closing two holes. With similar methods in the upper half of the scale and again in the overblown octave, the skilled recorder player is master of all chromatic exigencies.

The concept of a 'whole consort' or choir of instruments of the same type arose early in the fifteenth century with the maturer, more harmonious schools of polyphony, and may have been partly inspired by the improved sound of the organ. The quartet of recorders (*fleutes*) that performed for Philip of Burgundy in 1454 probably included no recorder deeper than tenor. The bass was added later in the century following the corresponding extension of the range of parts in vocal compositions, and the early sixteenth-century consort typically comprised a treble, two tenors

(one for alto), and a bass. Similar consorts of flutes followed,
very beautifully made instruments, cylindrically bored in
one piece of boxwood. The sound of these flutes is full and
expressive, and a single flute seems to have been preferred
to a single recorder when making mixed or 'broken'
consorts with strings (as in Morley's *Lessons*, mentioned on
p. 166). From *c.* 1550 larger and deeper recorders were made
(it would have been impracticable with flutes), descending
down to *c*, even *F*, in actual sounds, and professional
players, who had best access to them, used often to perform
pieces on all the larger sizes together. The prominence
given to the little descant size today brings a false impression
of recorder-playing of the past, both of the consort period
and of Bach's day, when the treble was all-important.

Another introduction of *c.* 1500 was a consort of reed
instruments, *crumhorns* (Fig. 66), appropriate to indoor

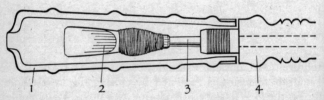

Fig. 66. Crumhorn, top end. Cap sectionized to show reed.
1, cap; 2, reed; 3, staple; 4, instrument.

music and giving variety beside the two kinds of flute. The
fourteenth century had already felt a need for a soft-toned
reed instrument and had found it in the *douçaine* or *dulzaina*,
of which very little is known. The crumhorn, however, is
well understood from some two dozen specimens preserved
in museums on the continent. Apparently adapted from
a German or Central European folk instrument related to
the bagpipes, it is cylindrically bored with the lower end
upturned (Pl. 21c), and employs a large double reed. A
useful feature is the cap fitted over the reed, with an opening

in the top for blowing into and tonguing against, giving the instrument the feel of a recorder and preserving the reed from rapid deterioration through excessive wetting. The tone has a strongly humming nasal quality, and since a cylindrical reed instrument gives low notes for its length, a bass crumhorn, descending to bottom *F* of the bass voice, need only be about three feet long (as against over six feet for a great bass recorder reaching the same note in actual pitch). The instruments are, however, inconveniently restricted in compass through their not being capable of over-blow to an upper register. Some modern German makers now reviving the crumhorn, along with cornetts, early flutes, etc., will provide one or two closed keys to extend its compass from a rather frustrating ninth to a useful eleventh – an addition for which there exist historically contemporary precedents, not with the crumhorn itself but with instruments closely akin to it.

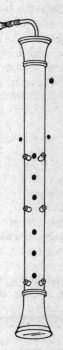

Many other reed instruments introduced in the sixteenth century pursued the same basic idea – cylindrical-bore double-reed instruments for consorts: *sordoni* (German *Sordunen*) or *courtauts* (Fig. 67) in which the bore ran down and up in a single pillar of wood; *bassanelli*, with plain top-to-bottom bore; and rackets (Fig. 68), with six or more bores cut in a short thick wood or ivory cylinder, connected in series and so enabling a note as low as *F'*, the lowest but one of the double bass, to be produced from an instrument scarcely twelve inches tall. Though built in consorts, these instruments appeared on the scene late in the century when blended wind consorts of

FIG. 67.
Courtaut
(sordone)
(after
Mersenne)

*mixed* instruments became increasingly fashionable, and in the vocal polyphony that musical directors drew so largely upon for their instrumental repertory, the deep, soft buzz of one racket among recorders, cornetts, etc., made a better effect than a whole consort of them.

Not one of these reed instruments outlived the fashions for which they were created; by the end of the seventeenth century they were curiosities already listed in catalogues of private museums, through which most of the extant specimens have come down to us. A mid-sixteenth-century invention of lasting value, however, was the *fagotto* or

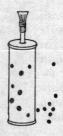

Fig. 68. Racket
(dots beside instrument
indicate holes on rear side) (Mersenne)

*dulzian*, in English 'curtal', the prototype of the bassoon. Here, too, a doubled-back bore was incorporated, but this time it was a conical bore readily overblowing to the octave register (Fig. 69). Again consorts were built but little used, the instrument proving more valuable as a bass to other instruments. As late as the 1680s, before the re-modelled or classical bassoon replaced it, works by Buchner and others include a 'fagotto' (i.e. curtal) in an otherwise stringed orchestra. Some establishments preferred the deeper-pitched *Quart-fagott* descending to *G'* (the ordinary one went down to *C*), and it was almost certainly one of these that Bach employed in Cantatas 31 and 155 (1715–16). It is now hard to imagine the effect of Ulrich, Bach's Weimar fagottist, in the wild *obbligato* of Cantata 155 on this deep instrument, but as far as one can judge in their dry, leaking condition today, the old curtals gave a warm, human sound, and would have spoken evenly and fluently when they were new.

To go back a little, the complement to the chamber or *bas* music of the Renaissance was the *haut* (loud) music, in which the shawm was predominant (Pl. 21a, b). We have already referred to its deafening sound in the Arab world (p. 54). In Europe it has been no milder: 'the loudest of instruments, excepting only the trumpet', wrote Mersenne. Its power is due in the first place to its reed and the manner of mouthing it. The reed, fan-shaped, wide-tipped, and narrow-stemmed, is mounted on the metal tube or 'staple', which fits into the instrument (Fig. 70, right, d). Most oriental players disdain control of the reed, letting it vibrate freely inside the mouth with the lips pressed to a wide disc mounted upon the staple. The instrument is held high like a trumpet, a posture which, as one knows from many earlier jazz clarinet-tists, encourages uninhibited blowing. The European shawm reed is of harder

FIG. 69. Curtal (fagotto, dulcian)

material, prepared like all Western double reeds by folding over a strip of seasoned cane, shaping and binding the ends together, and paring down and finally separating the tip (Fig. 70 a–e). The European shawmist presses the lips to a wooden 'pirouette' (g) which permits lip-control without appreciably reducing the reed's amplitude of vibration. Today, four shawms, two trebles and two tenors (with large metal bells, Pl. 21b), all fitted with modern mechanism, are always to be heard in Catalonia, leading the bands that play for the sardana dance.

Historically, the shawm's unique qualities must have been fully developed by the times of the earlier Caliphs, when the Roman tradition of ceremonial ensembles of trumpets was expanded to produce vast military bands of trumpets, drums, and cymbals, to which shawms were able to contribute a more positive melodic element than the long Arab trumpets could ever have done. The band was

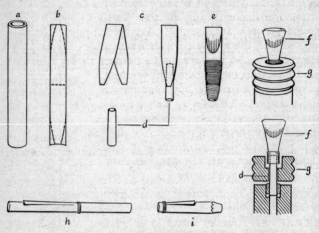

FIG. 70. (a–e) Double reed making (bagpipe)
(f–g) Catalan shawm reed with pirouette
(h–i) Single reeds

adopted in Europe at about the time of the last crusade – the 'pypes, trompes, nakers, clariounes, that in the bataille blowen blody sounes' in *The Knight's Tale*. Just after Chaucer's time, the band's wind section came to be employed in *haut* music for dancing, played polyphonically with the trumpet taking one of the lower parts (through which it soon became a trombone; see Chapter 11). Shawms meanwhile began to be made in different sizes, culminating in the bass shawms or 'pömmers' of the sixteenth century and first half of the seventeenth, through which period the band was civilian rather than military, still including a trombone and also, mollifying the sound with their incomparable sweetness, cornetts. After this, shawms were displaced in all fields, except locally, by the oboe. Their only flourishing survival is now in Spain. The popular Macedonian *zurla* is also a shawm but of an Asiatic pattern.

Though today shepherds pipe less and villages mostly have the radio, many ancient pipes are still with us as toys. The display of toy musical instruments along the foot of a music store's window is interesting in every country. Here we can mention but a few. In Barcelona one should find a prettily-turned boxwood 'French flageolet', with its characteristic arrangement of holes – four for the fingers and two for the thumbs; in the last century it soared to fashion as the 'Quadrille flageolet' during the popularity of that dance. In Britain, the 'English flageolet' with six holes has now been displaced by cheap recorders, though the primeval European flageolet lives on next to 'nigger bones' (virtually the Latin *crotala*) as the penny whistle (*fistula*), as also does the plastic panpipe (*syrinx*). The Swanee whistle, scored for by Ravel in *L'Enfant et les Sortilèges*, is also made by Indian children as a bamboo bird-pipe, while another type of flute – the 'globular' flute of earthenware known in Egypt and prehistoric China – is common in Italy as a Carnaval whistle, *ocarina*, made in the form of a bird. One blows into its tail and sometimes a couple of fingerholes are provided for making fragments of melody. About seventy years ago it was developed as the now familiar musical toy with nine holes, and in 1939 a consort of them achieved fame in Bing Crosby's 'When the Sweet-potato Piper plays'. A religious procession in southern Italy may still show an assortment of rattles, clappers, scrapers, bells and whistles preserving their full folklore functions of raising an exorcizing clamour; and here the strange grunting of a friction drum should be heard above the rest – possibly to remind British spectators of the little cardboard friction drums with resined thread, sold at fairs at home within the last few years if not still today, as toys for reproducing farmyard noises, just as they are in India and Japan, while the full-size ritual friction drum numbered among the sound-producers for the early *musique concrète*.

Most folk instruments can now be heard on records, for which the lists in Kunst's *Ethnomusicology* (see Bibliography, 'Primitive Musical Instruments') are helpful, as well as those issued by the International Folk Music Council, London; while the British Institute of Recorded Sound, London, has far from neglected the wide fields of folk and primitive music. One needs also to examine the instruments themselves, useful British collections being those of the Pitt Rivers Museum, Oxford, and the Horniman Museum, London. But no collection in this country can hope to rival the Instrumental Museum of the Conservatoire Royal de Musique, Brussels. This immense collection, systematically built up by Victor Mahillon (1841–1924, and truly the Father of Organology), also contains original examples of almost all the sixteenth-century wind instruments mentioned in this chapter as well as of their stringed contemporaries. It is unquestionably the first place that anyone with a special interest in musical instruments must visit.

# 10. *The Woodwind*

JAMES A. MACGILLIVRAY

THE flute, oboe, clarinet, and bassoon formed the wood-wind of the classical orchestra, and are directly or indirectly the parent forms of the subsidiary members that have at various times entered the group. They are instruments of strongly individual character, differing radically in their sound producers, acoustical behaviour, and fingering systems, and they are also used variously in bands of many kinds. But as their main historic function has been to play together as a section of the orchestra, and as they have constantly influenced each other at all critical stages of their development, a collective treatment is the clearest and most concise method of describing them.

Though the history of flutes and reed instruments is a very long one, and though European musicians have made and played pipes called 'flutes' and 'hautbois' since the Middle Ages and the Renaissance respectively, the orchestral woodwind instruments are of more recent origin than is often realized.

The *oboe* (Fr. *hautbois*), around which the woodwind section was developed, was a newer instrument in Bach's time than the saxophone was when first used in jazz, and as great a novelty to Purcell as the *Ondes Martenot* to Messiaen; and from a modern aspect, the oboe of those times, though possessing no mechanism beyond three simple keys, was much nearer to our present instrument than to earlier instruments known by the same name in France and England up to the middle of the seventeenth century. The oboe first appeared at the court of Louis XIV of France shortly before 1660. The royal musicians, organized in the various bands of the Grande Écurie du Roi, had been employed primarily for traditional outdoor ceremonies, and played the old instruments, led by the shawm, which had essentially belonged to the open air – and also of course to the partly open theatres of the Shakespearean type. But these musicians played too for the king's entertainments in the palace, and the changing taste which made this increasingly their more important function was given a new impetus by the appointment of Lully as *surintendant* first of the king's chamber music (1655) and later of ballet and opera. Following the fashion of his native Italy, Lully immediately banned the old wind instruments from indoor performance, with the exception of the rather monotonous recorder, which was left as the only contrast to bowed and plucked string tone.

The musicians of the Grande Écurie, some of them on intimate terms with the king, were among the most privileged and famous in Europe. Many were composers, all played several instruments, and some were already well-known instrument makers. (One was also a world famous botanist, and another received a pension from the London Chess Club as the leading master of his day.) It was among these players that the oboe was created, either as a prestige measure to increase their part in the more refined music of the court, or in response to a demand for greater tonal variety for wind instruments. It has been shown by Josef Marx that the inventors were almost certainly Jean Hotteterre and Michel Philidor. As only the former is recorded as an instrument maker, Philidor may merely have helped in testing and reed-making, or may have conceived the idea and entrusted the realization of it to the hands of his craftsman colleague.

The new 'French hoboy', as it became known for a time in England, was made, unlike the shawm, in three separate joints, which facilitated more exact boring (Pl. 22b). The bore was narrower, the bell was smaller and internally flanged (evidently for tonal reasons, since the lowest note, $c'$, spoke through two vent-holes in the bell neck), and the fingerholes were much smaller. The shawm's characteristic jangle of overtones was thus replaced by a more restrained 'classical' tone, and the cross-fingerings, remaining essential to the technique, greatly improved. The

C key was fish-tailed as it had been on shawms and the new E♮ key was duplicated, in each case for the benefit of the 'left-handed' player (i.e. one who plays with the left hand on the lower joint, as many peasant pipers do today). The double reed (Fig. 71) was made narrower than that of the shawm and also long enough to give control of the

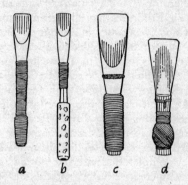

FIG. 71. Oboe reeds: (a) English *c.* 1800; (b) modern. Bassoon reeds: (c) English *c.* 1800; (d) modern German. All slightly less than half size.

lowest notes in *pianissimo*, while the abolition of the 'pirouette' made the reed fully lip-controlled and kept it farther forward in the mouth to permit more effective tonguing. The small French bagpipe, *musette*, was at this time a favourite in aristocratic circles, in the hands both of noble amateurs and the professionals of the Hotteterre–Philidor circle, and it was from the skill lavished on the manufacture of these beautifully constructed and decorated little instruments that the craftsmanship which went to create the new oboe was no doubt largely derived. The shawm, on the other hand, remained to the end within traditions of manufacture going back to the thirteenth-century *faiseurs de flûtes*, who were members of the guild of chair-leg makers.

The first hundred years or so of the oboe's existence were

in many ways its golden age. It was often the only and always the principal upper woodwind instrument in the orchestra; at first largely to double the violins in order, it was said, to give clearer articulation. But it rapidly gained independence, and internationally celebrated virtuosi, who included Sammartini, Besozzi, and Fischer, were more numerous than they have been at any time since. Curiously enough, music historians have long and staunchly agreed that the old oboe was congenitally out of tune and capable only of a stentorian and hideous caterwauling. Even Vaughan Williams wrote (in Hinrichsen's *Musical Year-Book* 1952): 'I should like to see Mr Goossens confronted with one of those gross bagpipes which in Bach's time stood for an oboe.' Yet it was for this very instrument that Bach wrote his most telling *obbligati* and Mozart his unisons with the soprano voice in its tenderest moments; so that if the oboe sounded as execrable as the historians have claimed, must we not completely revise our notions of these great composers' competence? But we should not forget that even with later and modern standards of playing, the claim of each generation that its favourite player was the first to reveal the beauties of his instrument ever persists; it merely means that some fashion has changed, while criticisms such as Burney's of bad woodwind intonation are still the commonest criticisms of performance among musicians today.

Until quite recently, any practical experiments that were attempted with old oboes were made in ignorance of eighteenth-century fingering and with a modern reed. The latter is a millimetre or more too narrow. It is only with a reed at least the size of that now used for the cor anglais that one can explore the possibilities of the old oboe. The whole compass is then controllable, and after a little practice one is conscious of making substantial lip-adjustment only on the flat low *f'♯* (which was not cross-fingered) – though the *b'♭* may be rather stuffy. In the second octave all semitones speak evenly and in tune, and although high notes above *d'''* may be risky on an otherwise good reed, the sensational top $f'''$s of Mozart's Quartet are quite practicable. The maximum volume is considerably less than on modern instruments, while the minimum at which one can play fluently and with safety is perhaps a little louder; but the penetrating low notes which are a lifelong trial to the modern second oboist in pianissimo are easier. The tone is less brilliant, less incisive and dramatic, but fuller and warmer, with an infinite nostalgic charm. The writer has found that many listeners spontaneously express a preference for it, though to some extent this may be due to its relative unfamiliarity. *Vibrato*, largely banned by the Romantics as detracting from the full, dramatic style they required, was quite usual in the earlier period: Mozart's remarks about Fischer even suggest that its abuse was already becoming a scourge. The fingering is certainly difficult, having few of those alternatives which alleviate cross-fingering difficulties on the recorder, and many of the baroque sonatas and concertos now played by young students were originally virtuoso pieces. But despite the difficulty of achieving unfailing smoothness of performance, the early enthusiasm for the oboe was natural and inevitable. The Grand Écurie had produced a wind instrument second only to the violin in power of expression, and its emergence was decisive in establishing a mixed combination of wind and strings as the normal orchestra thenceforth.

In open-air music, for which the shawm would on the face of it appear to be the more suitable, the new instrument rapidly triumphed, and the French *Douze Grands Hautbois du Roi* became the standard form for a military band for more than a century; 'Grands' referred to the eminence of the players, and is not to be confused with the expression 'Great Hobby' used for a time in England to distinguish the old instrument (shawm) from the new. For the bass, two of these twelve musicians played the bassoon.

The history of the *bassoon*\* up to this point is similar. Resembling its own predecessor – the one-piece curtal

---

\* Fr. *basson;* Ger. Ital. *Fagott, fagotto.* N.B. Dutch, Danish, *bazuin,* *basun* are words allied to Ger. *Posaune* and mean 'trombone'.

(Fig. 69) – rather more closely than the oboe did the shawm, the bassoon (Pl. 23) is most easily visualized as a large oboe pitched a twelfth lower and extended in compass down to $B'\flat$ by means of a U-bend and a parallel ascending bore on which the holes and keys are controlled by the two thumbs. The impossibly wide finger stretch theoretically required for an instrument of this size is reduced by drilling the fingerholes at angles approaching forty-five degrees through a very considerable thickness of wood. This device, the slowly-expanding conical bore, and the strange resonating effect of the extension, contribute to a characteristic tone quality that has always proved extremely sensitive to attempts at acoustically more rational construction. Cross-fingerings respond even better than on the old oboe, largely because the holes of the extension, especially the right thumb hole, can be used to alter or steady various notes. Conceived as a bass to the oboe, yet sounding quite different, the bassoon anticipated the eighteenth-century taste for tonal individuality among the members of the woodwind family (in contrast to the matched consorts of earlier times). It was usually made of maple or pear wood in four joints of which only the lowest or 'butt' contains both descending and ascending bores, and the curved brass mouthpipe or 'crook' lacked the 'pin hole' now usual. The bassoon was dispersed throughout Europe in company with the oboe, which, so far as a bass instrument can, it approached in popularity as a solo instrument, far outclassing the cello in this respect throughout the eighteenth century.

The *flute*, as remodelled from the cylindrical flute of the previous era, may be another invention of Hotteterre and his colleagues. The new flute retained the cylindrical head joint, but the rest of it was conical, narrowing towards the foot. Like the oboe it was made in three joints, but from before the mid eighteenth century in four (Pl. 22). The full tube-length sounded $d'$, and the single key, for $E\flat$, was not duplicated since a left-handed player had only to rotate the foot-joint. Oboe and flute were both usually of boxwood, often dark-stained and handsomely mounted at the joints with ivory. On both, all notes outside the scale of D major, excepting E♭, had to be obtained by cross-fingering, but the important thing to notice is that this was far more effective on the oboe than on the flute, particularly in the low register. This largely explains the greater immediate success of the oboe, and its clear contemporary acknowledgement as a new French invention, whereas in France and England the flute continued to be called a 'German' flute, as its cylindrical predecessor had been termed German or Swiss.

Since the recorder responds particularly well to cross-fingering, has greater carrying power than one might think, and a compass only slightly smaller than that of the old flute, it is sometimes wondered why it was so soon superseded. The main reason was the increasing preoccupation with nuance and dynamic range that was soon to find Besozzi's 'prodigious *messa di voce*' on the oboe a nine days' wonder, and eventually established the pianoforte in place of the harpsichord: perhaps a 'shadow cast before' by the Romantic movement. With its fixed sound-generator, the recorder belonged to a vanishing world of simple formal phrasing and level organ-like dynamics. No special fingering or other expedient could produce with steady intonation the infinite graduations of volume of the violin and oboe virtuosi, and its passing was due to the very limitations which once more have made it attractive to those suffering from a surfeit of modern over-phrasing. The same problem also *does* exist for the flute player, but since his tone is directly controlled by the lips the tendency for pitch to vary with intensity can be counteracted: while the player projects the breath through the small aperture of his lips to strike the far edge of the embouchure hole, the angle of impact can be varied considerably, affecting the intonation of the note. Yet control of pitch remains a major difficulty for the modern flautist, and is responsible for the exaggerated jaw-movements used in rapid *crescendo* and *diminuendo* by some schools of playing. The unmistakably *personal* tone which is characteristic of all lip-controlled instruments must also have played a part in the rout of the recorder before the flute. A century earlier it had been held a disadvantage of the flute that it expressed the player rather than the music, but changing tastes had now made this a decisive advantage.

In technique, the flute had an inescapable bias towards the sharp keys around D major, on account of the unsatisfactory cross-fingerings especially in the low octave. One cannot of course judge solely by the experiments of modern players in their limited spare time just how much the old flautists may have achieved, but even Quantz, Frederick the Great's celebrated flute master, wrote that solos in the difficult keys should be played only when it was certain that the listeners were fully aware of the difficulties involved.

It has long been known that the *clarinet* was invented by J. C. Denner (1655–1707) in Nuremberg about the beginning of the eighteenth century. Yet in view of its reputation as a comparative newcomer, it should be noted that this is only forty or fifty years later than the date now accepted for the invention of the oboe. Many primitive reedpipes combine a cylindrical bore with a single reed of the bagpipe-drone type (see Chapters 1 and 9). But the clarinet, with its separate reed-blade bound to the mouthpiece, marked (like the oboe among the double reeds) the arrival of the fully lip-controlled instrument. This arrangement *may* have been one of Denner's ideas. He is also known to have improved an instrument with the confusing name *chalumeau*. This word (cognate with 'shawm') can mean a straw, a bagpipe or its chanter, and a number of other things. However, the small size (about eight inches) of the chalumeau, which began to appear in a few operatic scores after Denner's time, is always stressed by writers, and to produce sounds of bearable pitch it must therefore have been cylindrical in bore, performing as a 'stopped pipe', i.e. giving a note about an octave lower than its length would otherwise indicate (and it is shown thus in Diderot's *Encylopédie*, 1767). Though the existence of this chalumeau has not been traced before Denner's time, it seems likely that his work on this one-register seven-holed pipe did give rise to his clarinet. Probably an attempt to extend the single register one or two notes upwards by means of keys near the top accidentally revealed the principle of the 'speaker key', which enables another scale to be played at the twelfth above (the third harmonics, since with a 'stopped pipe' system the second harmonics or octaves are unobtainable). This leaves a gap or 'break' of four diatonic notes between the top of the lower seven-note scale and the bottom of the upper. In the earliest type of clarinet, of which an example by Denner survives, this gap is filled by extending the low octave upwards by a thumb-hole (uncovered for $g'$), and a key for $a'$ for the first finger of the left hand, which with the addition of the speaker (which still retains this double function today) gives $b'♭$. The scale of the second register (the twelfths) was extended downwards by means of a hole for the right little finger, giving $c''$ when closed. Since the clarinet was at first used more or less in imitation of the natural trumpet, the absence of $b'♮$ scarcely mattered, but it soon became available through lengthening the tube and fitting the now-familiar long B key to extend the upper register downwards by a semitone (Pl. 22b); the exact date of this improvement is not known. Two more keys (for $c''♯$ and $e''♭$, also giving the twelfths below) were added later in the eighteenth century, to complete an upper register only a little less even than that of the oboe; but a few of the low-register cross-fingerings remained very bad.

Clarinet embouchures have varied considerably in the course of time. In the classic French embouchure, the lips are stretched easily back over the teeth to form cushions between the teeth and the reed and the mouthpiece. The reed's vibration is thus controlled by a light muscular action when the mouth closes on the mouthpiece. Slight national and other variations have always existed, such as the former military technique of putting the upper teeth on the mouthpiece, fairly recently adopted by most serious players in England and America. (Since the last war this method has even been introduced at the Paris Conservatoire by Delécluse.) Early clarinettists, however, played with the reed upwards, controlled by the upper lip. This style survived in most parts of Italy until the present century, and is still sometimes found among professional players in Naples. But it is believed to have been through German players at Mannheim, among the first to play with the reed downwards, that the clarinet came to the notice of Mozart, whose penetrating insight into its possibilities raised it to the important position in the orchestra that it has held ever since. All in all, the woodwind of the early classical orchestra possessed a high degree of efficiency, though each within a rather limited sphere, and Mozart's widow lived long enough to find the players of thirty years later, with their mechanic-

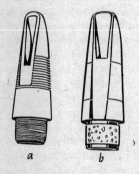

FIG. 72. Clarinet mouthpieces:
(a) Late eighteenth century;
(b) modern

ally improved instruments, musically and tonally inferior by comparison with her recollection of the old.

After the initial experiments in various, mostly high keys, the clarinet reached the orchestra as an instrument in C, giving in its upper register the same basic scale as the flute or oboe. The warmer toned B♭ clarinet, about three inches longer, became the favourite for concertos and for band or orchestral use from the middle of the eighteenth century. But D and A clarinets also existed, both to play with horns and trumpets in D, and for symphonies in sharp keys, and one result of this was to introduce the brass-instrument system of transposition into the woodwind – though it had already been used occasionally among recorders. This is a logical idea if one remembers that music is written for the player, not for the score-reader. The player in fact does *not* transpose; his music is transposed expressly so that he shall not have to. A moment's thought will show that if the music were written at actual pitch, then to play the scale of C on the A clarinet, he would have to use the same fingerings as for the scale of C♯ on the B♭ clarinet. He would therefore have the sensations of transposing, although sounding the same notes; and with several instruments, and therefore several different series of fingerings, the burden would be excessive. But with transposed parts the oboist can play the cor anglais with the *same fingering* for each *written* note; so can the clarinettist *any* clarinet, basset-horn, or bass clarinet, the saxophonist *any* saxophone, and so on. Most woodwind are transposing instruments except those 'in C', i.e. the flute, the oboe, and the little-used C clarinets and saxophones. The bassoon has always been played from parts at actual pitch, and is therefore regarded as being 'in C', though its basic fingerings are those of an instrument 'in F'.

\*

Some of these less usual instruments were well-known in the eighteenth century. Two of them were in some respects alike: the *cor anglais* and the *basset horn*, both pitched in F. They were, however, far too individually differentiated both in tone and in use to be properly regarded merely as 'tenors' to the oboe and the clarinet respectively. In construction, both were originally curved and leather-covered, but later angled with two straight joints connected by a knee-socket (Pl. 24). Their modern forms, however, are straight, the basset horn often with an upturned bell. The basic resemblance of the early curved shape to a goat-horn is obvious. 'Basset' was a common South German musical term for 'small bass' (the basset hound was so-called after its voice). 'Anglais', or rather 'inglese' – the Italian '*corno inglese*' being the earlier name – is harder to explain, though perhaps the instrument's soft and melancholy tone was thought to resemble the muted quality of English speech, which always amuses foreigners.

The precursor of the cor anglais was the tenor oboe, or *taille de hautbois*, in F. It had come into being at the same time as the oboe, which it resembled in all but size and pitch: a component of the French-style oboe-and-bassoon band mentioned earlier, and it so appears in Purcell's *Dioclesian*, where the band is used as a distinct unit. Some continental tenors, however, had globular bells, like every cor anglais. In Bach's works, *taille* is presumably this tenor oboe, with flared or globed bell according to the maker. Bach's *oboe da caccia* may or may not have been (nobody knows) a cor anglais or similar curved instrument, again with or without the globe; a well-known London player of the 1920s obtained a virtual monopoly of Bach engagements by having a flared bell made for his cor anglais, which he affixed in a quiet corner of the bandroom before playing 'oboe da caccia'. When asked point-blank by a conductor the difference between the two instruments, he replied 'Five guineas a concert'.

Bach's other variety of oboe, the *oboe d'amore* (Ger. *Liebeshoboe*), was pitched a minor third below the oboe. It was used by Telemann in 1722 and for the first time by Bach a year later. On this, old German bells are globular, old French ones straight. Having completely died out later in the eighteenth century, the oboe d'amore was revived for Bach performances by Mahillon, the well-known Brussels maker. It should be mentioned that the globular bell, so arresting a visual feature of these deeper oboes, has little acoustical effect, as compared with no bell at all, beyond rounding the tone of the lowest note, and as compared with a flared bell, giving slightly less brilliance. It also appears in the deeper-sounding pipes of some bagpipes, and its presence on deep oboes may stem from some folk tradition. It does, however, save extra length, and also breadth, which probably enabled it to survive the period of acoustical rationalization which coincided with the introduction of new harder woods, most of which have a quite narrow usable core. African blackwood, in particular, would rarely provide a flared bell wide enough for a cor anglais-sized instrument without cutting into the inferior and often discoloured outer wood.

For the basset horn we can name the probable inventor: Mayrhofer, of Passau in Bavaria, *c.* 1770 (though many of the early players were Bohemian). It has a small bore for its length (only about a millimetre wider than that of the average clarinet of the time) and an extension of its compass down to its low C (sounding *F*), which in the old curved and angled instruments incorporated a characteristic 'box' in which, to reduce total length, the bore is twice doubled back on itself before entering the bell (Pl. 24). The surviving Mayrhofer instrument (at Hamburg, Museum of Hamburg History) has but one key for this extension, adding only the C to the normal clarinet compass, but most old examples also have a D key and some also the two chromatic keys, all worked by the right thumb. The deep and sombre tone of the basset horn greatly attracted Mozart towards the end of his life, after which it remained for some time a standard component of the German military band. Danzi wrote an agreeable sonata for basset horn and piano, and Mendelssohn two Konzertstücke for clarinet, basset horn, and piano which are today undeservedly neglected. Later it almost died out, yet it was used in England for some solos in Balfe's *Bohemian Girl*. Mahillon revived it for Mozart's works, as the oboe d'amore was revived for Bach's, and this enabled Richard Strauss to use it in several operas, though his example has seldom been followed. The extinct globe-belled *clarinette d'amour* was usually in G, sometimes A♭ or F. The analogous *flûte d'amour* in A seems to have been used mainly for variety in flute recitals.

Among *double bassoons*, pitched an octave below the bassoon, Stanesby's 'basson grosso' made for Handel's Fireworks Music, though according to Burney not played at the performance, was featured at the Handel commemoration in 1784, and was played by Eric Halfpenny on television a few years ago (by courtesy of the National

Museum of Ireland, where it is preserved). Otherwise, the early history of the double bassoon, or contrabassoon, was confined to Vienna, where it was played in military bands. It reached the West with Beethoven's works, but seems to have been regarded as troublesome until the time of Wilhelm Heckel's reconstruction (c. 1880), with which, and with the larger orchestras of the late nineteenth century, it became a regular member of the woodwind. Small tenor and even treble bassoons are also found; a work was written for them by J. Kaspar Trost (see the *Galpin Society Journal*, XI). A speculation that they were used to teach boys is confirmed by a living London bassoonist who learnt the bassoon in this way in a Sicilian orphanage.

At the other end of the scale, the small flute or *piccolo* (Fr. *petite flûte*, Ital. *ottavino*) proves rather elusive historically, though Gluck scored for it and some conical eighteenth-century specimens survive. More is known about the *fife*, which up to the 1850s in England and the present time in Germany retained the earlier cylinder bore and absence of keys. It was mostly played in its easiest tonalities with no accompaniment other than side drums.

\*

The next phase in woodwind history, coinciding roughly with the working life of Beethoven, is marked by the steady addition of keys to gain fluency in all tonalities, though at first without any important change in the type of key used. This met the demand for freer modulation in orchestral music and the needs of the military band in its emergent 'concert' role, playing transcriptions of orchestral works and operatic selections. (As early as 1782 Mozart had been commissioned to transcribe *Die Entführung* for military band.)

First of all, the field of operations of the flute – the most home-bound in tonalities – had to be enlarged. The decisive step was taken in England about 1760, and four-keyed flutes soon became common (making six keys with the frequently-added extended foot joint for low C and C♯, Pl. 22). This lacked only the *c″* and duplicate F keys of the system which reigned until Boehm's invention of 1832, and is still used in most drum-and-flute bands. Since the new keys were identical in principle with the old ones, it is often wondered why they were not thought of earlier. The musette of the French courtiers had been provided with chromatic keys since the middle of the seventeenth century. Moreover, the Hotteterres were in a sense primarily bagpipe makers, and Jean Hotteterre himself was officially a bagpiper in the Grande Écurie. So it seems clear that their launching the oboe and the flute in the first place as cross-fingered instruments was a matter of deliberate choice. Some of the reasons which must have led to this choice remained valid until

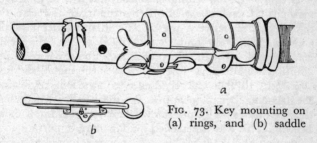

*a*

*b*

FIG. 73. Key mounting on (a) rings, and (b) saddle

1810 or even 1820. The old type of key was of sheet brass with a solid leather pad, rotating on a brass pin fixed through ridges in the wood and closing a rimless hole (Fig. 73a). Closure was far from hermetic: the leather was porous, the fall of the key imprecise, and the flat brass spring usually sluggish in action. An increase in the number of such keys, especially in the upper part of the instrument, must therefore necessarily involve a certain sacrifice of tone and efficiency. The musette, not being lip-controlled, had a greater need for keys, since there was no means of humouring cross-fingered notes, while the objections to keys were less valid since the instrument did not figure in ensemble music of a sensitive and exacting standard. But with the oboe in its early days, for example, it could hardly have been foreseen that a need for facility in the remoter tonalities would one day over-ride loss of resonance and certainty of response in those tonalities which were already good. It is significant that the leading players, masters of an existing technique and by their position least able to tolerate cracked notes and impaired *pianissimo*, were those most prone to conservatism. The beginning of the nineteenth century, however, was on the threshold of a period of inventions which left no excuse for tolerating any difficulty for which a theoretical solution could be found, and which produced by the middle of the century multi-keyed instruments practically identical with those of today, for which composers write complex passages in extreme registers and in six or seven sharps.

It cannot be too strongly stressed that it is in improved methods of *construction* of mechanism that the essential difference lies between the woodwind instruments of the eighteenth century and those typical of the nineteenth century and today, not merely in *ideas* about where to put additional useful keys. Just before 1800 the metal 'saddles' (Fig. 73b), till then scarcely used save in the long keywork of the bassoon, began to appear on the smaller woodwind; the key rotates on a stout screw-headed pin held in a metal bearing. This was superseded – a far more important step, beginning about 1806 – by metal pillars soldered to a footplate screwed to the wood; a hard-drawn metal 'barrel', silver-soldered across the key itself, is accurately fitted to the cheeks of the pillars through which is screwed the hard steel rod on which it rotates. This arose of necessity in the manufacture of glass flutes by Laurent of Paris, but its advantages even on wood were soon obvious. The key falls more accurately, noticeable lateral play occurring only after long wear. In about 1840 the system was modified by screwing the pillars directly to the wood – a retrograde step with the sole advantage of economy. Advances made in the hand-forging of metals in Brussels and Paris between 1820 and 1830 enabled these fittings to be made strongly and efficiently, and began the trend towards centralization of the Western woodwind industry in these two cities. No less vital was the introduction by Ivan Müller (1786–1854), in his thirteen-keyed clarinet, of the kid pad stuffed with wool, set in a cupped key and closing a countersunk hole which presented a sharp edge to the pad. This lasted until the present pads of animal tissue stuffed with felt backed by cardboard were introduced in the 1860s. Finally, Auguste Buffet's needle springs with their rotary action gave a new flexibility to keywork design. The advances all round called for new and more stable woods to replace boxwood, which sometimes warps badly enough to throw complex mechanism out of alignment. Among these are cocus, rosewood, and the various grenadillas including the now favourite African blackwood, called *ébène* or *Mozambique* by French manufacturers but not to be confused with the unresonant ebony, despite occasional mistranslation in makers' catalogues. Yet the possibility of making a reliable keyed instrument in boxwood cannot be ruled out: Töttcher, in Germany, has made several solo recordings on a modern boxwood oboe.

Once these technological advances had made fully chromatic keywork compatible with airtightness, research into the bores, and the size and placing of the holes, could proceed in terms of tonal improvement without an eye to possible ill effects upon cross-fingerings. Brilliance would seem to have been the chief ideal of a period dominated at its peak by the dramatic and controversial figures of Theobald Boehm (1794–1881) and Adolphe (Antoine Joseph) Sax (1814–94). Boehm, trained in minute craftsmanship as a jeweller, was for many years principal flute in the Munich orchestra and a well-known soloist. Skilled also in science, he turned aside from his flute after his first reconstruction of it to invent an overstrung piano and an iron-smelting process that was used until modern times. Sax, a clarinettist of some distinction, was reared in the musical instrument making trade by his father Charles Sax in Brussels. Surrounded since his arrival in Paris by influential friends in the Army and the Conservatoire, and by no less eminent rivals who ceaselessly attacked him, he and his work are still matters of controversy (cf. p. 312). His improvements to the clarinet included the addition of the two right hand rings which turned the

fingering of Müller's instrument into that of the present
'simple system' still used in some orchestras and by many
learners.

The innovations of Boehm were the most radical ever
attempted in the woodwind field since the invention of the
oboe in the seventeenth century, while the exhaustiveness
of his acoustical research which preceded them remains
unparalleled. His work began during a visit to London,
when he had been greatly impressed by the powerful tone,
especially in the lower register, of the celebrated player
Charles Nicholson (1795–1837). To emulate it, it seemed
to his essentially scientific mind that the flute must be redesigned on entirely new principles. Some of the holes of

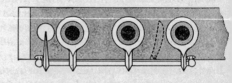

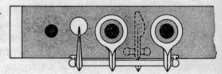

Fig. 74. Ring mechan-
ism on clarinet: (a)
Boehm system; (b)
simple system (brille)

Nicholson's flute were intentionally much larger than normal, but to extend their effect Boehm aimed at a whole
chromatic series of holes as large as possible and placed as
close as possible to their theoretically correct positions, all
of them standing normally open in order to secure an
approximation to an 'open end' for every note. To control
this with eight fingers and one thumb (for the right thumb
must hold up the instrument) a new system of fingering had
to be devised. He wrote: 'I decided to adopt the system of
ring keys', implying that the idea was already known –
indeed, it had been used in 1808 by an English clergyman
and later by the French clarinettist Lefèvre. The 'ring key'

(Fig. 74) enables a finger both to close the hole under it and to actuate a key at any distance from it through the agency of a long rod or axle. It was this system of rings or *anneaux mobiles* rather than his acoustical achievements that first caught the imagination of players and makers, and came to be thought of as 'Boehm's system', and the crux of his inventions. Boehm's arrangement, first applied to a conical flute (1832, Pl. 22a), remains with very slight modifications the fingering system of the flute today. His cylindrical bore with parabolic head, which followed fifteen years later in 1847, was yet more revolutionary; the holes are too large for the fingertips, so the rings are replaced by padded plates. Only the microscopic changes in bore of individual makers distinguish Boehm's flute of 1847 from our modern ones, while other systems still met in England (Radcliff; Rudall Carte 1867 model, Pl. 22a, etc.) have the same bore but mechanism altered to assist players used to the old fingerings. The Boehm flute was adopted very soon by the leading French and English players. Yet Boehm's own countrymen, Wagner included, were inclined to complain that the tone had been changed, and its dispersal in Germany was relatively slow. A London flutist who was still playing after the last war had in his boyhood heard eight-keyed flutes played in the Munich Opera, where Boehm himself had first played his new flute.

It may surprise players that the 'Boehm' clarinet is older than the Boehm (cylindrical) flute, and indeed older than the Albert or 'simple system' clarinet – if the '*clarinet d'après le système de M. Boehm*' exhibited at the exhibition of 1839 by Klosé (professor at the Paris Conservatoire) and the maker Auguste Buffet was indeed the Boehm-Klosé clarinet which was patented in 1844. (Klosé's Method for this instrument had already appeared in 1843.) The holes of Klosé's instrument were on the whole larger and more logically spaced than previously, but otherwise the influence of Boehm did not go far beyond the keywork. It was soon adopted in France, but in England, where the 1847 flute was quickly accepted, the Boehm clarinet was little used before the advent of Manuel Gomez, c. 1890, and its subsequent adoption by Charles Draper and George Anderson when students. Even in London orchestral circles twenty years ago there were still half a dozen players of the old system (or Clinton's modification of it). In the provinces and the army bands the Boehm was a rarity as late as 1925, when the wide use of the saxophone speeded up the change; the fingering is nearer, and the smoother emission of the Boehm clarinet makes it an easier doubling instrument in dance band and theatre.

In 1844 Buffet also produced a Boehm oboe, this time with some acoustical advice from Boehm himself, which accounts for the large bore and large size and low position of the holes. Though it is the only oboe designed on a logical basis it had little success save where loudness was the prime consideration. It was used for a time in French army bands, and also in Spain, where the writer heard it in a village band quite recently. French makers still export otherwise normal oboes with Boehm fingering to Spain and South America.

The modern oboe was evolved through empirical improvement of the older models. Brod set an extremely high standard in the quality of keywork; Guillaume Triébert (d. 1848) improved the already smallish French bore so that the series of conical sections approximated more nearly to a single cone. His son Frédéric (1813–78) freely applied Boehm's rings and axles, though not his fingerings. Both the present English model with thumb-plate and rings for B♭ and C, and the French 'Conservatoire System', which gives the same notes by means of the top ring on the bottom joint, were products of Frédéric Triébert's collaboration with Barret, a Frenchman who played at Covent Garden and taught at the Royal Academy of Music and Kneller Hall, and were publicized through Barret's still widely used Method. Some complex instruments made for Barret in the 1860s combined both the fingerings, with additions; experience with these no doubt prompted the present English insistence on simplicity of keywork, and dislike of automatic octave keys. Meanwhile, Germany and Austria

had led the advance in the earlier application of keys, but
largely rejected the new bores and the new technology. The
German industry, traditionally based on Markneukirchen,
continued to supply Northern and Eastern Europe, and
some lower-priced markets elsewhere, with instruments akin
to the eighteenth-century types (though bore resemblances
do not necessarily imply near-identity, particularly later
in the century).

With the bassoon, the picture is reversed. The colourful
instrument evolved by Savary, Triébert, and Buffet-Crampon in France had not radically changed from its eighteenth-century fingering and general character (Pl. 23).
The very different bassoon now used in most countries
originated in Germany. The fault with the early bassoon
lay not so much in its cross-fingered notes as in the uneven-
ness and instability of some of the notes of its simple scale.
About 1824, therefore, Carl Almenraeder (1786–1843),
assisted by the physicist G. Weber, undertook a thorough
revision of the positioning of the essential holes and keys in
order to obtain more positive and even response regardless of
any other consequences. Like other rationalized bassoons
since, the new model was attacked for having sacrificed the
tone. But some fifty years later, Wilhelm Heckel (1856–
1909) of Biebrich-am-Rhein, Wiesbaden, was able to claim
to have restored it without loss of the evenness and steadiness
that Almenraeder had achieved. The modern German bassoon is thus Heckel's (Pl. 23d), and it is now regularly
played everywhere save in France, Belgium, Italy, and
Spain, though it has generally supplanted the French
instrument in England only within the last thirty years. It
still retains a number of cross-fingerings (especially above
$d'$), but fewer than the French. On the other hand, various
problems connected with clean production of the tenor
octave make its fingering by no means as simple as may
appear on first trial.

Berlioz, Wagner, and others consolidated the position of
piccolo, cor anglais, and bass clarinet in the orchestra. But
the collapse of the vogue for huge orchestras in the 1920s and

the cessation of all initiative in military bands have left most of the less usual members of the woodwind family outside regular music-making. Of the instruments just named, the piccolo is fitted with Boehm's mechanism but has generally retained the old conical bore. Cylindrical Boehm piccolos, however, long familiar in Italy, are now being mass-produced at low cost. The *bass flute* in G (now increasingly called 'alto flute' in Britain, as it always has been in most other countries) was Boehm's ideal instrument, but his enthusiasm for it had little effect upon composers before the present century, and only Stravinsky has really done orchestral justice to its fascinating middle register. It has had some success as a recital instrument, while the 'special arrangement' orchestras have created a fashion for playing it close to the microphone. The true bass flute in C, an octave below the flute, appears in some Italian scores as *albisifono*. Although Rudall Carte have made more than forty of these instruments (Pl. 25a) and are now working on an improved model, it is not demanded by any work in the present repertory, though some American popular records have displayed the massed tone of over twenty flutes including both G and C basses.

Although Brod's *cor anglais moderne* of 1839 was of the modern straight shape, the eighteenth-century curved or angled form (Pl. 24a) persisted surprisingly late (at least until 1900 in Italy). A curved, leather-covered cor anglais was in the possession of a Bayreuth oboist when *Tristan* was first performed there, but this may not have been the one actually used in the performances. The composer's note in some early editions of *The Ring* that the '*Althoboe*' must in future be substituted for the '*Englisches Horn*' no doubt indicates the arrival in Germany of the straight instrument (though the use of both expressions in *Hansel and Gretel* may be a problem for the organological detective). A rare freak during the eighteenth century, the *baritone oboe* was tackled seriously by Triébert and other early nineteenth-century French makers, most of whom constructed it with a small bassoon-like butt joint and upturned globular bell (Pl. 24c).

It was not used orchestrally until the present century, when Lorée's straight model of 1889 became the new prototype. The *heckelphone* (Pl. 25c), at the same pitch (with an extension to low A) but with much larger bore and quite different tone colour, is said to be the result of a suggestion made by Wagner to Heckel. It did not appear, however, until 1904. Its reed resembled the smallest variety of bassoon reed. Strauss used it in *Salome* and *Elektra*, and Hindemith in an excellent trio with viola and piano. Confusion is caused in England by the expression 'bass oboe' (applied by makers only to an abortive experiment a fifth lower still). This is usually taken to mean the baritone oboe, but is found in the English editions of some Delius scores which, in the original German manuscript orchestral parts, specify heckelphone. Of the two, the baritone, with its smaller bore and reed, is the more readily mastered by a cor anglais player and the more manageable in *pianissimo* on the lowest notes. The more flexible and cello-like heckelphone is far more powerful, and is sufficiently differentiated from the cor anglais to be considered a new and interesting tone-colour.

Early *bass clarinets*, from *c.* 1780 onwards, may be regarded as curiosities. The solo in Meyerbeer's *Les Huguenots* is said to have been written for Auguste Buffet's instrument of 1832, but it was Sax who, in 1838 created the type used today (Pl. 25b), save in Germany, where a narrower-bore instrument is used, with a smaller reed. Though this last may blend better, it lacks the exotic quality of the Franco-Belgian design stemming from Sax. The *alto* (or *tenor*) *clarinet* (Pl. 24d), with larger bore than the basset horn, was used in British military bands in the pre-saxophone days, and is still found in large American and continental bands. Though neglected elsewhere, it records and broadcasts extremely well. It was used in the early Jack Payne band by Frankie Johnson, and sometimes in film studios more recently. But of all the instruments that are scarcely used at all, undoubtedly the most useful potentially are the *contrabass clarinets*. Of those in B♭, an octave below the bass clarinet, Fontaine-Besson's 'pedal clarinet' was the first to arouse much interest. Later models, of wood or of metal have been produced in Germany by Hüller and by Heckel, while in France a remarkable collapsible metal model, fitting into an alto saxophone case, is made by Leblanc, (Pl. 25b). Both this and Selmer's higher contrabass in E♭ are magnificent instruments, rich-toned, easily blown, flexible, and agile – by far the most effective of all the lowest woodwind instruments. The Leblanc contrabass, with mechanism ingeniously straddling the double tube, is, at the time of writing, exported to America at the rate of 25 a month. It was slow to arrive in Britain, but has been used by Stephen Trier in the London Symphony Orchestra, for instance with Stokowsky in the experiment of discreetly doubling the double basses in order to strengthen the fundamentals of their notes (the maestro has declared that he can hear little but overtones from double basses). Also in London, Frank Reidy has used this contrabass clarinet regularly in light music, especially with the Jack Parnell band on television, while Elizabeth Lutyens has given it the 'theme tune' in the music for a film. Leblanc has also made an *octocontrabass clarinet*, an octave lower still. Three octaves lower than the ordinary clarinet, it includes a low D sounding *C''*, a sixth below the bottom note of the piano. The tone is full and solid, though slightly suggestive of the larger Jurassic fauna.

It is often stated that Sax's intention in making the *saxophone* (1846) was to simplify the fingering of the clarinet by making it overblow to the octave. This seems unlikely. With his experience as a woodwind experimenter, he would have known that no conical instrument would sound like a clarinet, and that if a clarinet could in fact be made to overblow the octave, its compass would become greatly reduced, whereas in his earlier experiments he had aimed at extending it. It would seem in fact that his object was the one he achieved, namely to make a conical instrument of wide enough bore to provide a loud but not blaring 'middle' to the military band. The single-reed mouthpiece was then necessitated by the width of bore required even at the top end of the tube. As for his choice of metal, it must be remembered that he planned the saxophones as a family of instruments, and a bass saxophone would be impossibly cumbersome in wood. His success in making metal clarinets may have suggested that a family of large-bore instruments would be practicable. The family now runs: soprano in B♭; alto in E♭; tenor in B♭; baritone in E♭; bass in B♭; there are also the tenor in C ('C melody' saxophone), other aberrant forms in C or F, and the freakish sopranino in F, originally specified, but not now used, in Ravel's *Bolero*. Bizet and Massenet used the alto in the orchestra, and saxophones have long been used variously in military bands. In dance bands the alto, tenor, and baritone are regularly used, while the difficult soprano (Pl. 22c), made famous in jazz by Sidney Bechet, is now enjoying a small revival, and in capable hands is in many ways the most effective of the family in other kinds of music.

The saxophone's modern vogue began quite independently of jazz; 'novelty solos' were played on the tenor saxophone in the intermissions in at least one West End theatre during the First World War. This popularity has not, however, made it any easier to find adaptable players who can make it sound convincing in a symphony orchestra, where its prospects of being used extensively seem today less promising, despite the examples of Vaughan Williams, Britten, and others, than when Berlioz greeted it with such enthusiasm over a hundred years ago. Moreover, further enlargement of the bore has destroyed the 'woodwind' character and dynamics of Sax's own instruments.

It is the saxophone quartet that shows the instruments at their best. The recordings of the Quatuor des Saxophones Marcel Mule, formerly known as the Quatuor des Saxophones de Paris, led by the inimitable Marcel Mule himself on soprano, will be a revelation to most people.

The *tarogato* is a Hungarian instrument resembling a soprano saxophone of wood, with narrower bore and small fingerholes, invented towards the end of the last century to replace an earlier national instrument akin to the shawm family. It is still played locally in Hungary and Rumania, and frequently used for the shepherd's call in the Third Act of *Tristan;* it was given a solo in Johann Strauss's *Zigeunerbaron* overture, which is now played on either oboe or clarinet. The *Sarrusophone,* a double-reed instrument of metal, began badly with a court case in which Sax claimed that bandmaster Sarrus had infringed his patent of the saxophone, and lost his case. His powerful influence is said subsequently to have prevented the French army bands from giving it a fair trial. Brought out in 1856, and intended to supplant the oboe and the bassoon in large bands, its bores are smallish for an instrument expressly designed to be powerful. From alto downwards, the sarrusophones are doubled back in ophicleide shape. Only the contrabass (Pl. 24e) has had any success: in the orchestra as a substitute contrabassoon (though now only in Spain) and in the band of the Garde Républicaine and other large bands on the continent and in America.

Changes in keywork and mechanism since the Boehm–Buffet–Triébert period have been few, and on the whole unimportant. A few may be mentioned, such as the perforated fingerplates long used on Boehm flutes by the French and their imitators elsewhere. These are claimed to facilitate more delicate shades of tone, and effect some improvements in intonation, though they make pad-fitting more difficult (one well-known London player actually takes his instrument to Paris for re-padding). They do not provide additional fingerings, unlike the perforated plates of the Gillet-model oboe in which 'half-hole' plates are held down by various keys in order to give perfect trills in place of some which are difficult or not in tune on the model with open rings. Several London players use the Gillet system which is today the standard system in France and America. Clarinets with fingerplates had a vogue among jazz players of the 1930s, but have been felt to give rather stifled sounds on certain notes, while perforated plates have not been tried. Clarinettists for some reason have always been more insistent than other woodwind players on simple, sturdy mechanism, even at the expense of lightness of action. This must in part be due to their constant rapid changes, with consequent risk of minor accident, between B♭ and A instruments in orchestras and between clarinet and saxophone in dance bands; and also possibly to tradition handed down by army-trained players.

A novel system not open to the usual complaints of excessive complexity or extreme deviation from normal fingering habits is that of the saxophone *'le Rationnel'* of M. Houvenaghel, of Leblanc, Paris. It is based on Boehm's acoustics and principles of fingering. The third finger of the right hand, which Boehm used to turn the B♮ into a B♭, lowers *all* notes by a semitone from F upwards. Whole passages can be played a semitone lower by lowering this one finger; and by alternately raising and lowering it, chromatic passages can be played with the diatonic fingering. The fingering of top and bottom notes is also simplified. But the main point is that all normal fingerings are retained, so the player can learn the others gradually, without interrupting his work. The instrument looks scarcely more complex than a normal saxophone, and could possibly turn out to be the most important new woodwind model since those of Boehm. This *'système intégral'* has been applied to the contrabass clarinet, and a clarinet has been designed for M. Druart of the Garde Républicaine and Orchestre de la Société des Concerts du Conservatoire.

Methods of manufacture are also fairly conservative for high-grade instruments, though some firms now power-hammer their keys, and large saxophone bells are sometimes blown by hydraulic pressure. The English practice of using ebonite bushes for the raised holes of oboes and clarinets dates from the 1930s. Its main function is to permit the external turnery to be done in one operation, but it stands up to wear better than wood, and in practice rarely seems to justify the deprecation of continental makers, who use it only on the cheapest models. On saxophones the tone-holes are drawn from the body-metal as a matter of course. This is an old-established method with flutes also, and is now becoming far more usual, though some players mistrust it, claiming that the bore becomes minutely distorted and preferring 'Louis Lot' model instruments made to special order with soldered-on tone-holes. Die-cast keys are only for mass-produced cheap instruments. Pads remain a stubbornly conservative item, and with the labour involved in dismantling a new instrument under test in order to correct a leak or make some slight re-tuning of a hole, they have a considerable effect on the price. One clue to the production of really cheap instruments may lie in designing more easily dismantled mechanism and more quickly adjustable pads, rather than in quicker methods of producing the parts and steady debasement of materials. Recently, solid plastic pads have been used in America.

*

While violinists and pianists of merit become accepted throughout the world, ideals in the style of performance of woodwind-playing remain stubbornly national. Radio and the rest have only recently begun to create a perceptible trend towards uniformity: indeed, some schools of playing have actually diverged further during the era of mechanical reproduction, thus preserving the stimulus always felt by players and audience alike when orchestras take to foreign travel. But despite the real charm of this diversity, there is clearly a point beyond which exaggeration of styles of purely local appeal ceases to have any validity for the bulk of the repertory, which is after all international; and in the writer's opinion this point has been freely overstepped during the present generation. The composer as well as the player is entitled to his national point of view, and he still has his name on the programme. One must beware of the temptation to relate these differences entirely to national temperament, since they can sometimes only be attributed to the influence of individually brilliant players or teachers; this is borne out by the startlingly different approach to different instruments sometimes found in one single country.

But with this qualification it is broadly true that national character, voice habits, tradition, and to an even greater extent musical organization and conditions, have been decisive influences. In fact it is one of the interesting things about the woodwind that they provide the main clue as to how various nations really feel about music, since string players all over the world have taken to admiring the same masters. As for the institutions, in Germany and Austria musicians are appointed for life (after a trial period of some two years), usually to orchestras with long histories, and tone and style are valued most for their contribution to the woodwind ensemble. This long-term approach to the building of orchestras is usual also in Russia and Central Europe, and the prosperous-looking musician who has been living on a pension for years is familiar to Russians. In France and England, by contrast, the effects of a catch-as-catch-can existence are evident; one London orchestra has at the time of writing appointed its ninth principal oboist since 1946. British woodwind-playing tends to be frankly commercial, setting a premium on fashion as against continuity of style, and in the last generation of players it has become the least stable of all. Few of the leading players today, on any of the instruments, play with either style or tone in the least like those of thirty years ago. It is the new soloist who is most sought after, and interest in ensemble ceases once intonation, attack, and elementary balance have been secured.

While some French musicians enjoy an almost German sense of security with the Opéra or the Garde Républicaine as a main base of operation, full-time salaried symphony orchestras are unknown. The numerous Paris orchestras resemble some of the British orchestras of years ago, consisting of a body of players gathered together from studios, theatres, and cafés to play symphonies once a week. Entry to these orchestras is, however, properly controlled, and membership is usually of long duration, though hard economic facts enforce a certain amount of 'deputy business', which, *pace* the London critics, is known throughout Europe. As in London, soloistic qualities are chiefly valued, and intense competition leads to a commercial sense of values (though the saleable commodities are quite different from those of London). But strong teaching traditions prevent extreme deviations in style, and the light-textured wood-wind tones blend to each other with a logic of their own.

The French, with their live peasant roots (the musicians are hardly ever Parisians) show an innate preference for woodwind sounds that distantly echo those of village fête and *bal-musette*: the sounds of *cornemuse*, hurdy-gurdy, musette (and accordion too) – vibrant, brittle, and slightly nasal, like the French speaking-voice, and all richly evocative in a way that does not depend on professional 'expression' as understood in sophisticated circles. The celebrated French *raffinement* has been a sublimation of these qualities going back to the pastoral entertainments of Louis XIV and the bagpipe maker from Normandy who provided the orchestra with its first woodwind. And the probability is that French woodwind-playing has not changed greatly since then; reports of it in the nineteenth century, for example, fully support this view, provided one firmly grasps the fact that the word 'refined' in this context does not have its suburban-English connotation of 'sentimental, emasculated, dull'. English playing, on the other hand, seems ultimately in-spired by the sounds of the village organ, and the tradition-ally stifled, hooting head voices of cathedral singers (with an origin in speech habits considered socially desirable), a line of influences duly continued in the cinema organ and glutinous commercial dance bands of the period preceding the last war: a 'nice sound' (as they say), excluding any brilliance, vibrancy, or astringent quality which would be grievous to the entirely middle-class and largely feminine audiences who as customers are always right.

It is traditional to deal rather grudgingly with German woodwind-playing (though for a rare example of the oppos-ing view, see A. Baines, 1957). This opinion was probably becoming obsolete before 1914. Although spontaneous virtuosity of the French or Belgian sort is rare, the German qualities of seriousness and energy give a special authen-

ticity to classical performances, though foreign music sometimes sounds a little dull in tone and square in phrasing.
The clarinet, rather than the flute or the oboe, tends to be the
*prima donna* of the ensemble. German orchestral conditions,
pride in national tradition, and the clear line drawn
between symphonic and other music have all encouraged
continuity or even conservatism of style longer than in other
countries, but since the last war a considerable outside
influence has been felt. The arrival of the Paris-trained
French Swiss, M. Nicolet, as principal flute with the Berlin
Philharmonic may prove a turning-point – as did the arrival
of Barrère in America with his French flute tone. German
flutes and oboes now seem to aim at more physical charm
of sound, and a wide *vibrato* – wide even by current English
standards – is gaining ground.

Vienna remains untouched by this movement, and indeed
by the tendency to solemnity of the earlier German school.
Techniques of tone production resemble those of Germany,
though the sounds are subtly different. Central Europe
uses the French upper woodwind (the Czechs, both as
players and makers, were the spearhead of the movement),
but tones have a slightly Germanic solidity. This is also
broadly true of Holland, where French influence is often
mentioned but is not very obvious. Russians apply their
highly distinctive sense of melodic line to a tone and technique close to that of the older German school, though we
shall notice an exception with the bassoon. This seems at
first sight out of keeping with the Slavonic love of contrasting colours so well translated into sound by composers like
Rimsky-Korsakov and Stravinsky (whose works come to
life so magnificently with French tones), but gives excellent
results in the symphonies of Tchaikovsky.

Among the smaller countries, Belgium has made a unique
contribution to world standards of woodwind playing. A
generation ago, Belgians were playing or teaching throughout the world, including England and even France. Though
temperamentally akin to the French and possessed of the
same facility, the Belgian traditions are more distinct than

is sometimes supposed – an oboe darker, reedier, and formerly *vibrato*-less; a more ringing clarinet; and a more solid and restrained flute – though some players have now adopted an altogether French style. A natural facility is likewise common in Italy and Spain. The tones in the former country tend to be those which give an interesting tinge of colour in doubling a voice, rather than those of the licensed soloist. The clarinet occasionally retains its original slight pastoral asperity which is often implied even in modern Italian scores (e.g. the Shepherd Boy's music in the Third Act of *Tosca*). A distinctively American style of playing is now just beginning to appear with the rise of the first generation of American-born principals in the important orchestras. Their teachers, like Tabuteau and Gillet on the oboe, Barrère on the flute, were mostly of the less exuberantly French kind, and the present movement is towards continued restraint, with stress on blending rather than contrasting colours, but with the French roots clearly showing, even though many eminent clarinettists are of Italian origin. The magnificent Kincaid of the Philadelphia Orchestra combines French flute virtues with a more virile quality which is all his own, and which against all precedent sounds equally appropriate in Beethoven and in César Franck. American bassoon tone, with the German type of instrument, is highly characteristic – much further from the German tradition than the upper instruments are from the French.

The supremacy of French woodwind-playing, with the Belgian the only near rival, was internationally accepted in the West from before 1850 until recently, and over most of the world it still is, though the truly classical quality to be found in the records of the 1930s is now rarer. So far as any trend towards world uniformity has existed, it has amounted to a spread of French-type instruments and whatever may locally be conceived as the French way of playing them. The exception is the bassoon.

French and German bassoons, often referred to respectively as the 'Buffet' and the 'Heckel' after the makers who perfected the two systems, differ so markedly in musical character as almost to constitute instruments of different species. Though more complex mechanically, the Heckel bassoon is no easier to finger. It is, however, immensely easier to blow, and it solves most of the problems of intonation, rapid *legato*, and response to an average reed, which traditionally worried all but the most expert players of the intractable Buffet; and its smooth, buzz-free tone matched the trends among the upper British woodwind when London began to adopt it in the 1930s, largely through Archie Camden, who had always played it in Manchester where Richter required it in the Hallé Orchestra. There is no doubt that the change-over has improved the average standard, though nearly thirty years of excellent playing by our leading bassoonists have never completely dispelled the charge of inflexibility, and from audience-distance the Heckel may sound quite fixed in dynamic level. The Russians, however, extract from this type of instrument a dark and telling sound of haunting and peculiarly Slavonic pathos; and when the composer clearly intends grotesquerie they make no attempt to correct his taste. The French instrument has long ceased to be studied at all by intending professionals in Britain, yet the performances of those like Cecil James and Joseph Castaldini, who resisted the change-over, keeps open the question of whether, in the hands of a player skilful enough to control it, the Buffet is not the more sensitive instrument of the two. Its freer sound blends better, and gives more support as a bass, while in the hands of a true artist it displays a more flexible response to melodic line; also its variety of expression, from pathos to grotesquerie, is very much greater. Some players of the Heckel now have had second thoughts about the superiority of their smoother instruments. Nevertheless, there is absolutely no question of the Buffet ever regaining its ascendancy. The English players always used a rather smaller reed than the traditional French one in order to avoid the latent 'buzz', which even in good French playing often seems excessive to English ears. Of the many French players who cannot be criticized on these grounds (or on the other common charge of excessive *vibrato*) an outstandingly tasteful example is Maurice Allard of the Lamoureux Orchestra. His uncle Raymond Allard, the last of the great Buffet players in America, retired recently from the Boston Symphony Orchestra – the principal overseas outpost of the French tradition.

Since the visits to England of the soloist Fleury about sixty years ago there had been occasional waves of enthusiasm for the tenuous but clear tone of French flutists, with their sensitive *vibrato* and meticulous phrasing. Professional players, however, disliked the style, and it did not become a force in the London orchestras until its adoption by Geoffrey Gilbert about 1935. The silver flute, which has now become the emblem of the French school, had never entirely disappeared in this country since the early Boehm instruments arrived, but the few who used it played it with much the same tone and style as the usual wooden one. The traditional English playing is always described as 'big-toned and brassy', and probably inherited much of its character from the legendary Charles Nicholson. The more relaxed and smaller-toned style of Belgium and Holland, already an influence in some provincial centres, was introduced to London by Albert Fransella before the turn of the century, but the 'brassy' school (with its considerable hard work and lip-stretching) went on through the 1920s, its last great virtuoso being Eli Hudson. Robert Murchie, the most famous of the players between the World Wars, belonged technically rather to the new school, despite his almost violent power, clarity, and brilliance. Though now cited as a champion of the 'old school' or of the 'English style', it is probably true that, just as with Fleury though in an entirely different way, it was the exotic, un-English quality of this vital little man from Clydeside which took London by storm. The only surviving recording of Hudson (though it can give little idea of his power) shows his phrasing to be easy, fluent, and even soothing, where Murchie was thrilling, dramatic, and declamatory. There can be little doubt that the former was the native tradition.

The principal flutists of the London orchestras are now nearly all committed to the French style, with its still greater stress on ease of production, to which the thin-walled silver flute responds so well. Only one major force, the Philharmonia Orchestra, is left as the custodian of an anglicized Murchie tradition, though the wooden flute remains usual outside London, and is fairly common in broadcast or recorded light music. Though French works barely make sense with any other flute-playing, the French style does sound a little thin in some of the German Romantics (notably the last movement of Brahms's First Symphony) and it is unlikely that Beethoven or Tchaikovsky will ever again be played in this country with the authority of a Murchie, though of course in some other respects our present players are much better than any of their predecessors.

It is often remarked that although 'French schools' of flute-playing exist in several countries, they never quite sound the same as the French players, of whom Cortet was a particularly fine example (though like so many French flutists he latterly spent most of his time conducting). As no one can diagnose the difference, the essential ingredient is probably one of personality rather than of method.

The clarinet, according to Berlioz, though '*favorable à l'expression des sentiments et des idées les plus poétiques*', is '*un instrument épique . . . sa voix est celle de l'héroique amour*' and '*peu propre à l'Idylle*'. This penetratingly describes the unique character impled in the clarinet-writing of the Romantics from Weber to Strauss. Its disappearance is the modern history of the clarinet in a nutshell.

The traditional London tone, although one of the really beautiful things in music, had always probably lacked the 'epic' quality; perhaps it even suited the 'idyll'. It combined a crystalline texture with a strong colour, markedly contrasting with the other woodwind (rather as all clarinets do when paired in thirds, or when flattered by the old acoustic recording). Although more typical of the once-favourite Belgian 'Albert' clarinet, it survived on the Boehm with such players as George Anderson of the London Symphony Orchestra, and in a more incisive form with Frederick Thurston. This tone has probably always appealed to the English taste, even in the days when the reed was controlled by the upper lip and Thomas Willman (d. 1840) was said to sound 'like musical glasses'. But the phenomenon of Charles Draper (1869–1952) gave such a shock to our clarinet-playing that it has never since settled down to any sort of uniformity. With Draper, and his less picturesque but immensely telling tone, the dramatic or epic was raised to the highest degree possible on any reed instrument: the very spirit of nineteenth-century romantic playing, and the diametric opposite of the feminine-nostalgic quality now everywhere labelled 'romantic'. Unfortunately, the only feature of his tone that has seemed to influence later clarinet-tists was its sheer breadth, and subsequent efforts to broaden the traditional tone quality already mentioned above have often resulted in a rather hooting sound, too thick and heavy to allow clear articulation. There is, however, a distinctive Manchester tone, heard in London mainly in the light orchestras of the film, broadcasting, and recording studios. More neutral in colour, but less cloying, it retains in some ways a more classical and certainly a more international view of the instrument than is held by many symphony or concerto players.

The 'epic' tradition has fared scarcely better in other countries, and the generally pale and thin French and American tones do it no more justice than the inert and plushy English ones. Some German and Russian players do show a certain masculine and dramatic feeling (it is worth recalling that the clarinet was a German invention, as the oboe and bassoon were French). There is some dispute as to how far this difference is encouraged by the large-bore Oehler instruments, with their relatively small expansion just above the bell. The German clarinet is of basically simple-system design with a number of vent keys to correct the intonation, and is normally played with a narrower, more conical mouthpiece, and with a smaller, thick tipped, hand-made reed. Though players differ greatly in the merits they ascribe to the simple-system instrument, the writer is inclined to agree that all clarinets of this sort do in fact differ subtly from the Boehm – even the English Boehm, which has a similar bore-diameter to the Albert. The different size and placing of the holes could account for this, but tinkering with the bore of the Boehm to improve individual notes is more probably responsible. This suspicion is born out by the ripe and colourful quality of the early Auguste Buffet Boehms made before these *évasements* were 'perfected' to leave the 'cylindrical' clarinet conical for one third of its length.

The oboe, with which we began this chapter at the court of Louis XIV, is still French in design almost throughout the world. During the nineteenth century, German makers had developed the oboe along different lines, enlarging the upper bore and retaining the old flanged bell, but this type is now found only in Russia and, in a more conservative form, in Vienna. (The Russian Government, however, has recently ordered very large numbers of oboes of the ordinary kind from Paris.) A similar type, though not flanged, played with a large fan-shaped reed, is still made in Italy, but has not for some years been used in the leading orchestras. The small French reed, as distinct from the fan-shaped one of other nineteenth-century schools, still retains in France the dimensions given for it in Garnier's Method of *c.* 1794, but in England and some other countries which have adopted it this reed has become slightly smaller than its classic size – sometimes much smaller, or even tiny as in Russia.

In England from the 1920s the influence of Leon Goossens brought about a change in woodwind-playing (and not only on the oboe) more marked even than that of Draper and Murchie. His soft-textured tone and slow *vibrato*, in diametrical opposition to the hitherto admired Belgian style, were soon being cultivated by all the young players. It is interesting to note that this school of oboe-playing depended for years entirely upon the Liverpool reed-maker Thomas Brearley, who made reeds over the years with a consistency of quality equalled only in the celebrated bassoon reeds of Kurt Ludwig of Munich. Probably for the first time in history numbers of highly successful oboists (though not Goossens himself) disclaimed all knowledge of reed-making. Since Brearley's death the craft has been strongly revived among players, partly through a trend towards a wider conception of the instrument, fostered in some cases by studies in Paris, Amsterdam, or Vienna. Indeed in retrospect it now seems that those English players, like Alec Whittaker and John McCarthy, who kept alive more traditional and international ideas of the instrument have been greater influences than at one time seemed likely, and the styles of the younger oboists are now less stereotyped than in the 1930s. The reaction from enforced insularity during the war years and the wider dispersal of foreign gramophone records have also played a part.

The playing of the two artists last mentioned bore a strong resemblance to the French playing so well represented by Morel, who, however, like Bleuzet and Lamorlette at their peak periods some twenty or thirty years ago, used a very hard reed by any modern standards. As always, it is the ideas and physical gifts of the player which count; even widely differing methods may produce near-identity of tone, and vice versa. Today, thanks to modern conditions in which recording and broadcasting can swell the working day of the free-lance player to sixteen hours out of the twenty-four, a less fatiguing, softer reed is more often used in Paris, and this, together with the rather larger bore of the modern instruments of Marigaux and others (though Rigoutat and Jardé have begun to reverse this trend), represents the only serious break with tradition.

In some countries, notably France and Germany, woodwind tone and intonation have suffered through the incredible folly that has allowed a rise in playing pitch to approximately $a' = 444$ or $445$ v.p.s., against the desires of players and reputable makers alike. From the former Continental Pitch (*diapason normal*) of $a' = 435$, this rise, dating from since the last war, takes us half way back to the

old British High Pitch of evil memory, and has brought
many continental manufacturers to a state of chaos. A rise
in pitch that is allowed to proceed at this speed never stops
without a firm resistance that takes a generation to organize,
and one cannot expect any maker to turn out first-class
instruments if his design at a given pitch is likely to be out
of date as soon as it is perfected.

*

Lastly it may be noted that the clarinet, alone of the orchestral woodwind, has a vigorous life as a folk instrument,
notably in the Balkans and the adjacent parts of Central
Europe, the true home of the peasant clarinettist. The
Czechs often claim the clarinet as their national instrument,
but the most striking effects are produced in the thrilling,
racing dance variations of Rumania and Bulgaria. The
Bulgarians excel in sheer primitive vigour and virility, the
Rumanians (perhaps more under the influence of gipsy
professionalism) show a greater polish and variety which do
not detract from the uniquely exciting quality of this style;
and their electrifying technique never fails to astonish the
trained symphonic player with his firm anchorage to
written notes. The wild *glissandi* and general conception of
improvisation compel one to speculate whether some players
from the Balkans were present in the St Louis area in the
embryonic period of jazz, as the influences known to have
affected the Southern Negroes at this time provide no
antecedent for the type of clarinet playing they adopted.
At least one record of a Rumanian player was issued in
America before 1914, which suggests that there may have
been a vogue for the idiom. The underlying feeling of the
music, however, is quite unlike that of jazz, despite the
technical resemblance.

Pure gipsy blood and an inability to read music are said
to be the qualifications for success in a similar type of playing
found in Hungary.

In Central Greece the clarinet in C survives and is
usually played in combination with a violin and lute. The

style, utterly different from that of the countries to the north, is based on song-like rather than virtuoso dance figures, though there is much bagpipe-like preluding on the low register, and the tone shows subtly oriental undertones suggestive of pent-up emotionalism rather than the high-spirited wildness of the Bulgarians and Rumanians. The descending *glissandi* which characterize the Greek tradition occur chiefly in the low register, an extraordinarily difficult trick even if the lay of the mouthpiece is very open. This habit is also a feature of Turkish café and night club music, in which the clarinet is played in a loose-lipped 'sub-tone' style, with a great deal of *vibrato* and *portamento*. The effect, to the naïve Western ear, is one of extreme decadence.

*

Two final remarks may be added. The orchestral tradition of the last hundred years has encouraged players to work towards the perfection of a single chosen type of tone, contrast being valued *between* the different instruments. The present revival in concerto playing may create a demand for greater variety of effect within the range of the *individual* instrument, and some woodwind players have already gone far in this respect. There is little doubt that in this case the full purity of, say, French or English tone as produced by a specialist will be lost, but string players have always accepted a comparable compromise. Secondly, it seems to the writer that as we approach the culmination of a period in which attention has been paid chiefly to making playing easier, we may be near the beginning of a new revolution of which we cannot foresee the exact nature, and that the increasing interest of musicians in antique instruments, far from being a reactionary preoccupation with the past for its own sake, may, by drawing attention to individual virtues which have been sacrificed in the general progress, make a contribution to the music of the future.

# 11. *The Older Brass Instruments: Cornett, Trombone, Trumpet*

## CHRISTOPHER W. MONK

THE history of European brass instruments tells how men have adapted the mellow signal of the herdsman's horn and the martial blast of the regal trumpet to tunes and all kinds of music. The process, so far as we can trace it, began in the Middle Ages, and has only become really complete within the last fifty years. The ancient world used horns and

FIG. 75. Jewish shofar of ram's horn

trumpets but there is no evidence that they used them for music of any sort. It is true that some examples of the Danish Bronze Age *lurs*, cast in the shape of a mammoth tusk, have mouthpieces astonishingly like modern melodic brass instruments, but Roman mouthpieces, for the hook-belled *lituus* (Fig. 76) and the large hoop-like *cornu*, are wide and

FIG. 76. Roman lituus

shallow, like many oriental trumpets (e.g. those of Persia, Tibet, and China) on which players are content with the rhythmic blaring of one or two notes. The sheer sound, for the sake of what it may symbolize or convey, is all that is demanded from a brass instrument at this stage. The parts for the brass in our classical symphonies contain many memories of this, especially with the trumpets, which, when the works were composed, could take little thematic part in the music, yet are included in so many of the scores. Only the last century saw mechanical developments which gave every brass instrument a complete scale of notes throughout its range, enabling the composer to treat it like other instruments, without special limitations of note and phrase.

The chief differences within the brass group arise from an evolution from two prototypes: the horn of an animal and its reproduction in wood or metal; and the trumpet of cane or a hollow branch, with its modified reproductions in metal tubes. A resonant cooing note is produced from the wide conical bore of a simple cowhorn; all its conical-tube descendants give, or can give, a sound akin to it, reaching in the French horn the last stage of refinement. A sharper, harsher sound is made from the mainly cylindrical tube of a trumpet, though it is smoothed and amplified by a bell, primitive equivalents of which include half a gourd or a section of horn fixed upon the end of the tube. Most medieval trumpets retained an early funnel-shaped bell-expansion that is first seen on Egyptian trumpets of the second millennium B.C., but from the sixteenth century of our era a flared bell expanding in an exponential curve has usually been adopted and used on horns as well. These differences in bore are accompanied by no less important differences in mouthpieces. Six forms of mouthpiece are shown in Fig. 77. In simple horns where more than just a round hole was made, a conical cup was found suitable; this shape, improved with a wide, well-rounded throat (as with the horn), emphasizes and adds to the natural smoothness of the sound due to the conical bore. Trumpets were given the shallow cup already noticed, with its sharp-edged throat that emphasizes the opposite quality of harshness or brilliance given from the cylindrical tube. Our trumpets today, however, are usually given a deeper cup with a more rounded throat in order to reduce any stridency; conversely, in the horn family, cornets and bugles are given

much the same 'compromise' mouthpiece cup to help produce a brighter sound. Trombones have a similar but larger
mouthpiece, for playing in a lower register with smooth
sonority.

Sounds are made on all these instruments by much the
same means. The lips are buzzed or squeaked together
across the rim of the mouthpiece to cause the column of air

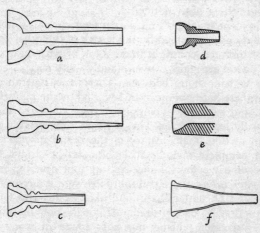

FIG. 77. Brass mouthpieces: (a) Trumpet, German, eighteenth century; (b) Trumpet, modern;
(c) Cornet; (d) Cornett;   (e) Mute cornett;
(f ) French horn

in the tube to vibrate. The teeth, slightly parted, support
the lips, which are drawn sideways by the buccinator
('trumpeter's') muscles of the face and set in motion by
a movement of the tongue. The tip of the tongue is put
lightly between the lips and suddenly withdrawn for a
heavy attack: for the normal attack it is withdrawn from
the base of the upper teeth, but from the palate for soft
articulation of notes, the player in effect pronouncing 't' or
'tu'. Rapid passages are managed by alternating 't' and

'k' in 'double-tonguing' and fast triplets by 'triple tonguing' 'ttk' (or 'tkt, ktk'). By adjusting the tightness of the lips and making movements of the back of the tongue and throat similar to those in whistling, it is possible to play *legato*, passing clearly from one note to another without any break in the sound; with practice this can be so rapid that trills are made with the lips alone. A picturesque effect sometimes called for is 'flutter-tonguing', involving simply the rapid rolling of the letter 'r'.

A simple, or 'natural' brass instrument has only a limited series of notes determined by the length of the tube. Bugle-calls, for instance, consist of these notes, or harmonics, here giving a good arpeggio, conventionally written $c'$, $g'$, $c''$, $e''$, $g''$, but with no notes between. The longer the tube, the more of these harmonics can be sounded by the player's lip tension, but seldom the complete range and even then a melodically limited scale. The attempts to solve this great problem are the main history of the brass: in what way could a complete melodic scale of notes be drawn from their peculiarly colourful and exciting tone-qualities?

The two earliest successful solutions were the *cornett* and the *trombone*. The latter has an unbroken history; the former has temporarily disappeared. Although not literally a 'brass' instrument, being normally made of wood, the cornett solved the problem by use of 'woodwind' finger-holes on a horn. An account of it is given largely with an eye to the future, since the need for it is now being acutely felt and cornetts are being made and played again in Britain, Germany, and America.

Little about it is familiar today. Even its name 'cornet' (Ital. *cornetto*, 'little horn') has passed to quite a different instrument, so that for distinction it is now conventionally spelt and pronounced 'cornett'. In late Saxon times holes were pierced in cow and goat horns so that tunes could be played on them; Scandinavian shepherds were still recently making this instrument (Fig. 78). The German name, *Zink*, and the French *cornet à bouquin* point possibly to tusks or goathorn as the original material; so does the slender curve of the cornett in its best-known form throughout its greatest period *c.* 1500–1650 (Pl. 26a and b). Curved cornetts were of hard close-grained wood like pear. A roughly-shaped block was halved lengthwise, and channels gouged in each half to make a conical bore when they were glued and bound together again. It was planed to an eight-sided shape and a single piece of leather was wrapped and glued round it, mainly to seal any leaks that might develop. The ordinary or treble cornett is about two feet long; descants (*cornettini*) were also made, and altos, tenors, and (rarely) basses.

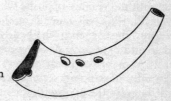

FIG. 78. Swedish cowhorn with fingerholes

There are normally six fingerholes and a thumbhole, though French cornett shown by Mersenne has no thumbhole. The fingers have to stretch very widely and the instrument is held obliquely so that they can fall more easily into position, the curve helping too. The fingering resembles a recorder's except that the thumbhole remains closed for both registers. Every semitone through two and a half octaves from *g* to *d′′′* is available, and with an agility scarcely exceeded by any instrument or the voice. There were also straight cornetts, turned and bored on a lathe in box or similar wood. A much-used 'mute cornett', so called because of its gentle veiled sound, was also made in this way save that a conical wide-throated mouthpiece was turned in the top of the instrument itself (Fig. 77e). The little separate mouthpiece of the other cornetts was commonly made of ivory, bone, or horn; as compared with other mouthpieces it had an unusually sharp rim to help hold the lightly-touching lips in position (Fig. 77d).

The sound of the cornett is not easy to describe. It is bright and clear, not unlike a well-trained chorister's voice; the cornett was in fact much used with voices in chapels and cathedrals, as were the trombones too. It has now been broadcast, and recordings of works by the Gabrielis, Monteverdi, and Schütz, using the cornett instead of a substitute, are beginning to appear. It is an instrument that not even an experienced musician can quickly master, and the player's lips have to do much more to focus the pitch and give equality to notes than on other brass. But with experience this turns out to be a great merit, not a handicap, for as with the violin – opposite which the cornett was often played (Pl. 18a) – all depends on the player's direct physical 'feel', and the cornett in the hands of a gifted musician can be true and expressive as few others can be. Nevertheless, after 1650 or so the finest players were being attracted to the rapidly developing techniques of the violin, and also, a little later, to the oboe with its rather fewer technical difficulties, and its aura of novelty. J. S. Bach, Handel, and Gluck, however, made some use of the cornett in the next century; Bach for instance included it in eleven cantatas. They expected a good deal from their players, even though the instrument was mainly used to support voice parts, but it had fallen into disuse even among the conservative German town-musicians by the end of the eighteenth century and was a rare curiosity in the next. Today with the renewed interest in music of its best period, the cornett is needed once more. No other instrument can reproduce its once much-loved sound in these scores, or blend so perfectly and expressively with the human voice.

While on the cornett fingerholes solved the problem of the complete scale by progressively shortening the sounding length of the tube, exactly the opposite – a telescopic slide progressively lengthening the tube – achieved the same result for the trombone. Such a slide could only be fitted to cylindrical tubing, in fact to some kind of trumpet. By the beginning of the fifteenth century the tubing of the straight medieval trumpet had been considerably lengthened and folded into a long flattened *S*-shape. It is fairly clear from many paintings of the period that some of these had been given a telescopic mouthpipe and were joining other instruments in polyphonic court music. These were presumably the *trompettes des ménestrels* referred to frequently in Burgundian records. The player appears to have steadied the wide-rimmed mouthpiece against his lips with one hand and slid the instrument bodily along the mouthpipe with the other, so managing to perform slow tenor and contra-tenor parts. The trombone (Old Fr. *sacqueboute*, and Engl. sackbut, Ger. *Posaune*) quickly followed as an improvement on this: the mouthpipe was fixed by a cross-stay to the tubing alongside, and the whole first loop was made to slide while the rest of the instrument was held still; moreover, only half of the old 'shift' was needed to lower a note by a given amount. By 1500 it looked recognizably the same as it does today. The example in Pl. 26d is dated 1557 and still has the old conical bell; its bore of ·492 inches is what we would now call 'medium wide'.

The principle is simple. The ordinary or tenor trombone is pitched in B♭, i.e. with the slide right in ('first position') it gives $B'♭$ as the fundamental and sounds the harmonics $B♭, f, b♭, d', f'$ ($a'♭$ rather flat), $b'♭, c'', d''$, etc., as shown in minims in Ex. 1. When the slide is pulled out a few inches ('second position') the fundamental becomes $A'$ and the harmonics are correspondingly lowered a semitone. A few inches more ('third position') lowers everything another semitone, and so on down to the seventh position, as far as an arm can comfortably reach. This gives $E$ as the bottom note of the trombone's *continuous* scale, leaving a gap down to the less-used fundamental or 'pedal' notes from the first-position $B'♭$ downwards.

A flexible lip is needed in the upper register where no lower positions need be used, and here jazz players, for instance, mainly display their remarkable virtuosity. In *legato* playing, the lower one descends the more often have big shifts of the slide to be concealed by skilful tonguing (though some awkward shifts can be avoided by alternative positions). But the complete control over intonation that the player commands with the slide makes up fully for such difficulties. Really there was very little wrong with the trombone from its beginning. Even the nuisance of big shifts has been partly removed in the last hundred years by a thumb valve which brings into play a coil of extra tubing to lower the pitch from B♭ to F (Pl. 26e) and so introduces fresh alternative positions (e.g. *c* and *B* are brought from the awkward sixth and seventh positions to first and second); it also supplies the missing notes above the pedals (Ex. 2).

Ex 1. Arabic numerals show harmonics
Roman numerals are slide positions

Ex 2.

Trombones have been made in different sizes: alto, tenor, bass, and sometimes contrabass. The alto has been dropped for some time from orchestras in general and is only now reappearing, and the bass survives chiefly in Britain. The tenor has always been the most popular. Up to the seventeenth century, extra lengths of tube, or 'crooks', were made for insertion so that the alto could be partly used as a tenor, the tenor as a bass, and so on – but slides are then usually too short for a seventh position. Experiments with valve systems have not been highly successful, since the beauty of a trombone owes so much to the slide; mounted musicians, or those in crowded theatre pits abroad, do however find some benefit in them.

The musical character of trombone-playing, with its relevant details of construction, has undergone tremendous change. In the 'sackbut' days of the sixteenth and seventeenth centuries the instrument was regularly in consort with cornetts or viols, violins, recorders, organ, and voices, and was expected to be as gentle as any of these could be. The rule for trombonists was stressed by Mersenne: the temptation to play it like a trumpet should be firmly resisted and the manner of the human voice cultivated. Mersenne particularly mentions its gentleness. Speer (1687) praised it for the same things and remarked that it needed so little bodily strength that a boy of eight could perfectly well play it. In solemn passages by eighteenth-century masters like those in *Saul* or *The Magic Flute* the playing would have been of this softly harmonious, vocal kind. Such parts are not common, however, for the eighteenth was not the trombone's great century. With purely instrumental styles developing, the decline of the princely chapels and the appearance of new and attractive brass instruments like the horn, the trombone was felt to be old-fashioned. The re-organized military bands at the end of the century rediscovered it but their needs changed its character. Berlioz described it with enthusiasm as 'menacing and formidable', able to 'break forth into frantic cries or sound its dread flourish to awaken the dead or to doom the living' (*Instrumentation*).

Yet in Germany, more particularly in Austria, the old idea of the trombone never really died. It lived, for example, in Beethoven's funeral *Equali*. The enlarged bore and bell which the German makers adopted towards the end of the last century show it too: they preserve some of the suave vocal quality even in the great volume of large orchestras and bands. Wide bores are common in German and American orchestras, where the tenor with a thumb valve has largely displaced others, and an especially large-bore instrument is used for bass trombone parts. Medium-wide bores have been almost universal in dance bands and British orchestras. The French tend to keep narrow bores, and have long used deep, nearly conical mouthpieces, to round off the tone in loud passages. What really counts though, as always, is the musician and what is expected of him. It was a far cry from the gently-blending agile vocal 'sackbut' to the 'wild clamour of the orgy' in the last century. There are now signs that a third epoch has begun, in the superbly skilful and smooth playing of the best dance band players of our time. Experiment has also begun today to produce suitable 'sackbut' instruments for the older music.

*

It seems at first strange that the slide was so rarely used with treble instruments. Slide-trumpets have appeared at various times since the Renaissance, mainly in England (see below, p. 289), but they have played only a small part. An early reason for this was that the cornett was far more satisfactory, while the trumpet was strictly reserved for the trumpet guilds. The latter formed an exclusive caste of

Ex. 3

musicians who developed brilliant flourishes without attempting to imitate vocal melody, exploiting the 'natural' instrument to the full. From the sixteenth century the celebrated *clarino* technique, developed especially in Germany, with its free use of harmonics up to the 16th or even 18th (Ex. 3), made possible diatonic fanfares, melodies, and specially written dance tunes and trumpet tunes harmonized by two or more lower trumpet parts with a timpanist invariably supplying a tonic-and-dominant bass (even though he may not appear in a score). Its first great document is Fantini's *Modo per imparar a sonare di tromba* (1638) in which many fanfares and dances are printed.

By 1500 the trumpet had its typical form (Pl. 27) with about seven feet of brass or silver tubing folded in one long loop. This placed it in C at the old high pitch, which became equivalent to D at eighteenth-century concert pitch (which accounts for the key of most of Bach's and Handel's choruses and arias with trumpets, though the instrument could be lowered a tone or more by crooks). The trumpet was decorated with 'garnishes' at the joints in the tubing, the 'ball' at the bell-joint, and the 'garland' round the bell-mouth. The bore (about ·4 inches) was less than that of a modern instrument (about ·45 inches in today's 'narrow bore') and was cylindrical to about a foot from the bell; the bell, too, was smaller (about 4 inches instead of $4\frac{1}{2}$ to 5). The mouthpiece had the old hemispherical cup with a rather small sharp-edged throat as a rule; rims were often broader and flatter than today, to make a comfortable airtight seal for strongly tensed lips without requiring undue pressure (Fig. 77a).

The 'natural' intonation of certain harmonics no doubt gave purely trumpet music a distinct character akin to that today of French *trompes de chasse* and Swiss alphorns, since the eleventh harmonic lies midway between F and F# while the thirteenth is a very flat A. In an orchestra the players could 'lip' these notes in tune, and the eleventh harmonic was sounded as F or F# as required. In this *clarino* register the natural trumpet has a particularly beautiful tone. Certainly, we are used to hearing the *clarino* parts of Purcell, Bach, and Handel played with great skill and beauty on modern instruments that are quite different; the real trumpet is rarely heard in the orchestra, save occasionally in Germany, and in England and now America. The vibrant modern instrument is difficult to subdue, perhaps because it offers less resistance. The real trumpet is richer and softer in a way that prompts the player to a different style of playing. It cannot stand up so well against large bodies of instruments or voices; if it is overplayed it will bray in the lower register and scream in the upper. It will, however, produce a clear flute-like quality which blends admirably with a small body of singers or players and will not overpower a moderately strong solo voice. Bach wrote several arias, now commonly avoided because of problems of balance, for two or three trumpets matched with a solo voice and a *continuo*. The doubts and evasions about the trumpet part in the Second Brandenburg Concerto have arisen from the same causes. The instrument that Gottfried Reiche played for Bach at Leipzig, and Valentine Snow for Handel in London, need not be conspicuous even in small-scale works, though it can stand out in solo parts as brightly and sweetly as could be wished; it can be played high and quietly without losing certainty and fullness, as tends to happen with any but the very best players today. The lower or *principale* register was meanwhile cultivated by other players.

The reasons for the decline of *clarino* playing at the end of the eighteenth century are fairly clear. One is the disappearance in the turmoil following the French Revolution of the numerous small courts which maintained players. Another is that the restrictive domination of trumpet guilds had forbidden any wide popular use through which the old technique might have survived. Only the less enterprising technique of military players could be counted upon. Moreover, the rapid increase in size of orchestras also meant that a *clarino* trumpeter had either to overblow and make an unpleasant noise or be almost inaudible. So by the time of Beethoven trumpets were reduced to simple parts centred more on the lower notes, and used to heighten emotional sounds, or to provide strong but restricted orchestral colour. On the other hand, there were no longer guilds to obstruct experiments to give the trumpet a complete scale. Two of these can be passed over quickly: the '*demilune*'

trumpet used a little in the second half of the eighteenth
century and early nineteenth, with the bell turned so that
hand-stopping could be used as on the horn; and the 'key
trumpet' with four brass keys of woodwind pattern opened
to shorten the tube. In either case, too much brilliance was
lost. The key trumpet was reported in Vienna in 1801, and
Haydn's well-known concerto is written for it; the instrument should not be confused with the more successful key
bugle (see Chapter 12).

A third experiment returned to the telescopic slide. Slide
trumpets continued to lead a shadowy existence in Germany
up to the time of Bach (his *tromba da tirarsi*) – a solitary
specimen dated 1651 survives in Berlin, a natural trumpet
with a sliding mouthpipe. In England, when the cornett
declined, a better design made a brief appearance in the
1690s – the 'flat trumpet' used by Purcell in the funeral
music for Queen Mary, and probably so-called because it
could play in minor ('flat') keys. Talbot (*c.* 1697) records the
details of a flat trumpet belonging to Purcell's principal
trumpeter, John Shore: a conventional trumpet with a slide
in the loop nearest the player. The slide could fill some
of the gaps between the fourth and eighth harmonics,
make certain semitones, and correct the natural intonation
of the eleventh and thirteenth harmonics. No more is heard
of it until 1798 when it reappeared very little changed (with
a spring for returning the slide, Pl. 27b) in the *Compleat
Preceptor* by John Hyde, a leading exponent. Though melodies in many keys could be played, it never progressed far
beyond being treated virtually as a natural trumpet. The
standard nineteenth-century natural trumpet was built in F,
and crooks were provided for E, Eb, D, and C. The slide
trumpet was equipped with them too; as late as 1906, when
it was fighting for its existence against the valved trumpet,
a Tutor described crooks as 'indispensable accessories',
despite the obvious inconvenience of changing them each
time the key of the music changed. On the whole, it may be
said that this slide trumpet preserved the best qualities of
the natural trumpet in a time of transition, reducing its

defects to a minimum. Only when the tone and style of the natural trumpet were finally abandoned, the slide trumpet lost its place, and it was never widely adopted outside England. One can best regard it as the last of the old instruments rather than the first of the new.

The trumpet was rescued from increasing musical insignificance by valves, of which Stölzel and Blühmel appear to have been the inventors, in Germany about 1815. Valves and their history are described in the next chapter, and it suffices to notice here their common form. Three pistons are controlled by the right hand. Each, when depressed against its spring, admits an extra loop of tubing in order to lower the pitch of the instrument by a specific amount and thus instantly to make available a new series of harmonics. The principle is shown very simply in Ex. 4 (in which open

Ex. 4

notes are shown in minims, valved notes in crotchets), the three valves adding their loops as follows:

First valve (loop length ⅛th of main tube) lowers pitch by one tone.

Second valve (loop length $\frac{1}{15}$th of main tube) lowers pitch by one semitone.

Third valve (loop length ⅕th of main tube) lowers pitch by three semitones.

In practice, this last interval is generally made by pressing the first and second valves together, the third valve being mainly used in combination with one or both of the others when the player requires to fill the larger gaps which exist between the open notes in the lower part of the compass (Ex. 4). An inherent fault in the system is that when valves are thus used in combination, the notes tend to be sharp. The reason for this is a simple matter of proportion. For example, on a 4-foot-long tube, six inches must be added to lower the pitch a tone (first valve) and about three inches to lower it a semitone (second valve). When the first valve is already down the resulting 4 feet 6 inches of tubing needs *rather more* than before to lower it a semitone, so that the note produced with the first and second valves will be a little sharp unless the player is very careful. The sharpness is more noticeable when the longer third valve is used with one of the others, and even more when all three valves are used together. Various devices have been introduced, notably a finger-operated third- or first-valve slide, but as in earlier times the chief remedy against faulty intonation lies with the player's ear and lip.

Lingering pride in dying traditions delayed the acceptance of valve trumpets even though many varieties were offered through the nineteenth century; most were in F, keeping the pitch and also the crooks of the late classical instrument. Military bands often had a pair of valve trumpets in E♭ and their rather dull parts are still sometimes found in arrangements used today. Full acceptance only came through the challenge of the cornet, a valved development of the circular continental post horn described in the next chapter. No old tradition hindered the rapid exploitation of the cornet; novel and brilliant feats of virtuosity became possible because it used mainly the wide-spaced second to eighth harmonics which allowed great certainty and attack; the increasing efficiency of the valves led to its adoption by many orchestral players in place of the trumpet, especially during the later years of the last century.

Trumpets at higher pitches than F had already been made in the 1820s, almost as soon as valves appeared, but found little favour. The 1880s brought second thoughts, and trumpets in high A, B♭, and C, offering the same technical advantages as the cornet, were being produced, German makers having taken the lead. Further to help reproduce the flexibility of the cornet, a taper near the mouthpiece later on became standard, while the hard tone of the earlier short trumpets was modified by using a deeper and more conical mouthpiece than the traditional hemisphere. Thus these instruments which have in turn displaced cornets in the orchestra are not in fact essentially so very different from them. Most are built in B♭ and employ the same notation as the cornet, which is an octave higher than that for the old trumpets, partly through bugle and post horn tradition, and partly to bring the most-used harmonics conveniently on the stave (Ex. 5). A certain amount of

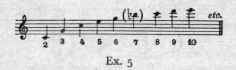

Ex. 5

dignity and more of the old tone is lost by the shorter tube, but a fine orchestral player can reduce the loss to a minimum while gaining at the same time a brilliance and accuracy that has probably never before been attained. Most important of all, an entirely new conception of the trumpet as a *complete* instrument with no serious limitations of notes and phrasing has been accepted. Richard Strauss was one of the first to realize this, followed by Debussy and others. Wagner's experiments must not be overlooked. The best-known deal with 'bass trumpets'; his 23-foot idea proved unmanageable, but every large opera house uses an instrument in C or B♭ pitched an octave below the ordinary trumpet to play the special parts he wrote in *The Ring*.

Following up the innovation of Kosleck, a brilliant German player of the 1870s and 1880s, *clarino* parts are now usually played on a short D trumpet, which used to be made straight but is now folded; some misleadingly call it a 'Bach trumpet'. It has a singularly lovely sound and can hold its own against very large forces. There are still smaller trumpets in F, used mainly for the Second Brandenburg Concerto, with a striking but rather dry sound, and even tiny trumpets in B♭ above that, which ensure accuracy but offer little else. In spite of much interest in the problem there are still few satisfactory instruments for playing clarino parts in anything approaching the original manner; the gentler sounds of the old long trumpets are missed sadly and are needed too for the recreational chamber music the French write particularly well. New metals are being tried to modify brittle and blaring sounds (or sometimes to produce them) and electrolysis has provided a valuable way of making tubes and bells entirely uniform.

The mute (Fig. 79) has been used since at least the seven-

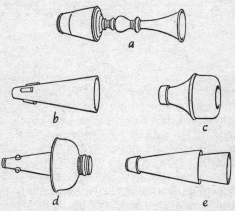

FIG. 79. Trumpet mutes (a) after Mersenne; (b) straight; (c) wow-wow; (d) cup; (e) clear-tone

teenth century. First a pear-shaped block of wood was used and later a hollow cone of wood, fibre, or leather constricted or closed at the wider end. Pushed into the bell it produces an echo of distant beauty as in Debussy's *Nuages*, comic chattering in Ravel's orchestration of Mussorgsky's *Pictures from an Exhibition*, or bleating sheep in Richard Strauss's *Don Quixote*. Jazz players, whose uninhibited experiments have already passed on exuberant *glissandi* to serious music like Bartók's Violin Concerto, use mutes of every possible shape and kind, including those made of headgear, and on trombones also. They will certainly affect still further the course of things to come, and what better symbol can there be of this assimilation into all kinds of music than the spectacle of the former instrument of kings and princes literally putting on a bowler hat and 'going to Town'?

# 12. *The Horn, and the Later Brass*

### R. MORLEY PEGGE

IN his monumental Tutor, published in 1824, the great French virtuoso and teacher, Louis-François Dauprat, says of the horn that 'notwithstanding its imperfections' (he was of course speaking of the horn without valves, for the valve horn, still in its infancy, had yet to reach France) 'it is of all wind instruments the most beautiful in respect of timbre and intrinsic quality of tone, while the feelings aroused by its charm are generally admitted to be irresistible'. To a large extent this is still true, though there are people who consider that some of this charm was whittled away by the universal adoption of the valve and has been still further undermined by the comparatively recent substitution of the heavily mechanized wide-bore German horn for the more refined, though more difficult, French type of instrument. But we should first look at the instrument's history.*

Leaving out such ancient instruments as the Scandinavian Bronze Age *lur* and the Roman *cornu*, which had certain horn-like characteristics but which disappeared with the civilizations of which they were a manifestation, the earliest form of *musical* horn, as far as we know, was the close-coiled helical horn. This horn, which probably originated in Central Europe about the middle of the sixteenth century, had a bore and bell akin to those of the present-day English bugle, and a deep funnel-like mouthpiece, the shank of which fitted over the mouthpipe, instead of into it as it does on present-day instruments. The use of these helical horns never seems to have been very general, though they were employed to some extent for hunting in Germany and in France, where they were called *cors à plusieurs tours*, and also no doubt in Italy. Their significance in the musical

* Fr. *cor, cor d'harmonie*; Ital. *corno*; Ger. *Horn* or *Waldhorn* (whence Russ. *valtorna*). N.B. Span. *trompa* (cf. Fr. *trompe*, the circular hunting horn).

development of the horn appears to have been overlooked by musicologists, probably because no specimen seems to have found its way into any major collection of musical instruments, which is perhaps not surprising since there is no evidence that the horn was ever used musically in combination with other instruments before the early years of the eighteenth century. On the rare occasions when horns are met with in the seventeenth-century theatre (e.g. in Cavalli's *Le Nozze di Tito e di Pelei*, produced in Venice in 1639, and Lully's *La Princesse d'Élide*, first performed at Versailles in 1664) they are simply used for fanfares illustrative of scenes of the chase.

The first of these early helical horns to attract the attention of a musician was a specimen in the hunting-accoutrement section of the Staatliches Historisches Museum at Dresden, the musician in question being that unrivalled authority on the history of brass instruments, the late W. F. H. Blandford. Two such instruments were examined and the smaller and older of the two is illustrated on Pl. 28a. It measures $6\frac{1}{2}$ in. across the coils, has a tube length of about 5 ft. 6 in., and gives the harmonic series of A♭ approximately (the pitch was determined by a rather hasty trial). It appears to have been made in or about 1575. At least six notes could have been obtained with ease on such an instrument, while on later and longer examples the range would equal that of the contemporary trumpet. Such horns may well have been used for fanfares harmonized in parts, though there is no evidence that they were ever employed with instruments other than their own kind. It is, however, extremely probable that the lower parts of the Cavalli and Lully fanfares were played on large helical horns.

About 1650, and almost certainly in France, a new type of horn appeared. It was a horn of much smaller bore than the helical horn and made in the form of a hoop, first in two coils and later (about 1690) in a single coil (Pl. 28b). This was the true parent of what we now know as the French horn, and in its original form it appears to have reached England from France in the wake of the Restoration, probably soon after the reinstatement of the Royal Buck-hounds in 1661. At all events an advertisement in *The Loyal Protestant and Domestick Intelligence* for 7 March 1681/2 of the London maker William Bull mentions '*French* horns', leaving no doubt that the term was already quite a familiar one.

Yet the early musical development of the horn owes nothing either to France or to England. For that the entire credit must go to Germany, in particular to Bohemia and Saxony, the 'French' horn being originally introduced into Bohemia by Graf Franz Anton von Spörck, to whom, when he first met it in Paris in 1681 at the end of his grand tour, it was a complete novelty. This, coupled with the fact that the earliest known score to include horns in the orchestral sense – Keiser's opera *Octavia* (Hamburg, 1705) – labels them '*cornes de chasse*', lends considerable weight to the belief that the instrument did well and truly originate in France, a view that has been hotly contested at least once.

Since the hoop diameter of the earliest horns of this model was only about 8 in., they had to be carried slung from a baldric; they were blown with the bell pointing upwards, in the same way as the small arcuate bugle horns that had long been in use in the hunting field. This custom persisted, even in the orchestra, to a large extent during the eighteenth century and until the practice of placing a hand in the bell became universal. With the advent of the larger hooped horn in the early years of the eighteenth century the instrument was held horizontally, at least shoulder-high. Apart from Bohemia, where, under the enlightened patronage of Von Spörck, a mellower quality of tone seems to have been cultivated, it may be assumed that the playing in general was pretty rough. In 1717 Lady Mary Wortley Montagu, writing from Vienna to her friend Lady Rich, says: '. . . the music good, if they had not the detestable custom of mixing hunting horns with it, that almost deafen the company'.

In England, although Handel and other composers used it rather exceptionally in the orchestra with trumpet players doubling on it when required, the French horn was chiefly used for the purposes of entertainment in the pleasure gardens and on the river, two performers playing duets being the usual thing. Rich men of family and fashion sometimes included in their retinues French horn players, often Negroes, to add *panache* to their equipages, but scarcely any use was made of it in the hunting field. France, on the other hand, restricted its use almost entirely to the chase and did not admit it to the orchestra before about 1735.

In its simplest form, still today that of the French *trompe de chasse* (sometimes *cor de chasse*), the horn is a slender conical tube, coiled in one or more circles, which expands very markedly in the last twelve inches or so to end in a widely flared bell. Its length could be anything from about eight to about eighteen feet, according to pitch. Thus a 10 ft 11 in. horn sounds the harmonic series of $G'$, one of 12 ft 3 in. that of $F'$, and so on. Since without mechanical aids a brass instrument will sound only the notes that comprise the harmonic series of its tube length, a separate horn was required at first for every change of key. The nuisance of having to carry round several horns had been overcome by about 1715 by the application of the crook system that had long been in use with the trumpet. With this system the fixed mouthpiece was replaced by a socket into which rings of tubing of various lengths could be fitted, and thus, with an adequate supply of crooks, one horn could be put into any key. Originally a set of crooks consisted of two master-crooks into which the mouthpiece fitted, and four couplers of assorted lengths which were placed between the master-crook and the instrument itself. One or other of the master-crooks – as a rule one was made in a single coil and the other with two coils – could be used either by itself or in any combination with one or more of the couplers. Individual crooks for each key seem to date from the closing years of the eighteenth century.

About the middle of the same century there occurred one of the most important innovations in the entire history of the horn. The Dresden horn player Anton Joseph Hampel (d. 1771), while experimenting with mutes, found that the introduction of a cotton pad into the bell of the horn lowered the pitch progressively as he pushed it farther in until, when the pad was in as far as it would go, the pitch suddenly rose a semitone. More experiments showed him that the same results could be obtained by the use of his hand alone. It thus became possible to produce a number of notes outside the harmonic series of the crook in use, while at the same time the roughness that is to some extent inherent in the instrument was smoothed off and the tone acquired that veiled, mysterious quality which is – or at any rate was – the chief asset of the horn. With the old system of crooks the distance between mouthpiece and bell necessarily varied with each change; this made it ill-suited to the demands of hand technique, so Hampel redesigned the instrument with crooks that fitted into the centre of the hoop, the original fixed mouthpipe being restored. The first instrument of the new model was made by the Dresden maker Johann Werner. Not entirely satisfactory, it was subsequently improved first by J. G. Haltenhof, of Hanau-am-Main, out of whose improvement came the tuning slide, and then by Raoux in Paris. This type of horn, as perfected by Raoux, became the instrument *par excellence* of the virtuoso soloist, then about to enter the heyday of his popularity, comparable to that of the leading violinists of today. The more notable of these horn virtuosi included Giovanni Punto (1748–1803), the Bohemian artist for whom Beethoven wrote his Horn Sonata and who was the most famous of all; Rodolphe, who introduced the hand horn to Paris in 1765; Spandau, of The Hague, who played in London in 1773; Leutgeb, for whom Mozart wrote four horn concertos and some chamber music; Palsa and Türrschmidt, the celebrated duettists; the Petrides brothers, followed by Puzzi, who settled in England; and a host of others.

The insurmountable drawback to the hand horn was the great disparity of tone and power between the open and the heavily stopped notes, which no degree of skill could quite succeed in disguising. This disparity was particularly marked in the hands of any but the finest performers, while the lower octave was practically useless even in the most

competent hands. Until about the end of the eighteenth
century horn players were strictly divided into two distinct
categories, first horns, or *cors-alto*, and second horns, or
*cors-basse*. On the medium crooks (F, E, E♭, and D) the
range of the former would be from the fourth (written as *c'*)
to the twentieth harmonic (*e'''*) and even higher, while the
latter covered from five semitones below the second harmonic (*c*) up to the sixteenth (*c'''*), and it was by no means
uncommon for the principal in a major orchestra to be a
'second horn'. With, or a little before, the turn of the century there grew up a third category known as *cors-mixte*, who
specialized in a limited range of about an octave and a half,
from the fourth to the twelfth harmonic (*g''*). This is the
range in which a reasonably homogeneous tone quality
could be obtained throughout, and it was the *cor-mixte* who
settled on the F crook as the best for the purpose and used it
regardless of the key of the piece. There is an important horn
*obbligato* in Spontini's *La Vestale*; the solo horn part is written
for the F horn, although the key is E♭ and the horns in the
accompanying orchestra are in E♭.

The deficiencies of the hand horn were to be made good
in Germany about 1815 by the invention of the valve, described in the second part of this chapter. The early valve-
horn players used their valves as a substitute for changing
the crook, playing their parts with hand horn technique
except when the required crook change was not forthcoming
with the two or three valves at their disposal; in that case
they acted like present-day players and simply transposed
the part with the aid of the valves. This combined hand-and-
valve technique probably accounts for the occasional
occurrence of crook changes from one bar to the next, a good
example of which may be seen in Wagner's familiar Introduction to the Third Act of his comparatively early work
*Lohengrin*.

In nearly all major symphony and opera orchestras
throughout the world the players now use either the so-
called 'double horn', or an ordinary single horn pitched in
high B♭ and with one or two extra valves. The double horn

is, as its name implies, a combination in a single instrument of an F horn and a B♭ horn, each complete with its appropriately tuned valve slides; a fourth valve, operated by the thumb, allows the player to switch instantly from the one to the other. The ever-increasing strain thrown on the player in the performance of modern music has made inevitable some change from the older and simpler horn. The French horn in F, in almost universal use up to about thirty years ago – in England with the French model with piston valves – is extremely difficult to play, and all but a few of the finest exponents were liable to crack far too many notes. The modern type of horn has therefore proved an immense boon to players, and the benefit of the technical

side of horn-playing is very great. The example above should help to make this clear, for it is the close proximity to each other of the harmonics above the eighth, necessitating extreme accuracy of attack as well as considerable muscular effort, that makes the F horn so liable to mishap in the upper register. Some German players go still further, having begun to use a horn pitched in high F, an octave above the normal F horn.

The F/B♭ double horn was first put on the market about 1899 by the well-known maker Kruspe, of Erfurt. A device embodying the principle on which the double horn is based was patented by Gautrot, of Paris, in 1864 under the name of *système équitonique*; this, however, was conceived as a 'compensating system' to improve the intonation of certain notes on instruments of the euphonium class, and though applied to the horn for a different purpose, that purpose was one of no practical advantage. Different forms of double horn mechanism are now employed by various makers, but space forbids description of these devices, all of which, in the end, achieve the same result. In England it is used in horns of the German pattern ('German horn'), with their larger bore, rotary valves, and (it must be added), coarser tone (Pl. 28f).

In spite of the addition of valves to the horn, the hand in the bell still has an effective part to play, for it serves not only to keep in check the instrument's natural roughness of tone but also to ensure perfect intonation. It also serves for a certain type of muting demanded when the part is marked 'stopped', '*sons bouchés*', '*gestopft*', or '*chiuso*', or simply when the sign $+$ is placed over a note or passage. This effect is obtained by closing the bell as tightly as possible, which causes the pitch to rise a semitone and obliges the player to transpose the passage accordingly. Some horns are provided with a supplementary half-tone valve to obviate the necessity of this transposition. Most composers, from Berlioz onwards, have made use of the peculiar pungent tone quality of the stopped notes.

Ordinary mutes, usually made of cardboard covered with rexine but sometimes of metal, do not affect the pitch. One exception, however, a small brass mute shaped like two truncated cones joined together at their bases, does raise the pitch a semitone; it is intended for the production *in the low register* of the 'stopped' effect, almost impossible to get with the hand alone.

### THE LATER BRASS

It now remains to say something about those brass instruments whose chief use is in the military or brass band, and which have not already been dealt with in the preceding chapter. One of these, the tuba, has also an important place in the modern orchestra, and another, the so-called Wagner tuba, has its own special use in the orchestra but finds no place in the normal kinds of wind band.

All are essentially the fruits of the invention of the valve (c. 1815), but they nevertheless have roots in the past, the most important being the serpent, of late sixteenth-century origin, and the eighteenth-century bugle-horn.

The *serpent* is a conical wooden tube about eight feet in length, folded in serpentine form to render it manageable and sounded by means of a cup-shaped mouthpiece inserted into a longish brass crook (Pl. 29a). Gaps in the scale of the full tube are bridged by uncovering six large fingerholes. Generally described as 'the bass of the cornett family', the serpent has both a technical and a structural resemblance to the cornett (p. 280), but in fact the ambits of the two instruments rarely seem to have overlapped, in spite of a co-existence lasting nearly two centuries: only perhaps now and then in France were they ever played in the same band.

The serpent owes its origin to the efforts of a French canon, Edmé Guillaume of Auxerre, to improve upon an unsatisfactory type of large cornett, about the year 1590. Its original purpose was to accompany plainsong in churches, and this indeed appears to have been its sole function until, about the middle of the eighteenth century, it found its way into wind ensembles in Germany, spreading thence into military bands all over Europe. It was, however, known and used in England before the end of the seventeenth century. The earliest serpents are said to have been made of two completely shaped halves hollowed out from the solid wood, but two specimens recently taken apart reveal different methods. One of these, an eighteenth-century French example, had one half shaped and hollowed out of the solid single piece of wood and the other half built up in four sections, the whole then being glued together and bound with strong paper and then with leather. The other specimen, a nineteenth-century English serpent, was found to be entirely made up of sections, so placed that their junctions do not lie opposite to each other, glued together and covered with canvas and finally with leather. Both instruments have heavy brass ferrules round the neck where the crook is inserted, the English specimen also having, as is typical, an ornamental brass band round the bell. English serpents intended for military use sometimes have the bell turned slightly outwards, as the result of a suggestion traditionally ascribed to George III. The mouthpieces of the church serpents were strictly hemispherical, with a fairly narrow throat and an exceedingly thin rim, but those of the nineteenth-century military serpents were usually deeper cupped and had wider rims. The mouthpieces were commonly made of ivory.

Since it is no longer possible for anyone today to play the instrument at more than amateur level, we cannot hope to get much idea of what it sounded like in the hands of the major virtuosi a hundred and fifty years ago, such as André, of the Prince Regent's band, Frichot, inventor of the bass horn and sometime serpentist of the 'Antient Concerts' orchestra, Abbé Aubert or Abbé Lunel of Notre Dame, Paris, and one or two others. As far as can be judged nowadays, the tone is rich and rather 'woody' in the lower register, weak and rather windy in the upper reaches. By its very nature the serpent is so flexible that good intonation depends entirely on the musicianship of the performer, and it is assuredly poor musicianship that was responsible for the bad reputation it got in certain quarters. Closed keys, usually three on early nineteenth-century examples, were first added about 1800.

The earliest known attempt to make the serpent more convenient to handle was that of Régibo, serpentist at the church of Saint Pierre in Lille, who made a serpent in three joints modelled on the lines of the bassoon. All we know about it, however, comes from his advertisement in Framery's *Calendrier Musical* for 1789. The next to emerge was the *bass horn* (Pl. 29c) invented by Frichot, a refugee from the French Revolution who came to London in the early 1790s; it was first made commercially by Astor, about 1800. Usually made of brass, or of copper with brass embellishments, and very exceptionally of wood, the bass horn had three, or sometimes four, closed keys. A true serpent, it had all the acoustical defects of that instrument, and although very successful in England it was never adopted on the continent. An enormous variety of upright serpents, some of them with dragon's head bells and even wagging tongues, appeared in the first half of the last century. Here are a few of the better-known types: *English*: Hibernicon, Serpent-cleide; *French*: *Serpent Piffault, Serpent Forveille, Ophibaryton, Ophimonocléide*; *German*: Russian bassoon, *Chromatisches Bass-horn, Bass-Euphonium*.

Turning now to the *key bugle* and the *ophicleide*, in former times the bugle was more properly called the 'bugle horn' (i.e. the horn of a 'bugle', in Old French a young bull). During the eighteenth century some copper and brass bugles were still made in the old oxhorn shape, while others had

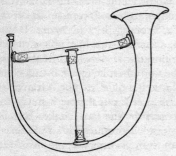

Fig. 80.
Hanoverian bugle-horn

a coil in the middle; they were variously used as watch-men's horns, post horns, etc. Hanoverian and English Light Infantry Regiments adopted them as duty and signal instruments (Fig. 80), sounding calls similar to those of the present day, and in 1814 the bugle became the badge of all the English Light Infantry. It assumed the folded trumpet shape about 1800.

There is a story, probably apocryphal, that a bugle with a hole in it was sent to Joseph Halliday, Master of the band of the Cavan Militia then quartered in Dublin, who, noticing that the hole affected the pitch, then and there conceived the idea of an instrument with five closed keys which he patented in 1810. On this a complete chromatic scale from $c'$ to $c'''$ could be played. Halliday sold his patent rights to the Dublin maker Matthew Pace, who appears to have made the first key bugle, which, as a compliment to H.R.H. the Duke of Kent (Commander-in-Chief of the British Army), became known as the Royal Kent Bugle. Very soon a sixth (open-standing) key near the bell was added, and in due course one or two more, for trills; six, however, was the standard number. The instrument was usually built in C, with a small round crook to put it into B♭ when required. Keys proved far more effective on the wide-bore bugle than they had on the Viennese key trumpet brought out nine years before Halliday's patent, and in the hands of a good player the key bugle was capable of great agility. As the first fully melodic treble brass instrument, it immediately became very popular for solo work until superseded about the middle of the century by the cornet. It was introduced to the continent during the last phase of the Napoleonic wars, and at a military review held in Paris by the Allies after Waterloo the Grand Duke Constantine commanded John Distin, solo key bugle in the Grenadier Guards band, to have a replica of the instrument made for him. Distin had his bugle copied by the Paris maker Halary (J. H. Asté) who, in 1817, himself produced a whole series of key bugles of which the most important was the *ophicleide*.

This bass bugle, much more efficient than serpents or bass horns, soon replaced them in large orchestras after its initial success in the stage band used in Spontini's opera *Olympie* (1819). In France and England it became the indispensable companion of the trombones, and was only displaced by the weightier-sounding tuba in the latter part of the last century. Ophicleide solos, played by Prospère, were a feature of Jullien's Promenade Concerts in the 1850s, and an occasional ophicleide solo – generally an arrangement of 'O ruddier than the cherry' – was not unknown at the early Henry Wood Queen's Hall Promenade Concerts. Ophicleides were normally in C or B♭, with eleven keys, of which that nearest the bell stood open, giving, when closed, a semitone below the key note. In England, the heyday of the ophicleide was roughly from 1830 to 1890.

\*

The invention in Germany, about 1815, of valves opened up a completely new era in ensemble music. It endowed with a homogeneous chromatic scale of anything up to four octaves brass instruments which hitherto had been able to sound only so much of the harmonic series germane to a single tube length as their proportions and the skill of the performer allowed. Thus, not only were the resources of the horn and trumpet vastly increased, but the way was open for the creation of whole new families of brass instruments.

Valves may be of two kinds: *descending,* which lower the pitch, and *ascending,* which raise it. The former (see p. 290) is the more common kind. But whereas a descending valve loop is brought into the circuit only when the valve is depressed, the loop of an ascending valve actually forms part of the primary tube, depression of the valve cutting out the loop and shortening by so much the length of the air-column. Apart from the thumb valve of the F/B♭ double horn, which in most models cuts out about three feet of tubing and puts the F horn into B♭, and the ascending whole-tone third valve used on horns in France, the ascending valve is seldom or never used nowadays. To circumvent the sharpness in pitch which the player has to contend against when valves are used in combination (p. 291), various compensating devices have been tried out, the most successful being D. J. Blaikley's 'Compensating Pistons', patented in 1878 and still used by Messrs Boosey & Hawkes for their best-quality larger instruments. Some details of this and other compensating systems, as well as a fuller account of the development of the valve, will be found in Grove's *Dictionary of Music and Musicians,* fifth edition (1954).

The invention of the valve, which had been foreshadowed some twenty-five years earlier by the double 'Chromatic Trumpet and French Horn' patented in London by Charles

Clagget, is generally attributed to two Silesians, Heinrich Stölzel, a horn player, and Friedrich Blühmel, apparently an amateur bandsman, who took out a joint patent in 1818. Which of the two was actually first in the field has never been satisfactorily cleared up, but the weight of such evidence as is now available tends to favour Stölzel, who demonstrated it in Berlin in 1815. It was taken up by the makers Griessling & Schlott, and the probability is that it was tubular; the valve described in the 1818 patent was rectangular, and may well have been an improvement on Stölzel's valve suggested by Blühmel. It was soon eclipsed by the slender tubular valve, the bottom of which served as a windway, and which is always known as the 'Stölzel valve'. Cheap cornets with these valves were still being made in France up to the outbreak of the First World War. An interesting though more or less abortive valve was patented in 1824 by an English farmer and brass worker, John Shaw. This system he called 'transverse spring slides', and it owed nothing whatever to any continental device. It embodied two original features, both subsequently used in modified form by continental makers, namely twin pistons and ascending valves, the first being seen in the so-called Vienna valve, while the second was used by Sax for his instruments with six independent pistons and Halary for his horn with an ascending third valve. The Vienna valve, which has nothing in common with the transverse spring slide beyond the twin piston, is said to have been invented by Leopold Uhlmann, of Vienna, on the strength of his patent, granted in 1830. In its improved form (Pl. 28e) it was very successful and was widely used for brass instruments of all kinds, especially in Austria and Belgium. It still survives on Viennese French horns, but even there it is having to give way to the rotary valve which is particularly suitable for the now ubiquitous double horn.

The rotary valve was probably invented by Joseph Riedl, also of Vienna, who patented his *Rad-Maschine* in 1832. This valve did away with the awkward angles and windway constrictions of the Stölzel valve, and it remains today in all essentials exactly the same as when it first appeared. Its original operating mechanism was an articulated crank, controlled by a watch spring enclosed in a small drum. This is still the commonest type of actuating mechanism, though another popular system is the so-called 'American' or 'string action', first heard of in a patent taken out in 1866 by the Schreiber Cornet Manufacturing Company of New York.

The first serious improvement to the piston valve was the Wieprecht-Moritz *Berliner-Pumpventil*, a short, thick valve with all the windways in the same plane. This appeared in Berlin in 1835 and was copied in Paris about five years later by Sax. In 1839 the Paris maker Périnet brought out the valve which, with minor modifications, is the piston valve which is universally in use today. As regards relative efficiency there is nothing whatever to choose between modern piston and rotary valves. The first are preferred in France, Belgium, England, and the United States, though in these last two countries rotary valves are used for French horns, following German practice. Elsewhere the rotary action is almost universally used. The choice is just a matter of locality and fashion.

The transition from the key bugle to the valve bugle or flugel horn was an obvious step. In England the flugel horn is seldom used outside brass bands, but on the continent it is a leading instrument in military bands, and alto and soprano (E♭) instruments are used as well as the ordinary B♭ flugel horn. No less obvious was the application in France, of valves to the circular continental model of post horn (*cornet de poste* (Fig. 81) or *cornet simple*) which thereupon became the *cornet-à-pistons*, known in England as the *cornopean* or *cornet*.

FIG. 81. French cornet de poste

Artistically the cornet got off to a

bad start from which it never really recovered. If, when it was first made, there had been in regular existence a short B♭ trumpet, it is at least possible that the cornet would never have appeared at all. An aura of vulgarity, wished upon it, doubtless unwittingly, by its godfather Dufrène, who introduced it to the Paris public in 1830 at the Champs Élysées concerts and at balls, has bedevilled it throughout its somewhat chequered career. The touchingly vulgar solos in *Petrushka** and in Tchaikovsky's *Swan Lake* show up only too well the instrument's fundamentally plebeian nature.

During the middle years of the 1820s Spontini, then chief Kapellmeister to the King of Prussia, sent to Paris some instruments with the valves that had lately been invented in Germany. At once the Paris instrument makers, and in particular Labbaye and Halary-Antoine, set about improving the mechanism. One result was their application by Halary in 1828 to the *cornet de poste*, as mentioned above, at first using two valves only, and a range of shanks and crooks from high C down to E♭ or even lower. Other French and Belgian makers followed suit, and in the early 1830s Embach in Amsterdam and Köhler and the brothers Charles and Frederick Pace in London began making what in England became known as the cornopean.

Many of the early French cornet virtuosi were horn players originally, notable among them being J. Forestier, cornet soloist of the Musard concerts and horn player at the Théâtre Italien; J. H. Maury, horn player at the Paris Opéra and professor of the cornet at the Conservatoire; and F. A. Schlotmann, a front-rank performer on both instruments. To this connexion with the horn were probably due the longer crooks, said to have had a particularly mellow tone, and the nearly conical mouthpiece. After a time it was trumpeters rather than horn players who took up the cornet, discarding the long crooks in favour of the more

* In the 1949 revised version the cornet solo in Tableau 3 has been transferred to the trumpet. One misses that touch of essential vulgarity in the cornet tone that helped to depict so vividly the fairground scene.

brilliant C or B♭ instrument as better adapted to show off the fireworks of which it is capable. Arban, the author of the standard Tutor for the cornet, was a pioneer of this school.

In the hands of a sensitive artist the cornet has always been popular. Koenig was the Number One attraction of Jullien's Promenade Concerts; Isaac Levy, 'The Demon Cornet Player', was a star performer with a large following, while those old enough to have heard Sousa's band before the First World War are not likely to forget the astounding cadenzas played by his solo cornettist Herbert Clarke. There are many other names that might be mentioned, but the very nature of the instrument ordains that what lingers in the memory is less their rendering of fine music than the seeming ease with which these virtuosi mastered the most formidable difficulties.

If the provision of valves to the soprano instruments was fairly straightforward, the same cannot be said of the replacement of serpents, bass horns, etc., by valved equivalents. The modern instruments now coming under notice are: (a) Those chiefly used in military and brass bands – E♭ tenor horn (Amer. Fr. *alto*; Germ. *Althorn*), B♭ baritone (Amer. *tenor*; Fr. *baryton*; Ger. *Tenorhorn*), B♭ euphonium (Amer. *baritone*; Fr. *basse*; Ger. *Baryton*), E♭ bass or bombardon (Fr. *contrebasse*), and B♭ bass, usually described as in BB♭, the double letter here denoting a large bore which favours emission of the lowest notes. In Germany the first two are often made in oval form. All may be made in circular form, circular basses being called 'helicons'. In America the last three are also made with the bell pointing forwards. (b) The orchestral tubas (p. 314). (c) The Wagner tubas (p. 315).

(a). Not much is known about the earliest of these instruments. A price-list of wind instruments issued in 1826 by the Mainz music publishers B. Schott's Söhne includes but one '*ventil*' instrument, and that a trumpet. Stölzel's (Berlin) price-list issued two years later includes a *Basshorn oder Basstrompete in F oder Es* (i.e. E♭) and a *Tenorhorn oder Tenortrompete in B;* these would appear to be the equivalents of a small bore bass in F or E♭, and a baritone. Neither seems to have attracted much attention at the time, any more than did the 'chromatic bass folded like a bugle horn, with three movable stops' seen in Percival's St James's Street manufactory by a correspondent of *The Harmonicon* (July 1830) – an instrument which may of course have been a foreign importation, but yet may well have been an experiment made by Percival's enterprising and ingenious partner John Köhler, later of Henrietta Street, Covent Garden.

The first such instrument to gain any real notoriety was the Wieprecht–Moritz five-valve *Basstuba* in F patented in 1835 together with the improved *Berliner-Pumpen* valve. Wieprecht had already caused considerable stir by introducing valved instruments into the band of the Prussian Dragoon Guards, of which he was bandmaster, but it was not until the advent of Adolphe Sax, who settled in Paris in 1841, that the world at large really became cognizant of these things.

There were other instruments of a similar class to those of Wieprecht in Germany in the middle and late 1830s, and some of them, like the *néo-altos* and *bombardons*, found their way to Paris before 1845; there were also the French-made *clavicors* (Danays/Guichard patent of 1837). Sax, however, thanks to influential backing in musical and political circles, was granted French patents for his *Saxhorns* and *Saxotrombas*. Amongst his backers was General de Rumigny, who became chairman of the Commission appointed in 1845 to carry out reforms in the French army bands so, when these reforms were put into effect, Sax was able to get a high proportion of his own instruments included in the official instrumentation. Inevitably he fell foul of the old-established French makers, whose chief customers were the army bands, who naturally made concerted efforts to get Sax's patents revoked. The litigation that ensued lasted ten years, neither party coming out of it all with much credit.

Incalculable harm was done to the French musical instrument industry, and in the end a number of makers, including Sax himself, were ruined. There seem to have been good grounds for the reaction of the French makers, for the Sax instruments differed but little from those already on the market which, as far as their general characteristics were concerned, were considered to be public property. Three things in particular contributed to Sax's spectacular success: better valves (he used an apparently pirated copy of the Berliner-Pumpen, much superior to the Stölzel valves with which the older instruments were equipped); a completely coordinated family instead of a hotch-potch of instruments from multiple sources; and last but not least, influence in the right quarters. The Sax combination was certainly a great advantage for marching bands, but at the cost of a deadly monotony of timbre, as can be appreciated today by comparing the music of the full military band with that of the purely brass band.

Among the few leading brass players whom Sax did not antagonize were the English Distin family, who formed a brass quintet consisting of John Distin (mentioned earlier in connexion with the key bugle) and his four sons, which already had a solid following in England and made successful continental tours. Sax made them a set of saxhorns with which they further enhanced their reputation both at home and abroad. There is no doubt that the rapid expansion of the amateur brass band movement in England about the middle of the last century was due in no small measure to the success of the Distins with their saxhorns. One of the sons, Henry, set up in business in London in 1846, first as an importer of instruments made by Sax and later as a maker in his own right. Every member of the bugle horn family, from the E♭ tenor horn to the BB♭ bass, was well established before mid-century; nothing more was needed beyond some further improvement in valve mechanism and, for mass production, in manufacturing processes. The patent files between 1818 and (say) 1875 bear eloquent witness to the amount of ingenuity expended in the search for the perfect valve. Today the valve is doubtless as nearly perfect mechanically as it is ever likely to be, but research nevertheless goes on, chiefly in the metallurgical aspects.

The term *bombardon* was first applied to a species of bass ophicleide with twelve keys brought out in the early 1820s by Wenzel Riedl, of Vienna. About ten years later the same maker produced, under the same name, a sort of large valved trombone. Of these original bombardons only the name survived, to be adopted by makers everywhere just as ophicleide, also originally a trade name, had been some years earlier. In 1845, the year in which Sax patented his saxhorns, the first very large CC and BB♭ basses were brought out by Červený (Königgratz) on the lines of Wieprecht's *Bass-tuba*, the same maker introducing, some forty years later, the monster basses used in German wind bands and known as *Kaiserbässe*. The original Sousaphone, first made in 1908 by G. C. Conn, of Elkhart, Ind., for Sousa's famous band, was a very large-bore upright bass with a kink in the bell which pointed upwards, but sousaphones have since had a vastly wide bell pointing forwards.

(b). If the wind-band basses have become stabilized in the E♭ and BB♭ models, it is far otherwise with the orchestral tuba. In England most players use a tuba in F, though some prefer one in E♭. America and Italy, on the other hand, favour a larger instrument in CC or BB♭. The standard German orchestral tuba, like its English counterpart, is in F, though there is also a six-piston model in F♯, the Séha system. No details of this instrument are available at the moment, but as H. Séha was at one time attached to Sax's workshop and also professed the six-valve trombone at the Brussels Conservatoire, it looks as though this tuba is a hangover from Sax's instruments with six independent ascending valves, which would account for its being 'in F♯'. France has its own special type of orchestral tuba which is, in fact, a very large bore euphonium in C with six valves by means of which its downward compass is extended chromatically a full octave below the normal fundamental, giving it the phenomenal range of four octaves from $C'$ to $c''$. The valves operate thus:

First   valve lowers the pitch by one tone
Second  ,,     ,,     ,,     ,,   ,, a semitone
Third   ,,     ,,     ,,     ,,   ,, two tones
Fourth  ,,     ,,     ,,     ,,   ,, two-and-a-half tones
Fifth   ,,     ,,     ,,     ,,   ,, a semitone
Sixth   ,,     ,,     ,,     ,,   ,, three-and-a-half-tones

This instrument is a development of the five-valve tuba used at the Paris Opéra between 1880 and 1892, when Courtois added an extra semitone valve (now the fifth) to serve chiefly as a transposer to facilitate fingering in sharp keys. It was this instrument that Ravel had in mind when he gave the tuba the well-known solo in 'Bydlo' in his orchestration of Mussorgsky's *Pictures from an Exhibition*.

When a tenor tuba is called for, as in Strauss's *Don Quixote*, an ordinary euphonium is used.

(c). *Wagner tubas*. 'Tuba' here is really a misnomer, the proper name for these instruments being *Wagner-Tuben*. It is possible that the mistake had its origin through the German conductor – presumably Richter – pronouncing the word 'tube' in the German manner (which would sound like 'tuba') when *The Ring* was first produced in London. This may not be the correct explanation, but it is a plausible one. These *Tuben*, conceived by Wagner to bridge certain gaps in the brass tone, are made in two sizes, in B♭ and F, at the same pitches respectively as the B♭ and F horns and using the same part of the harmonic series. In bore they are midway between the horn and the saxhorn, and they are intended to be played by horn players using their own mouthpieces. They are fitted with four valves, the purpose of the fourth being to improve the intonation of the lower octave. Wagner himself uses them only in *The Ring*, where they are played by the second quartet of horns, horns 5 and

7 playing the B♭ instruments, and 6 and 8 those in F. Some later composers have employed them, however, such as Bruckner in his last three symphonies, Richard Strauss in *Elektra*, *Die Frau ohne Schatten*, and the *Alpine* Symphony, and Stravinsky in *The Firebird* (original version).

Before taking leave of the brass, a short notice may be accorded to a few instruments that have never been adopted into the musical family.

Double, and even triple, instruments with separate bells but only one mouthpiece and set of valves have appeared from time to time ever since 1851, when Gisborne (Birmingham) brought out a combined cornet and flugel horn, and McNeil (Dublin) a combined trumpet, cornet, and flugel horn. In the 1880s the American maker Conn coupled a trombone with a euphonium, and Besson (London) brought out his 'doublephone', an instrument of similar character. The 'cornophone', patented by Besson (Paris) in 1890, except for the fact that its bell curved backwards over the valves, resembled the saxhorn. Cornophones are still sometimes used in France to replace Wagner tubas in symphony orchestras. A real curiosity that appeared in the early 1900s was an instrument by Sudre, the 'Sudrophone', made in all the usual sizes. This astonishing instrument, shaped rather like an ophicleide, had a gold-beater's skin membrane which, when brought into the circuit by means of a supplementary valve, was said to have produced a cello-like effect. The catalogue issued by the maker in 1905 contains as a frontispiece an amusing drawing by Willette of a schoolgirl playing a sudrophone to the obviously vocal accompaniment of her pet fox terrier.

Substitutes for the French horn, itself difficult to play and by no means ideal for the marching band, have come on the market, notably the tenor cor (Amer. mellophone) in F and E♭, which is virtually a saxhorn shaped like a French horn but using only the lower series of harmonics; it is generally made right-handed.

This list is by no means exhaustive, but there have been so many versions of what to all intents and purposes is the same instrument that we can only bid farewell to the brass by saluting that forerunner of the euphonium, the Somerophone, subsequently re-named the *Hellhorn*, with the words 'A hellhorn by any other name would sound as euphonious . . .'

# 13. *Free-Reed Instruments*

### JAMES HOWARTH

DURING the period 1818–48 an entirely new group of
musical instruments came into being in Europe: the group
today represented by the harmonium, the accordion, and
the harmonica. Too late in arrival to be found regular
places in the classical genres of music, they have won their
successes in other fields of the art. They are all sounded by
the so-called 'free reed' – a metal tongue that is screwed
or riveted over an accurately-cut aperture in a metal frame
and is caused to vibrate by air pressure supplied by the
mouth or by bellows. The pitch of each reed is determined
by the length and thickness of the tongue, which is tuned
by filing – near the tip to sharpen or near the fixed end to
flatten. Each tongue is 'sprung up' from its frame; its arc
of vibration is from the top of the frame to twice the height
at which it is sprung up (shown by dotted line in Fig. 82),

FIG. 82. Concertina reed: (left) Assembled,
with components on right; (right) the same,
showing mode of vibration

and it will vibrate only when the air stream flows through
the reed from this side, though the flow is caused equally
effectively either by direct pressure or by suction.

In the portable instruments, accordions and harmonicas,
the reeds are grouped in pairs, one arranged to sound on
the 'press' or 'blow', the other on the 'draw'. With 'single
action', as in harmonicas and some accordions, the two
reeds of a pair are tuned to sound adjacent notes of the

scale. The result, on the accordion, is that upon pressing a finger button, thus admitting the wind to one pair of reeds, one note is sounded on the press, but another on the draw. In the earliest designs, also the simple 'Melodions' of today, a single row of ten buttons thereby suffices to provide over two diatonic octaves, while for the left hand two keys or 'basses' control two pairs of reeds giving a bass note and its chord, the tonic on the press, the dominant on the draw. The single-action accordion has, however, been given an increased scope in Germany, Austria, and Switzerland, where it is today still popular, by adding to the original or C row, a second or F row arranged to give the notes common to both scales by the opposite movement of the bellows. Further additional rows of buttons supply accidentals and further alternatives, and modern basses are incorporated. The piano accordion and the concertina, however, are 'double-action' instruments, the two reeds of each pair being tuned to the same note, which is thus made available from a single key or button with both directions of movement of the bellows.

*

The introduction of the free reed is generally traced to the interest shown by a number of musicians and scientists towards the end of the eighteenth century in the mouth-organ of the Far East. This has a history of three thousand years, being first recorded in China c. 1100 B.C. The Chinese mouth-organ *sheng* and its closely similar Japanese form *sho* (Fig. 83) are numbered among these nations' classical instruments, the sho still contributing its silvery, high-pitched chords above the strange ensemble of the ancient Japanese court music, while an actual specimen of the sixth century A.D. is preserved among other Sino-Japanese instruments at the Imperial Treasure House at Nara. These mouth-organs employ brass reeds, each tongue cut with extreme skill by a scriber and a knife in the actual metal of its frame. Each reed is cemented over a slot near the base of a wooden pipe,

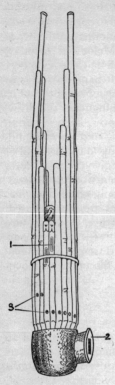

FIG. 83. Japanese
sho (mouth-organ)

camphor-scented and carved to resemble bamboo, and closed at this lower end. Higher up, the pipe is pierced with a vent slot (of which two are on the outside of the pipe (Fig. 83, 1), the others being on the inside). Each pipe thus provides a tuned air-column, to which its reed is acoustically coupled. The pipes rest in sockets in a lacquer windchest (originally a gourd), from the side of which protrudes the mouthpiece (2). As the instrument has so far been described, when it is blown all the pipes would sound together. But in fact all would be silent, since their fingering holes (3) remain uncovered. These destroy the acoustic coupling of reed and pipe; to make a pipe sound, its fingering hole must be closed with finger or thumb, and this is how the instrument is played. The reed tongues are not sprung up, but are extremely flexible and vibrate equally freely whether the player exhales or inhales through the mouthpiece. Elsewhere over Eastern Asia, from Assam to Indo-China and in Borneo, are many different, cruder forms of this mouth-organ, possibly representing earlier stages of its development. Their bamboo pipes, from one to about twelve in number, are waxed into a gourd. Their reeds are cut in thin brass or copper, and their pentatonic scale is usually deeper-pitched than on the sheng, e.g. *e*, *g*, *a*, *b*, *d'*, *e'*, and the natural reediness of their tone is pleasantly mellowed by the resonance of the pipes, which are fingered both separately and in chords; Sachs has truly described the harmony of the Laos mouth-organs as 'one of the most attractive musical styles in the Orient'. In some examples, the reeds are made from thin plates of bamboo, which can be cut with a knife of bamboo, so that the Oriental mouth-organ *could* antedate the Metal Age, though on grounds of distribution Sachs has assigned it to the Metal Age strata of his scheme.

In 1777, so the story goes, Père Amiot, among other things the author of a valuable book on Chinese instruments, sent the present of a sheng from China to Paris. In the course of its transcontinental journey, as much as on arrival at its destination, it aroused interest and touched off various experiments, first in the incorporation of free-reed stops in small organs and notably through the physicist Kratzenstein, the organist and teacher G. J. Vogler (a teacher of Weber), the firm of Érard in Paris, and later, also in Paris, Grenié in his *orgue expressif* of 1810. But the full story of the Western free-reed instruments may have another side to it. It is suggested for instance by Klier, a noted authority, that the Austrian and German products of 1818–21 in which our popular free-reed instruments first saw light may have owed less to the metal tongue which is blown than to that which is *plucked*. Two instruments employing the latter have been noticed in Chapter 1: the African *sansa*, of which a European equivalent may be found in the Swiss musical box, and the European *guimbarde* or Jew's harp. Compound guimbardes with as many as six differently-tuned tongues have been made in Austria, and *c.* 1814 a Bavarian maker, Eschenbach, was experimenting with a keyboard version of the plucked reed (though a later model of his had bellows). It thus remains something of an open question as to what extent the wind-sounded instruments were conceived as improved shengs or as blown guimbardes. The truth may well contain elements of both, while the practice of playing tunes on a birch bark held in the mouth, reported from the Harz Mountains, suggests another possible precursor.

The first of the Austro-German series, as far as is known,

T — L

was Haeckl's *Physharmonica*, i.e. 'bellows harmonica' (Vienna, 1818). It was a small reed organ foreshadowing the harmonium. (Up till that time the term 'harmonica' had denoted the Glass Harmonica, for which Mozart wrote the Quintet K.617 of 1791 – a series of tuned glass bowls rotated on an axle by a treadle and sounded by touching the rims with the fingers. Today in Italy Haeckl's word, as *fisarmonica*, means a piano accordion.) The father of the *Mundharmonica* (mouth-organ) and the *Hand-harmonica* (accordion) is generally recognized to have been C. F. L. Buschmann (1805–64) of Berlin, whose patents were taken out in 1821–2 for instruments variously named *aura*, *aeoline*, etc. Following Buschmann, Cyril Demian brought out his *Accordion* in Vienna in 1829, and in London in the same year Charles Wheatstone (1802–75) patented his 'Symphonium', a mouth-organ in which the reeds, one for each note and sounding only on the 'blow', were contained in a small metal box with blowing hole in the front and finger buttons on each side (Fig. 84). Wheatstone's work in this field was notable for its technological advances, shown for instance in his continual search for the best alloys for the reeds in order to give the steadiest pitch to the notes; the reeds for the Symphonium were first of silver (he even tried gold), quickly followed by steel. He experimented with bellows for this instrument, and his early bellows design, the Concertina, was perfected in 1844. Its octagonal, i.e. basically circular, shape was adapted as lending itself best to fraising the reed chambers on the lathe before the advent of suitable

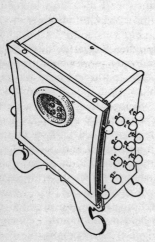

Fig. 84. Wheatstone's Symphonium, 1829

milling machines (Fig. 85). It had double action, the chromatic scale being divided between the two hands.

The first solo performer of note on a free-reed instrument, Giulio Regondi (b. 1822), had already been an accomplished guitarist at the age of eight; he made his name on the *Mélophone* (Jacquet, Paris, 1834), a bellows instrument built in approximately guitar shape, played across the knees, and provided with finger buttons for one hand, the other

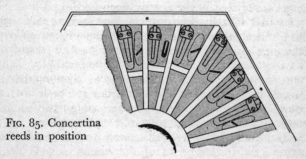

FIG. 85. Concertina
reeds in position

hand pumping the air from behind. Regondi also mastered the Wheatstone concertina, playing it on tour in Germany in 1846, astonishing the German critics, and writing for it two concertos. Another great artist on the concertina, around the 1870s, Richard Blagrove, was at first a violin soloist. After him came Alexander Prince, the greatest of all performers on the 'Duet System' concertina, in which a full chromatic scale is provided for each hand; he began as a boy prodigy, and was the first successfully to perform compositions like the Overture to *Tannhäuser* on the concertina.

Enlargements of the concertina, as in the Duet System, to increase the technical scope, boded ill for the instrument's future. Strength and ease of playing a free-reed instrument are governed by the relation between the pressure applied to the reeds and the area of the wind chamber or bellows. The concertina as originally made by Wheatstone was a small instrument, with small bellows area and a very powerful tone that could fill a large hall; the pressure on the reeds was a good two pounds per square inch. Larger models, made later, failed through containing too big an area when set against the limit of human strength applied to the bellows, and here the accordion scored, possessing an ideal shape for accommodating all the reeds within a small bellows area. (Still more on the harmonica the most intense pressure can be applied to the reeds, even up to an over-strong pressure that distorts their pitch, allowing the artist to obtain special effects.) Many of the virtuosi upon the large concertina in the last century used to pack the reed chambers with small pieces of cork or wood to reduce their size and obtain a more penetrating sound; an analogy to this may be found in brass instrument mouthpieces with their different sizes of cup (the 'reed' being here the player's lips), and in the narrowing of saxophone mouthpiece-chambers which some players demand in order to obtain a 'brass' tone. Different tone colours are obtained in harmoniums by applications of the same principle.

The great popularity of the *accordion* began in the present century (in England *c.* 1910) after various makers, notably Mariano Dallapé of Stradella, Italy, switched over to steel reeds, with their more steady pitch; for music with wavering pitch lacks the power to exert more than a fleeting hold upon an audience, and the older brass-reed accordions were suited best to domestic use and to accompaniments. Dallapé also adopted the pianoforte-style keyboard, which had been introduced earlier in both Vienna and Paris, and distinguishes the 'piano accordion', today the prevailing type. To this, couplers or 'registers' were later added, largely during the 1930s – though they had been known earlier, e.g. in some mélophones. The principal registers now include the unison or 'chorist', the octave below, and a tremulant obtained by admitting a bank of reeds off-tuned from the chorist reeds to cause 'beating'. Additional registers include the octave above, and a second tremulant off-tuned in the opposite manner from the first to give a fresh effect when the two are used in conjunction. These registers are brought into operation by stop levers placed above the keyboard and identified by conventional signs or by terms such as 'clarinet' (chorist only), 'violin' (chorist and tremulant), 'bandoneon' (chorist and lower octave), etc. (The Bandoneon, a solo instrument in Argentine tango orchestras, is itself a square-built button accordion invented by Band of Kleefeld, *c.* 1840; some models have double action, others single.) The left-hand side of the piano accordion has become equally complex, usually provided with up to 120 buttons, of which the first two rows give bass notes, arranged in musical key order, F, C, G, D, etc., but staggered by a major third between the two rows to facilitate scale passages in the bass. The other four rows give three-note chords respectively of major and minor triads, and dominant and diminished sevenths, all similarly following the cyclic key order. These chords are basically obtained from one chromatic set of reeds tuned from $g$ to $f'$ $\sharp$, but there are registers for the left hand, controlled by bar levers, through which (a) these chords can be duplicated at the octave and the double-octave above, and (b) the bass notes can be sounded over as many as five octaves, the button for C then sounding every C from $C$ to $c'''$.

Meanwhile, the German *Mund-harmonica* was especially taken up by the firm founded at Trossingen in 1857 by Matthias Hohner. An important addition to it was the slider stop, which switches the instrument to a second diatonic set of reeds tuned a semitone above the first. Many techniques for the harmonica are based upon masking unwanted reed-chambers with the tongue, and it is interesting to find that it is upon this little instrument (the one on which the performer possesses the nearest to direct contact with his sound-producers, the reeds, and the one which remains closest to the free-reed family's various presumed ancestors) that the highest peak of artistry has been achieved and the widest fame won, namely in the playing of Larry Adler, who has been described as one of the greatest living artists on any musical instrument, and for whom concertos have been written by A. V. Berger, Vaughan Williams, Gordon Jacob, and others. Among many variations upon the harmonica theme brought out by the indefatigable Hohner, the 'Melodica' is a chromatic mouth-organ held like a recorder and fingered with a miniature piano-style keyboard.

Among the early reed organs with keyboard and foot bellows, Green's *seraphine* (London, 1834) failed through harshness of tone. Debain, in Paris, patented the *harmonium* in 1848. At first this was quite small, mounted on a tripod, with a single foot pedal for the wind. The single pedal afforded a direct control of the wind pressure on the reeds when a certain valve was lifted (the 'expression' stop) to by-pass the wind-chest in which the pressure was normally equalized; thus with the valve open, all dynamic shades of expression could be obtained as they can be on the accordion and the other portable instruments. As a tremulant, a second set of reeds, slightly off-tuned to the main set, could be brought into action to make 'beats'. The harmonium later acquired other stops in an attempt to imitate the organ's variety of tone colour; sets of reed chambers of different sizes and shapes were provided, small-sized chambers, for instance, giving a trumpet or tuba tone. Improvements to the harmonium were made in Paris by Alexandre, and above all by the firm of Mustel, the greatest of the harmonium makers, whose beautiful workmanship brought the instrument to its highest perfection. Meanwhile in America the harmonium has pursued a somewhat different course, having generally been blown by suction. But in America as in Europe the harmonium has been losing ground to the smaller electronic organs, and thus one of the last to come is likely to be among the first to go as the Western musical world feels the impact of a new technology. Today it is in India that harmoniums are most valued – to supply a drone.

# 14. *The Orchestral Instruments of Percussion*

## JAMES BLADES

THE instruments of percussion in the symphony orchestra fall into three groups known to players respectively as the timpani or kettledrums; the percussion with indefinite pitch, including side and bass drums, cymbals, gong, triangle, tambourine, castanets, etc.; and the tuned percussion, including glockenspiel, tubular bells, xylophone, marimba, and vibraphone. Of these, the timpani (Fr. *timbales*; Ger. *Pauken*) demand our first attention, for these instruments take pride of place where percussion is concerned.

The two sizes of Arab kettledrum have already been described (p. 34). The first of these to be seen in Europe were the small kind, *nakers* (from Arabic *naqqara*), brought over with other Saracen instruments in the thirteenth century. The direct precursors of the modern kettledrums, however, are the larger Arab instruments, hemispherical or egg-shaped, and used in pairs of approximately 24 in. and 20 in. in diameter. They were played mounted on camel or horse, reached the West from the Ottoman Empire during the fifteenth century, and inspired the European use of cavalry kettledrums, which in their turn began to be put to orchestral use in the seventeenth century to become, after considerable development, the important instruments which they are in the orchestra today.

*Kettledrums* were already in use in certain English cavalry regiments in the sixteenth century, their novelty attracting the interest of Henry VIII, who ordered the purchase of a number of Viennese kettledrums for playing on horseback, and the hire of skilled performers. Almost invariably played in company with trumpets – usually some twelve trumpets and one pair of drums – the drums constituted an ensemble that became a royal preserve and remained so for a long time (Pl. 27a); at the Restoration, the use of cavalry drums was restricted to the Household

Cavalry, though from the accession of James II every mounted regiment was equipped with them, while in Germany various imperial decrees had led to the establishment of the Imperial Guild of Trumpeters and Kettledrummers in 1623. The German drummers were renowned for their skilful and spectacular style of playing, its system holding a secret imparted only to initiates of the Guild. Court and other official composers had, however, benefit of their art, and during the seventeenth century began to recognize the possibilities of cavalry kettledrums, along with trumpets, as orchestral instruments.

The shape of the bowl and the single skin combine to render the tone of a kettledrum pure and distinct, and there is every reason to suppose that the original Arab drummers tuned their instruments to a definite interval. When Napoleon was in Egypt, Villoteau, his musical surveyor, recorded the large kettledrums as tuned to a fifth. In Europe, by the seventeenth century, the drums were equipped with screws to tension the vellums – a great improvement on the original method of bracing or nailing – and a general system of tuning a pair of kettledrums was observed, namely, to the keynote of the trumpets and to the dominant, a fourth below.

The factors which determine the pitch of a kettledrum are briefly as follows: (a) the diameter of the bowl of a kettledrum (which is usually made of copper and has a small hole in the bottom of the shell to release the excessive vibrations) decides the range of effective musical notes obtainable on the vellum or 'head' stretched across its open ends; a vellum that is tensioned too tightly has very little resonance, and one that is too slack has a tone, to use a professional expression, like a 'carpet'; (b) the difference in diameter between the two drums of a pair (usually from three to four inches) apportions the high and low notes, for a small drum gives a higher sound than a larger one, assuming that their skins are equally tensioned; (c) increasing or lessening the tension on a vellum by means of the screws alters its pitch; the tighter the skin is stretched the higher the note, and vice versa; lastly (d), the number of effective notes obtainable from a stretched vellum is also governed by its condition and thickness; one that is too 'stout' or has lost its resilience has a very limited range of pure-sounding notes.

In orchestras of the time of Bach and Handel, the drums were merely cavalry drums put to orchestral use, with a limited compass and a range of well-sounding notes that restricted their ordinary use to the trumpeter's keys of D and C. In the first key the two drums were tuned in fourths to *d* and *A*, and in the second to *c* and *G*, tunings which had arisen, together with a rhythmical style of playing, during the drums' long association with trumpets to which they provided a bass. (Some exceptional tunings are, however, recorded, as in a march written in 1683 in Paris by the brothers Philidor for two pairs of kettledrums alone, one pair tuned normally to *c* and *G*, but the other to *g* and *e*; it is reproduced in the *Galpin Society Journal*, ix, 1956.) Nearly always, the cavalry style is reflected in the orchestras of this period. Solo passages for the drums occur, an early example being in Purcell's *Fairy Queen* (1692), but composers hesitated to employ them in soft music, largely because most drum sticks then in use produced a harsh sound, having heads of ebony or similar wood (sometimes disc-shaped, as in Pl. 27). Moreover the drums themselves appear to have been equipped with very stout heads, no doubt because of the use of the hard-headed sticks inherited from cavalry practice. Yet the kettledrums had become firmly established in the orchestra and composers began to demand more of them. This necessitated an improvement in their sound and construction.

A small advance, with a Bach example, was to demand tunings in fifths (with the tonic below the dominant) to use the drums effectively in keys like G, the tuning here being *d* and *G*. In other keys, the relative position of tonic to dominant on the two drums was that which best fitted their respective ranges. After this time, increased size of the drums, together with better-quality vellums (possibly selected calf skins as used today) and minor mechanical improvements brought the combined range of a pair of timpani up to one octave, each drum having a range of a perfect fifth: on the larger drum from the low F (*F* to *c*) and on the smaller up to the high F (*B♭* to *f*), making possible the octave Fs in Beethoven's Eighth and Ninth Symphonies. That is but one amongst many of Beethoven's effects devised with the timpani. Others include the passage in the Ninth Symphony where he requires both drums (tuned to B♭ and *f*) to be struck simultaneously, and the celebrated tuning to *A* (natural) and *e♭* in *Fidelio*. His use of the 'roll' or tremolo is no less remarkable. A roll is the drummer's method of sustaining a note, and is produced on the timpani by a series of rapid, regular, single hand-to-hand beats. It had been rather sparingly written for by earlier composers, but Beethoven employed its thrilling sound in nearly every orchestral composition, and in many new ways.

Something more should now be said about the manner in which the timpani are played. In orchestral performance the drums are normally placed in front of the performer with the larger drums to the left. Cavalry drums remain to this day played as originally, with the larger drum on the right, and certain continental orchestral timpanists adhere to this style. The sticks strike the vellum between edge and centre, this spot producing the most musical sound. Whenever possible the timpani are played by hand-to-hand strokes: R L R L R L or L R L R L R . . . – the 'double beat' on either hand (R R or L L) being used only as the occasion warrants to avoid a difficult 'cross beat' (one hand crossing over the other) in extremely fast or very soft passages. At an average tempo the beating is illustrated by Ex. 1, *a* with the cross beat from the large to the small drum on the last two notes, or as *b*, with the cross beat from small to large drum. When the sticks pass from drum to drum in an elegant manner, the effect of cross beats is pleasingly spectacular, but they are not always practicable. To begin with, there is a limit to their speed through the risk of catching the sticks against each other when crossing very rapidly, and, in a continuous series of fast cross beats, of ending up in a tangle. Sometimes two drums are too far apart for a cross beat. But quite often the deciding factor is the volume of tone required, since the swing of the stick can add to the strength

of impact, so that when crossing at speed the drum is likely to be struck too heavily. Hence the player avoids the cross beat when playing Ex. 1 at speed or very quietly, and passes the sticks from drum to drum at those moments in the music when it is most convenient, as indicated in Ex. 2.

To cross over at speed and play *all* the strokes extremely quietly is an ever-present problem to the most accomplished performer; the double beat on either hand is, however, permissible on the two quavers of Ex. 1 and 2 when there is felt to be no alternative.

Beethoven's immediate successors required changes of tuning not only between movements but also during the course of a movement, a number of bars' rest being given to enable the timpanist to tighten or slacken the vellums the required amount by means of the tensioning screws. The timpani in use at that time were still fitted with square-top screws requiring the use of an independent unattached tuning handle and rendering the work of re-tuning slow and laborious. Improvement was sought and resulted in the introduction of the attached T-shaped tensioning screw, which allows pitch changes in considerably less time. After Beethoven, though Weber had written a part requiring the use of three kettledrums, it was Berlioz who was responsible for the next major developments. Already in the *Symphonie Fantastique* (1830) he scored for two pairs of timpani to be played by separate performers, and the four drums sound chords, each of four performers playing a separate instrument. Further, he submitted that the instrument should produce a more musical tone than previously, and in his *Instrumentation* he criticized the old-fashioned drum sticks, suggesting the more frequent use of sticks with leather and sponge ends. This suggestion, readily adopted, without doubt revolutionized orchestral timpani-playing.

From the middle of the last century, further demands, especially for more rapid changes of pitch, led to mechanically-tuned kettledrums. Using principally a system of tensioning by means of one handle only or pedal, these long remained in an experimental state, but by the end of the century the difficulty of placing the tension evenly on all parts of the vellum had been reasonably well overcome, and a drum tuned by a turn of the handle only, or by a foot pedal, was being used with success on the continent and was attracting the attention of British composers. Pedal-tuned timpani or 'machine drums' (Pl. 30a) are essential for works with rapid changes of tuning or *glissandi*; the later types are extremely efficient, and in many orchestras are completely replacing the older hand-screw drums. A modern orchestral set of three kettledrums has instruments with diameters of $29\frac{1}{2}$ in., 26 in., and 24 in. respectively, giving a combined range from $E\flat$ to $g$. Additional drums are added when required. An excellent example of modern writing for three kettledrums is the solo passage that opens the percussion variation in Britten's *Young Person's Guide to the Orchestra*, while interesting patterns for four timpani are found in Bliss's Piano Concerto and Walton's First Symphony. Notes lower than $E\flat$ and higher than $g$ are asked for only occasionally, and call for the use of an extra large or very small drum.

Re-tuning the kettledrums during the course of a piece is a very difficult thing to do, because the notes on the drums have quite often to be altered to suit a change of key that is to *follow*, which means that the timpanist must be able to tune his instruments to fit a completely different key from that in which the orchestra is playing. The process is rendered doubly difficult since it must be inaudible to all but himself; it calls for an extremely light touch on the drum with the stick (or a flick of the fingertip) while listening with the ear close to the vellum. The ear is the deciding factor in tuning the timpani; there is no set rule that a given number of turns on the handles one way or the other will raise or lower the pitch of the vellum precisely to the note required, nor will the gauges fitted to certain types of machine drums give more than a close approximation on calf vellums. Some skins require a different degree of tension from others, and changing temperature – a bugbear to timpanists – adds its own complications. In very damp weather or in a humid atmosphere, the vellums tend to slacken and greater pressure is required to tighten them to the desired pitches; in dry weather, not only is less tension required in the first place, but the vellums tighten considerably of their own accord. These considerations keep the timpanists very busy, constant adjustments being necessary to counteract the continual sharpening or flattening of his instruments brought about by the varying atmospheric conditions. The weather is also responsible for many broken vellums; frost or a sudden heat wave may cruelly destroy a player's favourite 'timp skin', even during performance. This necessitates the speedy fitting of the spare head, which is normally kept at hand already lapped on to a hoop (an operation demonstrated, for the side drum, in Pl. 30d). To fit it is only a matter of a few minutes' work. Apart from breakages, the life of a timpani vellum depends upon the condition of the hide in the first place, the best-quality calf skins retaining their elasticity for a year or two. Goat skins are a fair substitute. Plastic heads possess commendable qualities. They are little affected by atmospheric conditions, rendering the tuning gauge practical. Opinions differ as to their tonal qualities, many players preferring the sound of the calfskin.

A timpanist's stock-in-trade includes several pairs of drum sticks with heads of different weights and textures. The heads are of hard, medium, of soft felt, lamb's wool, wood, and ivory, each producing a different tone on the drum. The normal sound is made with medium or soft felt heads, harder or softer sticks being used when a composer asks for them in the part ('with hard sticks', etc.). But within the normal range, the timpanist uses his discretion as to the type of stick required, rapid passages demanding a more brittle sound than slow passages, and so on. Occasionally the timpani are muted, by placing a piece of felt or soft cloth on the vellum to reduce the vibration and give an extreme *staccato*.

Throughout the period of the orchestral development of the timpani, the cavalry drums which were their inspiration have not ceased to be used by mounted regiments. Sometimes they were so much increased in size that they were mounted on a chariot or carriage, as the 'great kettledrums' of Artillery Regiments in the first half of the eighteenth century; a fine pair with diameters 42 in. and 38 in. respectively are preserved in the Rotunda Museum, Woolwich. Even when otherwise restricted to guild or royal use, kettledrums were always an accepted prize of war. A pair captured from the French at Dettingen, formerly exhibited in the United Services Museum, London, are especially well-preserved drums, with brass bowls 24 in. and 21 in. in diameter and vellums tensioned by square-headed screws. Drums were also presented to the Blues by George III and to the 1st and 2nd Life Guards by William IV. The banner is still carried on these drums, on solemn occasions draped with a black cloth, though the battle honours are on the 'shabracque' or saddle cloth. Mounted kettledrummers continue to play their instruments in the traditional spectacular style, and in certain routines, for example musical rides, the drums play a bass or 'fourth trumpet' part just as they did in the seventeenth century. In state processions it remains the privilege of the Household Cavalry to act as Sovereign's Escort. The officiating regiment is headed by the band, to whom the Director of Music gives instructions by way of the kettledrummer who rides immediately behind him. At a sign from the director's baton the kettledrummer gives two quick beats on the drums, which is the signal for the trumpeters to raise their instruments into playing position. This is shortly followed by another sign upon which the kettledrummer plays two three-pace rolls, a five-pace roll, or other flourish in the tempo of the tune to be performed and the band then begins playing. For 'cease playing', the kettledrummer transmits the director's sign to the players by giving two very loud beats at a certain point before the end of the tune. In infantry and other marching bands, similar directions are conveyed by the bass drummer and side drummers.

\*

Among the players of the remaining instruments of percussion, the principal player is responsible for the side drum (as well as for certain tuned percussion instruments), while bass drum and cymbals are played by separate performers who rank as sub-principals. These three players constitute the normal strength of the section apart from the timpanist, and they deal as far as is possible with the smaller instruments of percussion – triangle, tambourine, castanets, etc. – extra players being engaged as the occasion demands.

A tradition no less glorious than that of the cavalry kettledrum accompanies the history of the *side drum* or 'snare drum' so long associated with Regiments of Foot. The side drum is descended from the medieval double-skinned drum, tabor or tabret, in pictures of which one can already observe that feature which is responsible for the side drum's uniquely snappy sound, namely the 'snares'. These consist of a number of gut or wire strings stretched across the lower skin or 'snare head' (Pl. 31a), which vibrates against them with a sharp sound when the upper skin is struck (the 'batter head'). The medieval instrument, which was quite small, was subsequently increased in size, mainly during the fifteenth century, from which time onwards it was played chiefly with the fife – a combination which has been as important to the infantry as trumpets and kettledrums have been to the cavalry. It was constructed like the military drum in use today, having a cylindrical shell and having the two skins braced by a rope (Pl. 30b). With its larger width and deeper shell, and its shorter, heavier sticks, the side drum up to the eighteenth century would have had a rather dull, tubby sound, different from the crisp tone of its present-day counterpart. Nevertheless, it gained occasional admittance into the orchestra, and an early instance is in the opera *Alcyone* (1706) of Marin Marais. Gluck, Rossini, and Berlioz are among subsequent composers who employed the side drum, and by the end of the nineteenth century it was firmly established as an instrument of the orchestra. A fine use of side drums with wind instruments alone is in 'La Rejouissance' in Handel's *Fireworks Music;* no part is written, the drummers having the privilege of elaborate improvisation.

Ex. 3

The side drum is a particularly difficult instrument to play. To perfect the legitimate long roll requires considerable practice of the 'Mammy-daddy' or double beat on alternate hands – a technique quite distinct from the single hand-to-hand beating used in the roll on the timpani or the rapid single-beat tremolo used in modern style dance playing. The 'Mammy-daddy' beats are played very slowly and firmly at first and held at a slow tempo for as long as possible, from thirty seconds to two or three minutes. With practice, the beats gradually close together and in time make a purring sound on the drum, known as a close roll. The beats on the side drum are often ornamented with grace notes known as 'drags' and 'flams'. The drag (Ex. 3a) consists of two faint beats played in front of the main stroke (sounding 'dr't'); the flam (b) is one faint beat in front of the main stroke (sounding 'plut'). The 'paradiddle' beat is interesting, and is played as shown in Ex. 3c (which shows also the manner of writing for the side drum, on the third space of the stave). It is also used on the timpani.

At a steady march tempo, with eight strokes on the drum in each bar, the sound of the paradiddle is fascinating, especially if a slight accent is placed on the first beat of each group of four. The long and numerous strokes, rolls, the various grace notes, single double and triple beating, and paradiddles (including strokes, flam, and drag) constitute the basis of the side drummer's technique.

The sticks used for playing the side drum (which is normally placed at an angle of forty-five degrees) are of hickory or lancewood; they are about 15 in. in length and taper towards the tip or head, which strikes the vellum. The vellums are made from selected calf skins or plastic material. Side drums vary in depth according to the player's taste, but a fairly deep model (Pl. 31a) is generally used in symphony orchestras. The snares can be instantly released, enabling the drum to be quickly muted or to be used to imitate a native drum or a tenor drum if need be. During orchestral performance it is customary to release the snares when the instrument is not being played, otherwise they are inclined to vibrate on the skin when the timpani or other instruments (particularly the horns) play notes that produce sympathetic vibration from the snare head.

The *tenor drum* is a somewhat larger instrument than a deep-model side drum, and is without snares. As a rule it is played with soft sticks. It is occasionally used in the orchestra, but it really belongs to the full Corps of Drums of regimental military bands, which includes side and tenor drums, bass drum, but not the cymbals, and demonstrate marching drum technique of the highest order. A remarkable standard of military band drumming is attained by the Basle drummers and the drummers of the Garde Républicaine, who are .

drawn from certain families in which the art is passed from father to son.

The *bass drum*, also known to all as the 'Big Drum', is a firm favourite with composers, conductors, and players alike. It is a friendly instrument, its deep note blending admirably with the other orchestral instruments in music of almost every description. It is a comparatively recent addition to Western music, wherein it dates from the middle of the eighteenth century when European military bands were being increased to include percussion instruments on the lines of the Turkish military music – bass drum, cymbals, triangle, and sometimes also tambourine and the Jingling Johnny or Turkish Crescent. This 'Turkish music', as it was then commonly called, grew extremely popular, and the presence of most of these instruments in the orchestra and military band of today shows that its spirit is with us yet. Mozart uses it, introducing bass drum, cymbals, and triangle in *Die Entführung aus dem Serail*, and Haydn a few years later in his 'Military' Symphony. Using the same instrumentation, Beethoven includes it in one or two of his later compositions, notably in the finale of the Ninth Symphony. The bass drum in use at this period was generally described as the 'Long drum' (Pl. 30c); it resembled a very deep side drum (but without snares) and it was played in a horizontal position and struck either with heavy knobbed sticks on both sides, or alternately by a stick on one side and a switch of twigs on the other, this second method producing an interesting rhythmic sound that anticipated the similar effects now made by the modern dance drummer; in Turkish and Balkan folk music one may still hear the big drum, *davul*, beaten with a knobbed or hooked stick on one side and a light cane on the other. The long drum was later replaced by the large shallow bass drum, giving a superior tone, which led to more frequent use of the instrument in orchestral compositions; the bass drum had been employed by classical composers mainly as a means of suggesting military atmosphere, but by the middle of the nineteenth century it was joining the timpani and the side drum in the orchestral ensemble. After Berlioz, Wagner and Verdi wrote important parts for the bass drum and demanded the long sustained note of the instrument, played by means of the roll.

The orchestral bass drum used normally today has a narrow wooden shell and only one vellum, and average 34 in. in diameter. Alternatively a double-headed bass drum is used. Each type has its merits. The single-headed bass drum is more easily controlled, since the vibrations of the vellum can be checked while the instrument is being struck. For ordinary orchestral purposes the best tone is produced from the bass drum by striking the vellum between edge and centre with a felt-headed stick; the centre of the drum is struck only to obtain certain effects or when playing recurrent *staccato* beats, as in quick-march time. A pair of sticks similar to the soft-headed timpani sticks is used for playing sustained notes, these being executed in the same way as the tremolo on the timpani. The music for the bass drum is written in the first space of the clef and is normally printed together with the music for the cymbals. While it is not complex as that for the timpani or the side drum, it cannot be taken any less seriously, as a glance at the score of Stravinsky's *The Rite of Spring* will show.

\*

Those splendid instruments the *cymbals*, which played such an important part in the ceremonial and religious music of Antiquity and have been heard in the West since the Middle Ages, richly deserve the place they hold in the percussion section of the orchestra. Cymbals are sounded by being clashed one against the other, or by a single cymbal being struck with soft- or hard- headed drum stick. The accepted rule is that they are clashed together unless the music specifies something different, as 'with soft sticks' or 'with hard sticks', or a suspended cymbal rolled with timpani sticks. Occasionally the cymbals are rubbed together. In much modern music the cymbal notes are indicated by a diamond or cross with a tail, but when the cymbal part is written in the same copy as that for the bass drum the second space of the stave is used (Ex. 4). A pair of good cymbals (which can vary in diameter from 14 in. to 20 in.), properly clashed by being stuck across each other, will ring for a considerable time, and hence their vibration must be skilfully controlled to ensure that the shorter notes sound well but are of no longer than the correct duration. In Ex. 4, for instance, the long and short notes must be properly distinguished by the player, who damps the vibration where necessary – particularly on the final quaver, which must be played *sec* by his drawing the instruments smartly to his body. When the cymbals have to be played as softly as possible it is permissible to touch one with the

Ex. 4

edge of the other. In his Sonata for Two Pianos and Percussion, Bartók asks that the edge of the cymbal be touched with the blade of a penknife (and the side drum be played with knitting needles – two interesting examples of this great master's precise sense of sonorities). In modern works in general, an additional cymbal suspended on a stand, called a 'loose' or 'suspended' cymbal, is necessary to enable the player to cope with the various qualities of tone and effect that are demanded.

A socket for holding a cymbal is usually provided on the bass drum, making it possible for the two instruments to be played by one performer. They are so played in concert performances by military bands; one cymbal is fixed to the bass drum and is struck with the other cymbal, this being held in the left hand, thus leaving the right hand free to play the drum (which is here normally played with a double-headed stick which allows the player to perform a tremolo by deft movement of the wrist). In symphony orchestras the cymbals generally require the full attention of an expert player, but the above arrangement is sometimes essential, as in Stravinsky's *Petrushka*.

The cymbals in use today are of Turkish origin. Many have been manufactured under a secret process by the Armenian family Zildjian (which means 'cymbal maker') who have retained the secret in the family for over three hundred years. Branches of the family continue to make the cymbals, both in Istanbul and in America. In recent years, however, certain British and continental firms have spent a great deal on research in the making of cymbals and gongs and are now manufacturing instruments that are meeting with world-wide approval.

Chinese cymbals have a different shape and tone, and are generally struck with a beater instead of being used in pairs. The 'ancient cymbals' scored for by Debussy in *L'Après-midi d'un faune* are small instruments which, unlike the other instruments of this group, are tuned to definite notes. Their use was inspired by the discovery of 'finger cymbals' of the oriental pattern in Ancient Egyptian tombs. These, about two inches in diameter, are secured to finger and thumb and manipulated in much the same manner as the Spanish castanets, though not with the same rapidity. Ravel, in *Daphnis and Chloë*, calls for them under the classical name *crotales*, which denoted small clappers in general.

The *tam-tam* or *gong*, from Eastern Asia, has been used in the orchestra to assist a climax, or with its ominous note to suggest sadness or despair. The Chinese large flat tam-tam with shallow rim is from three to four feet across and gives a sound of indeterminate pitch with tremendous sustaining power. It is expensive and precious, made by a process known only to a few, and the best instruments are engraved with a dragon, the number of its claws proclaiming the rank of its owner. Burmese gongs are heavier, with wider rims. Only a few tam-tams of the best quality have reached England from China, and these are possessed by established symphony orchestras or in private hands. The J. Arthur Rank Film Company have permitted divulgence of the fact

that the arresting notes apparently produced by the
Herculean figure in their screen trade-mark consist of an
expertly recorded superimposition of strokes delivered on
an orchestral tam-tam.

(The ingenious *steel drums* recently introduced in Trinidad
are polytonic gongs, each made from the end and part of the
sides of an oil-drum. The end is hammered slightly concave
and softened by heat. Various sectors are then marked out
with punched grooves, after which each sector is tuned to
a different note by the depth and fashion of the indent.)

Of the smaller instruments of percussion the *triangle* is one
of the most important: a rod of high-grade steel, bent to
shape, and suspended by a piece of fine gut to allow maximum vibration. It is struck with a metal beater which, for
performing a tremolo, is held inside the triangle and moved
rapidly from side to side. Single beats are played either outside or inside as desired in the circumstances. The instrument seems to have first appeared in Italy in the fourteenth
century, and from then until the eighteenth century, when
it was first used in the orchestra, it usually carried three or
more jingling rings, distantly recalling the sistrum of
Antiquity. Its place in the 'Turkish Music' has already
been mentioned, but it would be unfair not to recall also its
celebrated solo in Liszt's First Piano Concerto and the
gentler parts it plays in 'Anitra's Dance' in Grieg's *Peer
Gynt* music and in other well-known works.

Ancient frame drums (Hebrew *tof*, Graeco-Roman *tym-
panum*, etc.) were tambourines without the jingles. The
medieval *timbrel*, one of the instruments that appeared in
the West during the later crusades, possessed the jingles let
into the frame which contribute so much to the interesting
sounds obtained from our *tambourine*. Often the timbrel is
shown with a snare as well, and in such cases no doubt had
two skins; but a single-skin tambourine makes a more convenient instrument for the dancer, and this was its principal
role up to the time of its Western ensemble employment,
which was first in military 'Turkish music' and later in the
orchestra for marking rhythms in many kinds of descriptive

music. It is played by striking the vellum with the finger-tips, knuckles, or palm of the hand, according to the volume of tone required; or by shaking it to produce a continuous sound from the jingles. The latter may also be set in motion by the friction set up through the rubbing of a moistened thumb over the vellum.

*Castanets* are a Mediterranean variety among the number-ous clappers or *crotala* known to history. They consist of two round and hollowed pieces of ebony or similar wood, which for normal orchestral purposes are attached to each side of the similarly-shaped end of a length of hardwood, the other end of which tapers to form a convenient handle. The instrument is shaken, or tapped on the hand or the knee, in various rhythms to give characteristic colour to Spanish dances.

'*Effects*' is the term given in the percussion section to the remaining instruments – wood block, sleigh bells, cowbell, rattle (or ratchet), anvil, whip, thunder-sheet, and so on – all of which are called upon now and then to play a part in orchestral music. In the drummer's music they are clearly named, and their notes are usually written in the top space of the stave, or directly above it. The playing of them, as also of the tambourine, etc., is distributed between the percussion players, who decide, if a problem arises, in a comradely way who can best manipulate each instrument at the moment when it is required.

*

Turning now to the tuned percussion, we find that from the latter part of the last century there has been a steady increase in the orchestral use of the percussion instruments with definite pitch.

The *glockenspiel* (Pl. 31b) is the most frequently used of this group. It is a 'metallophone' with steel bars arranged in two rows in the manner of the piano keyboard – an arrange-ment followed also in the xylophone, marimba, etc. (though it is interesting to note that in the European folk xylophone formerly played in the Alpine regions, the *Hölzernes Gelächter* mentioned in Germany in the sixteenth century, the individual bars lie parallel with the player's body and their two rows extend away to the front of him). The normal compass of the glockenspiel is two and a half octaves, written from *g* to *c'''* but sounding two octaves higher. A sweet, bell-like tone is produced from the instrument by striking the bars in the centre with beaters having knobs of hardwood, rubber, or pyraline. A short solo is occasionally given to the glockenspiel, but as a rule it is employed to support a melody or to bring the colour of small bells into the orchestration by means of arpeggios and so on.

A 'piano-action' glockenspiel is occasionally used, and is required, for instance, by Mozart in *The Magic Flute*. In this, the bars are struck by means of keyboard mechanism, but in general the tone is interfered with by the noise of the mechanism and by the fact that the steel bars are enclosed within the body of the instrument. This form must not be confused with the *celesta*, invented by Mustel of Paris, which is similar in design but has a softer sound. (Though the celesta is a percussion instrument in the strict sense, it is not included in the orchestral percussion group; usually it is played by an extra player who is a pianist.) The *lyra-glockenspiel* is a glockenspiel intended for use in military bands on the march. Its steel bars are held in a vertical lyre-shaped frame carried on a staff, the weight of the instrument being taken on the player's belt. It is used in some bands today, both in England and abroad, and has great carrying power, being easily distinguished in the largest bands.

The *xylophone* has a series of wooden bars covering a compass of three to four octaves, sounding as written. It is played in the same way as the glockenspiel and with similar beaters. The tone of the upper notes is dry and chippy, but the lower notes are richer and more resonant, and can be made with softer beaters, especially if the instrument is resonated. In the typical present-day type of xylophone, the bars are fully resonated by metal tubes fixed below them. The bars themselves rest on strips of felt or rubber and are usually made of British Honduras rosewood, which gives a brilliant tone and is very durable. If for any reason a note should go out of tune, the pitch of the bar is either sharpened by reducing its length slightly or flattened by lessening the depth of the wood. The xylophone was used effectively by Saint-Saëns in his *Danse macabre* (1874) to conjure up the rattling skeleton of the 'Dance of Death', but it is only fair to point out that the instrument had been scored for in earlier works, besides having already become popular as a soloist's instrument in variety and garden concerts. In the orchestra an exemplary use of its dry tone is in Walton's *Belshazzar's Feast*, in which all the percussion parts are interesting, not forgetting the anvil's support to the line 'Praise Ye the God of Iron'.

The orchestral *marimba* is a deep-toned xylophone with a range of from three to four octaves, the latter ascending from *c'*, sounding an octave lower than the four-octave xylophone. It is played normally with soft-headed beaters and has been used in several modern scores. The *vibraphone* (Pl. 31c) is an enchanting instrument which continues to find favour with present-day composers (beginning possibly with Berg in *Lulu*, 1937) and must be included in the regular percussion group of the symphony and chamber orchestra. Designed in America *c.* 1920, its bars are made of a metal alloy much lighter than steel, giving a tone that is mellow and sustained. The bars are resonated with metal tubes whose upper openings are alternately opened and closed by means of fans rotating on a long axle turned by a clockwork or electric motor. Each resonator amplifies the note of the bar above it and the fan produces a *vibrato* in this amplified sound, which continues long after the note has been struck. The sweetest tone is obtained with soft-headed beaters, and the instrument is especially suitable for quiet, slow-moving solos, or for accompanying these with simple, harp-like chords and arpeggios, and also for the creation of an ethereal atmosphere in music of a romantic nature. Played in 'swing' style, the vibraphone is an important instrument in the modern small group. The speed of the fans can be controlled, and a pedal damping-attachment to prevent one note or chord from ringing into another completes the mechanism of the instrument.

*Tubular bells* or *chimes* are metal tubes of graded lengths set in vibration by being struck at the top with a raw-hide hammer or similar implement. They reproduce the sound of a church bell (though sometimes the sound of large bells, e.g. as required in *Parsifal*, is imitated by electrically amplified steel wires, or by discs of bell metal). Until recent years a diatonic octave in the key of E♭ was considered adequate for ordinary orchestral purposes and also, in the lighter field of music, for the performance of tubular bell solos, always written in this key. Later the scale was increased to include all thirteen semitones of this octave, the tubes hung in a straight row – an improvement on the set of eight but still having considerable limitations. Eventually this gave place to the modern chromatic set of eighteen tubes hung in two rows in keyboard fashion, with a compass from *c′* to *f″*. Like the vibraphone, the set of chimes is fitted with a damping mechanism for cutting out the sound as desired. The tubular bells are mainly used in orchestral works when the character of the music calls for them: the sad tolling of a distant bell, the tranquil sound of chimes, and the tremendous effect of pealing bells like that in Tchaikovsky's *1812 Overture*, which leaves no doubt as to the value of their support in the portrayal of joy and thanksgiving. A quite different chime is the Gong Chime native to East Asia; Puccini scores for it in *Madame Butterfly* and *Turandot*, and the Royal Opera House, Covent Garden, possesses a genuine Chinese instrument which is used when these operas are performed. The chimes and the other tuned percussion instruments are extremely difficult to play while reading at sight, the eye having to watch the instrument as well as the music and the conductor. Complex passages are sometimes memorized, allowing the instruments to be played with greater freedom, but even so a difficult part for glockenspiel, xylophone, or tubular bells is by no means a simple thing to bring off in performance. The music for the tuned percussion is, with few exceptions, written in the treble clef.

(Among non-orchestral chimes, church bells, with their elaborate art of change-ringing, form too large a subject to enter upon here, and so do carillons, like the famous chimes of Ghent and other Flemish cities, played from a keyboard. But we should notice *hand bells*. These comprise an octave or more of small bells, each with a leathered clapper pivoted to swing in only one direction across the bell. With two performers, each holds four bells by their straps, two in each hand and so grasped that a turn of the wrist in one direction causes one bell to sound its note, and a turn in the direction at right angles to the first causes the other to do likewise. By this means two performers play tunes on the eight bells, sometimes damping their sound against the clothing or a leather apron.)

\*

The instruments of percussion used in light orchestras are themselves similar in every way to those of the symphony orchestra, the difference being that certain instruments are less used, others more. Thus, the timpani do not figure so prominently, while the ordinary and tuned percussion are put to fuller use. In an orchestra of around thirty players it is customary to employ a timpanist and one or more percussion players, who together cope with all the instruments. But in small orchestras one single player is called upon to manage *all* the percussion instruments. For this, various expedients are sought, such as the foot-pedal beater for the bass drum, and the foot-pedal cymbal ('foot cymbal'), and also the placing of the instruments as close together as possible. A certain amount of tone is lost from the bass drum and cymbals, and in 'condensed' drum parts some effects must be sacrificed; but on the whole the parts are admirably arranged and performed, and a part like that in Ex. 5 presents no difficulty. For extremely rapid changes a plan of action is prepared in advance, and it is interesting to notice in this connexion that since Stravinsky's *L'Histoire d'un*

*soldat* (1918) serious composers have increasingly included
in their scores exact diagrams for the placing of the instruments when a single percussion player is to deal with a great
number of instruments.

Naturally the instruments of percussion play a vital role
in the dance orchestra, wherein special instruments now
include: a bass drum of the small pattern introduced for
dance music; the Hi-Hat cymbals; and usually two 'tom-
toms', and a cowbell. A notable feature of dance drumming
is the frequent use of wire brushes instead of drum sticks,
the steady swishing sound made by sliding the brushes
rhythmically across the side drum, together with neatly-
placed accented beats, providing an ideal accompaniment of

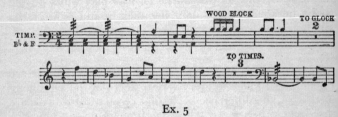

Ex. 5

the melody in many styles. A different kind of drumming is
heard in the fascinating 'Latin-American' music. Here, in
the rumba, the samba, etc., the form of the percussion instruments takes us back to the first chapter of the book, where
close equivalents to all the instruments will be found: the
*maracas* and the *cabaça*, gourd rattles; the *guiro*, a scraper;
the *claves*, percussion sticks; and the 'conga drum' and
*bongos*, single-skin drums of essentially primitive character
(Pl. 32a). The percussion dominates the music, the unyield-
ing beat of the low-toned conga drum and higher-toned
bongos (both played with the fingers) together with the
relentless clicking of the claves, guiro, maracas, and tambourine being further coloured by the cowbell and the
rhythm of the bass drum and the side drum, played without
snares but with the ordinary sticks in the irresistible manner

of the rumba – each of the instruments, in a large orchestra, entrusted to a separate performer.

The appeal of rumba and samba music lies in its apparent simplicity. All the rhythmic instruments with the exception of the bongos and the side drum keep strictly to their various individual patterns. There is no space to describe their intricacies here, but it is surely interesting and revealing that after all the noble musical instruments that have been described in the chapters of this book, developed through centuries of cultivated art, the simple and primitive instruments of the rumba and the samba are again a source of continual enjoyment and inspiration to a huge section of our community. That percussionists should have helped to bring this about is but one more contribution of their age-old tradition.

# Glossary of Technical and Acoustic Terms

AEROPHONES: instruments in which the primary sound-producer is vibrating air: hence, wind instruments, also bull-roarer, siren, etc.

AIR-COLUMN: the air within the tube of a wind instrument, vibrating as a stationary wave over the distance from the sound-generator to the distal end of the tube or the nearest uncovered hole, as the case may be.

ARCO: Ital. bow. In music, *col arco*, 'with the bow', as opposed to *pizzicato*, etc.

ARTICULATION: the pointing of music in performance.

BELL: in wind instruments, (a) the evasement of the wider end of the tube of a brass instrument, (b) the terminal joint, not necessarily evased, of a reed instrument.

BELLY: the upper plate or covering of the body of a stringed instrument, over or from which the strings are stretched.

BICHORD: having two strings to one note.

BRIDGE: a raised component through which the vibration of the strings is communicated to the belly or soundboard of a stringed instrument. With the lute, etc., it also serves as the attachment of the strings.

CANE: in this book, denotes the natural reed or bamboo which enters into the construction of many instruments.

CAPOTASTO: a clamp sometimes secured over the strings and fingerboard on lutes, etc., to serve as a 'nut' in certain techniques.

CHECK: in pianoforte action, the pad which catches the hammer in an intermediate position while the key is held down, the jack meanwhile returning ready to repeat the note after the key is released. The check also prevents rebound of the hammer.

CHEVALET: Fr. bridge.

CHORDOPHONES: stringed instruments.

CHROMATIC: a musical passage or scale in music in which two or more adjacent semitones follow one another.

CLOSED KEY: in wind instruments, a key sprung to close a hole.

COL LEGNO: striking the strings of violins, etc., with the stick of the bow. (Ital.).

COMPENSATING: in brass instruments, valve systems of compound design to minimize certain defects of intonation; but in double horns, valve arrangements designed to simplify and lighten construction.

COMPOSITION PEDAL: see p. 83.

CONSORT: sixteenth- and seventeenth-century English term (Fr., Ital. *concert, concerto*) for a group of instruments played together. A 'whole consort' is of instruments all of a kind.

COUPLER: in organs and harpsichords, a mechanism that enables stops to be played from a different keyboard from that to which they are directly connected.

COURSE: in stringed instruments on which some or all the strings may be duplicated, triplicated, etc., the term 'course' is used. Thus, a pianoforte may have a 'triple course' for each of the higher notes, a 'double course' for each of the middle, and a 'single' for each of the lowest. An 'octave course' (on lutes, etc.) is a double course with its two strings tuned an octave apart.

COVERED HOLES: in woodwind, padded plates on axles, replacing plain fingerholes or rings.

CROOK: in brass instruments, a length of tubing, usually coiled, that may be added to the tubing to lower the pitch by a definite musical interval. In woodwind, a metal tube by which the reed (or with large recorders the mouthpiece) is brought into reach of the player's mouth.

DAMPER: apparatus or means for checking the vibration of a string, membrane (drum skin, etc.), or hard vibrating substance.

DESCANT: in instruments, a modern English appropriation of Ger. *diskant* ('treble').

DIATONIC: music employing eight degrees to the octave, as in our simple major and minor scales.

DOUBLE: (a) an epithet derived from the organist's description of the sub-bass or 16-foot octave by double letters, CC, DD, etc., to denote an instrument of deeper pitch than the normal bass. (b) as applied to simple and early reedpipes and flageolets, two pipes played by one player.

DRONE: a single note, or consonant set of notes, sounded continuously or continually in accompaniment to melody.

EMBOUCHURE: in wind instruments, the muscular stance of the player's mouth. Often used also for the mouth hole of a flute.

EQUAL TEMPERAMENT: division of the octave into (logarithmically) equal semitones, introduced in the eighteenth century for keyboard instruments to avoid enharmonic confusion. Thus, tuning by harmonic fifths, starting from C, leads to values for F, B♭, E♭, A♭, etc. which are higher than required by harmonic ratios in the sharp keys for E♯, A♯, D♯, G♯, etc. In E.T., tuning by slightly narrowed fifths brings a serviceable mean value to every note of the chromatic scale.

ESCAPEMENT: in pianoforte action, the clearance between the string and the hammer after it has struck the string, while the key is held down. *Double escapement* is a complex mechanism which enables repetition of a note without complete release of the key to be made.

FINGERBOARD: a strip of wood or other material laid upon the neck of a lute or fiddle, or upon the soundbox of a zither, against which the strings are stopped.

FINGERHOLES: the holes in a pipe, uncovered by the fingers to make the different notes.

FIPPLE: the assembly of block and harp edge by which sound is generated in a flageolet or recorder, hence 'fipple flute' (a flageolet), etc. (Such has become the conventional usage, though strictly the word should denote the recorder's 'beak'.)

FLAGEOLET: O. Fr. diminutive of *flageol*, a flageolet or tabor pipe. Subsequently employed for small and toy instruments of this kind. In this book, a generic term for flutes with fixed sound-generating arrangement, whether by fipple or other form of block, or by equivalent primitive arrangements.

FLUE: in organs, a pipe, or rank of pipes, sounded on the fipple principle.

FREQUENCY: vibrations (cycles) per second.

FRETS: raised marks on the fingerboards of a stringed instrument to assist stopping the strings, usually made by placing gut loops or wood or metal ridges.

FRETTED: (a) provided with frets; (b) in clavichords, employing one string for two or more notes by arranging the tangents of adjacent keys to strike it in different places.

FROG: the block by which the hair is attached at the heel of a violin bow. Also called 'nut'.

FUNDAMENTAL: the lowest frequency of a given harmonic series; the pitch at which this sounds. Numbered '1' in the harmonic series.

GLISSANDO: lit. 'sliding'; a slide from one note to another, usually over a large interval and occupying most of, or all of, the time value of the first written note (cf. *portamento*).

GUIMBARDE: Fr. 'Jew's Harp'. In this book, a generic word for the instrument of this kind.

HARMONICS: accoustical, geometrical, or 'harmonic' divisions of a given frequency; as audible overtones, their relative strengths establish tone colour; or a harmonic may be selected by the player, by various means, to be heard as a positive note. The latter enters to a considerable extent into the playing many stringed instruments, especially violin, etc., and harp; considerably more in woodwind instruments ('overblowing'); and most of all on brass instruments, whose technique depends upon this almost entirely.

IDIOPHONES: percussion instruments, excluding drums or any other such that depend upon a vibrating membrane for the sound.

JEU: Fr. a 'whole consort'; a rank of organ pipes.

JOINT: commonly used in woodwind to describe each detachable section of the tube.

KEY: (a) the unit of a keyboard; (b) in woodwind instruments, usually a lever for covering a hole otherwise out of reach of the fingers.

KLAVIER: Ger. keyboard, or keyboard instrument.

LEGATO: lit. 'tied'; notes played without detaching one from another.

MACHINE HEAD: in guitars, double basses, etc., a head fitted with worm-and-pinion gears for turning the tuning pegs.

MANUAL: in organs, a keyboard for the hands, as opposed to one for the feet; also used for harpsichord keyboards.

MOUTHPIPE: in brass instruments, the section of tube into which the mouthpiece is placed. Also called 'leader pipe'.

MULTIPLE STOP: on violin, etc., a chord made by sounding two or more strings simultaneously.

MUTE: a device that may be added to a violin or wind instrument to lessen the volume of tone or to change its character, or both.

NATURAL: (brass instruments) lacking mechanism (slide, keys, valves).

NECK: the part of a lute, violin, etc., which is grasped by the hand that stops the strings.

NUT: (a) the fixed ridge which raises the strings of a stringed instrument above fingerboard or soundboard next to the tuning pegs or wrest pins; (b) the 'frog' (q.v.) of a violin bow.

OCTAVE: the interval embraced by the eight diatonic degrees of the scale; in nomenclature, octaves are reckoned from one C to the next above, either as shown on p. 22, or by the organist's expressions: 8-foot (C to b), 4-foot (c to b), etc., though these terms are also used in another sense in which '8-ft' denotes the keyboard compass as sounded at the normal pitch (i.e. as a singer or pianoforte sounds the notes), '4-ft' denotes causing these same notes on the keyboard to sound an octave higher throughout, and '16-ft' an octave lower throughout (and so on for 2-ft, 32-ft, etc.).

OPEN KEY: in wind instruments, a key that is sprung to uncover a hole.

OPEN NOTE: in brass instruments with valves, a note that is sounded without using the valves. Hence sometimes used to describe the notes of a 'natural' brass instrument. As an instruction in brass music, however, 'open' countermands 'muted'.

OPEN STRING: a string when it is not stopped (by the fingers or by mechanism).

OVERBLOWING: in woodwind, the upward extensions of the compass made by selecting harmonics above the fundamental.

OVERTONES: higher frequencies audible above the recognized pitch of a note being sounded. In a musical note of definite pitch the overtones belong mainly to the harmonic series; with sounds of indefinite pitch, as of cymbals, the overtones are inharmonic, i.e. dissonant.

PENTATONIC: music that employs, or principally employs, only five degrees within the octave (e.g. *Auld Lang Syne*).

PITCH: (a) of a note, its height or vibration frequency as sensed by the ear; (b) of performance and playing, the normalization of pitch for performance, usually in terms of the frequency of the note $a'$. At the present standard pitch (established 1939), $a'$ has 440 vibrations per second. Previously, similar standards (French $a' = 435$ v.p.s., Eng. 439 v.p.s.) had competed with various local high pitches, as Eng. $a' = 452$, which had grown up in the nineteenth century. In the eighteenth century, playing pitch was generally lower, around $a' = 422$, nearly a semitone below today's. But around 1600 pitch was in most places as high or higher than that of today; (c) of a type of instrument, its relation to another of similar kind in terms of the note made by a given string-tuning or pipe-fingering; the 'pitch' af the viola is a fifth below that of the violin, etc.

PIZZICATO: striking a string with the finger or thumb in an instrument that is normally bowed.

PLECTRUM: a blade or quill with which the strings are struck in some instruments. It may be (a) held between fingers and thumb, (b) worn in a ring on finger or thumb, and (c) incorporated into a mechanism as on the harpsichord.

PONTICELLO: Ital., the bridge of a violin, etc. *Sul ponticello*, bowing close to the bridge to give a thin sound.

PORTAMENTO: a slide made from one note to another after the first has been sounded for virtually its full time value.

PORTATO: a violin bowing, two or more notes being detached in a single bow stroke and indicated by dots under a slur. From this, an indication of semi-staccato in music for any kind of instrument.

POSITION: (a) in violin, etc., the fingering of the higher note of a string is systematized in terms of the position taken by the first finger of the left hand; e.g. in the 'first position' the hand is held so that the first finger stops the whole-tone above the note of the open string; the positions thence ascend following the diatonic degrees of the scale as obtained with the first finger, and thus the third position is where this finger stops *g″* on the violin E string; (b) in trombone, the position of the slide, from the first (with the slide drawn right back) to the seventh (with it fully extended).

QUART-, QUINT-: Old German expressions denoting an instrument pitched a fourth or fifth below or above the ordinary.

RANK: a set of organ pipes of a kind, making up one stop.

REED: the sound-generating component of reed instruments and organ reed pipes. (Also, of course, the natural material from which this component is in many cases made, but to avoid the possibility of confusion, this material is termed 'cane' in this book.) A reed is a flexible blade held fast at one end and placed so that it partly chokes the escape of air under pressure, which causes its free end to vibrate or flutter, bending inwards and outwards at a steady frequency. A reed with a single blade may be harnessed to a pipe in order to set its air column in vibration (as the single reed of clarinet, bagpipe drone, organ reed pipe), or be left without a pipe to emit a musical note at its own frequency (the free reed of an accordian, etc.). A reed with twin blades, bound face to face with a narrow passage between them, forms the double reed of oboe, shawm, etc. The term 'reed' is also sometimes applied to a flexible blade that is set in vibration by being plucked, as in musical boxes, guimbardes, and the African sansa.

REED INSTRUMENT: an instrument in which sound is generated by the vibration of a reed under air pressure.

REEDPIPE: in this book a simple pipe that is sounded by a reed. It may or may not be made of cane.

RE-ENTRANT TUNING: a tuning of strings that does not follow order of pitch throughout.

REGISTER: (a) a set of pipes in an organ or of strings in a harpsichord; (b) different parts of the compass of an instrument, having its most precise meaning in woodwind, where the different registers consist of fundamentals and of specific overblown harmonics.

RESONATOR: a term variously used. In acoustics, generally the body which is first set in vibration by the generating action, thus including e.g. strings, drum skins, the loose bars of tuned percussion instruments, the circular plates of gongs and cymbals, the air column of a wind instrument (also its reed, if present), and the free reed and plucked reed. In musical practice, resonator usually denotes a secondary resonator or amplifier, as the body of a stringed instrument, and especially the tubular or globular resonators attached below xylophone bars, etc.

RIB: (a) the side walls of violin, guitar, etc.; (b) the elements of which the vaulted body of a lute or older harp is built up.

SHIFT: a change of position (q.v.) in violin-, trombone-playing, etc.

SORDINO; SOURDINE: Ital., Fr. mute.

SOUND-BOARD, -CHEST, -TABLE, -SKIN, etc.: terms variously used in describing parts of the body of stringed instruments.

STOP: (a) a set of organ pipes or harpsichord strings ('register'); (b) the lever or slider by which a register is put into operation; (c) to 'stop' the strings of violin, etc. against the fingerboard or frets; (d) to raise or lower the pitch and alter the tone of notes on the horn by 'stopping' the bell with the hand.

STOPPED PIPE: an organ flue pipe that is stopped at the upper end; certain flutes, e.g. panpipes, also employ stopped pipes. The air column represents a quarter wavelength, and only the odd-numbered harmonics are produced.

SYMPATHETIC STRINGS: metal strings, not touched with the fingers or bow, provided on some stringed instruments to vibrate in sympathy with the stopped strings.

TAILLE: Fr. sixteenth- and seventeenth-century term for 'tenor', thus taille des violons, viola; t. des hautbois, tenor oboe. A contemporary Fr. term for 'alto' is haute-contre ('contralto').

**TAILPIECE:** the piece to which the strings of violin, etc., are attached at their opposite ends from the pegs.

**TAILPIN:** the button let into the bottom block of a violin, etc., to which the tailpiece is attached by a gut loop.

**TALON:** the heel of a bow; the bow hair close to the frog.

**TASTEN:** Ger. the keys of a keyboard.

**TASTI:** Ital. the keys of a keyboard, also frets.

**TENON:** the male member of a socketed joint on wind instruments.

**TONE COLOUR:** see Harmonics.

**TONGUING:** motion of the tongue employed on wind instruments for articulation.

**TRANSPOSE:** to sound music at a different pitch from that of the written notes.

**TRANSVERSE FLUTE:** *flauto traverso*, etc. The ordinary flute, with mouth hole in the side and held transversely.

**TREMULANT:** a regular wavering of pitch secured on various instruments by various means.

**TUNING SLIDE:** in wind instruments, a part of the tubing that is made extensible for purposes of tuning.

**TUTTI:** passages in ensemble music when all or most of the instruments play at once.

**UNA CORDA:** on the pianoforte, when depression of the left pedal causes the hammers to strike one string only for each note.

**UNISON:** besides its ordinary meaning, the term denotes on organ and harpsichord the normal or '8-ft' pitch, when the notes sound in the same octave as when sung or played on a pianoforte, and not an octave higher or lower, etc.

**VENT HOLE:** an auxiliary hole often provided in woodwind instruments to tune a note or adjust the bell note. A vent key is one by which a vent hole may be mechanically controlled.

**VIBRATO:** a wavering in either the pitch or the strength of a note, made by muscular action (with fingers, diaphragm, etc.) of the player.

**WREST PIN:** a tuning pin on a keyboard instrument. Wrest plank, the board in which these pins are held in keyboard instruments.

# Bibliography

## DICTIONARIES AND ENCYCLOPEDIAS

BLUME, F. *Die Musik in Geschichte und Gegenwart*. Kassel and Basel, 1949; in progress.

GROVE. *Dictionary of Music and Musicians*. 5th edition, ed. Eric Blom. London, 1954.

LAVIGNAC, A. and LAURENCIE, L. de la. *Encyclopédie et Dictionnaire du Conservatoire*. Paris, 1913, etc.

MARCUSE, S. *Musical Instruments: A Comprehensive Dictionary*. New York, 1964.

SCHOLES, P. *Oxford Companion to Music*. London, 1938, etc.


## GENERAL

AGRICOLA, MARTIN. *Musica Instrumentalis Deutsch*. Wittemberg, 1528, etc.; reprint, Leipzig, 1896.

BERLIOZ, HECTOR. *Instrumentation*. Paris, 1848; London, 1858.

BESSARABOFF, N. *Ancient European Musical Instruments*. Harvard, 1941; 1965.

BONANNI, F. *Gabinetto armonico*. Rome, 1722.

BUCHNER, A. *Musical Instruments through the Ages*. London, 1956.

CARSE, ADAM. *The Orchestra in the XVIII Century*. Cambridge, 1940.

*The Orchestra from Beethoven to Berlioz*. London, 1948.

DART, THURSTON. *The Interpretation of Music*. London, 1954.

DIDEROT, D., and d'ALEMBERT, J. de R. *Encyclopédie*. Paris, 1767, 1776. (Section 'Lutherie').

DONINGTON, R. *The Instruments of Music*. London, 1949.

EISEL, J. P. *Musicus autodidaktos*. Erfurt, 1738.

EDDELSHEIM, J. *Das Orchester des Lully*. Tutzing, 1961.

FORSYTH, C. *Orchestration*. London, 1914, etc.

GALPIN, F. W. *Old English Instruments of Music*. London, 1910.

*Textbook of European Musical Instruments*. London 1937.

GALPIN SOCIETY JOURNAL, London, 1948 – (in progress).

GEIRINGER, K. *Musical Instruments*. London, 1943.

HARRISON, F. and RIMMER, J. *European Musical Instruments*. London, 1964.

HIPKINS, A. J. and GIBB, W. *Musical Instruments, Historic, Rare and Unique*. Edinburgh, 1888; London, 1945.

KINSKY, G. *History of Music in Pictures*. Leipzig, 1929; Eng. translation, 1930; New York, 1951.

KIRCHER, A. *Musurgia universalis.* Rome, 1650.

de LABORDE, B. *Essai sur la musique.* Paris, 1780.

MAHILLON, V. *Catalogue descriptif ... du Musée instrumentale du Conservatoire Royal de Musique, Bruxelles.* Ghent, 1893–1912.

MAJER, J. F. B. C. *Museum musicum.* Schwäb.-Hall, 1732; reprint Kassel, 1954.

MATTHESON, J. *Das neu-eröffnete Orchester.* Hamburg, 1713.

MERSENNE, MARIN. *Harmonie Universelle.* Paris, 1636; reprint 1964.

NORLIND, T. *Musikinstrumentens Historia.* Stockhom, 1941.

PRAETORIUS, MICHAEL. *Syntagma Musicum.* Wolfenbüttel, 1619; reprint, Kassel, 1929.

QUANTZ, J. J. *Versuch einer Anweisung die Flöte traversiere zu spielen.* Berlin, 1752; reprint, Kassel, 1953. English transl. by REILLY, E. R., London, 1966.

SACHS, CURT. *Real-Lexikon der Musikinstrumente.* Berlin, 1913, 1962. *Handbuch der Musikinstrumente.* Leipzig, 1930; reprint 1967. *The History of Musical Instruments.* New York, 1940.

SCHLOSSER, J. von. *Alte Musikinstrumente.* Vienna, 1920, 1967.

SCHNEIDER, W. *Historische-technische Beschreibung der musikalischen Instrumente.* Leipzig, 1834.

SPEER, DANIEL. *Grundrichtiger Unterricht der musikalischen Kunst.* Ulm, 1687, 1697.

TALBOT, JAMES. *Musica.* MS., Oxford, Christ Church Library, Mus. MS. 1187. (See BAINES, A. *Galpin Society Journal,* I, 1948; DONINGTON, R. ibid., iv, 1951; etc.)

TERRY, C. S. *Bach's Orchestra.* London, 1932, 1958.

TRICHET, P. *Traité des instruments de musique (c. 1640),* ed. F. Lesure. Neuilly-sur-Seine, 1957.

VIRDUNG, SEBASTIAN. *Musica Getuscht.* Basel, 1511; reprint, Kassel, 1931.

WEIGEL, J. C. *Musivalisches Theatrum (c. 1720),* ed. A. Berner. Kassel, 1961.

WINTERNITZ, E. *Musical Instruments of the Western World.* London, 1966.

## ACOUSTICS OF MUSICAL INSTRUMENTS

BENADE, A. H. *Horns, Strings and Harmony.* New York, 1960.

CULVER, C. A. *Musical Acoustics.* Philadelphia, 1947.

von HELMHOLTZ, H., trans. ELLIS, A. J. *The Sensations of Tone.* London, 1875, 1885; reprint, New York, 1954.

JEANS, SIR JAMES. *Science and Music*. New edn. Cambridge, 1961.

LLOYD, L. S. *Music and Sound*. London, 1937, 1951.

MILLER, C. DAYTON. *The Science of Musical Sounds*. New York, 1922.

OLSON, HARRY F. *Musical Engineering*. New York, 1952.

RICHARDSON, E. G. *The Acoustics of Orchestral Instruments*. London, 1929.

SEASHORE, C. *The Psychology of Music*. New York, 1938.

WOOD, ALEXANDER. *The Physics of Music*. London, 1944.


### ELECTRONIC MUSICAL INSTRUMENTS

DORF, R. H. *Electronic Musical Instruments*. New York, 1954.

DOUGLAS, ALAN. *The Electronic Musical Instrument Manual*. London, 1949.

EBY, R. L. *Electric Organs*. Wheaton, Illinois, 1953.


### PRIMITIVE MUSICAL INSTRUMENTS

HORNBOSTEL, E. M. von 'The Ethnology of African Sound Instruments' in *Africa*, London, 1933, vi, p. 129 ff., p. 277 ff.

IZIKOWITZ, K. G. *Musical and other Sound Instruments of the South American Indians*. Göteborg, 1935.

KIRBY, P. R. *The Musical Instruments of the Native Races of South Africa*. London, 1934; Johannesburg, 1953.

KUNST, JAAP. *Around von Hornbostel's Theory of the Cycle of blown fifths*. Amsterdam, 1948.

*Ethnomusicology*. 3rd edn. The Hague, 1959. (This contains a bibliography of 4,500 items, many bearing on instruments.)

SACHS, CURT. *Geist und Werden der Musikinstrumente*. Berlin, 1929; reprint, Hilversum, 1965. *The History of Musical Instruments*. New York, 1940.

SCHAEFFNER, A. *Origine des instruments de musique*. Paris, 1936.


### ORGAN

APEL, W. 'Early History of the Organ' in *Speculum*, XXIII, 2, Cambridge, Mass., 1948.

BEDOS DE CELLES, F. *L'Art du facteur d'orgues*. Paris, 1766–78; facsimile reprint, Kassel, 1934.

BONAVIA HUNT, N. A. *Morden Organ Stops*. London, 1923.

CLUTTON, C. and DIXON, G. *The Organ: its tonal structure and registration*. London, 1950.

CLUTTON, C. and NILAND. *The British Organ*. London, 1963.

DUFOURCQ, N. *Esquisse d'une histoire de l'orgue en France*. Paris, 1931.

FLADE, E. *Der Orgelbauer Gottfried Silbermann*. Leipzig, 1926.

HILL, A. G. *The Organ and Organ cases of the Middle Ages and Renaissance*. London, 1883.

HOPKINS, E. J. and RIMBAULT, E. F. *The Organ, its History and Construction*. London, 1855–77; reprint, Amsterdam, 1965.

SCHLICK, A. *Spiegel der Orgelmacher*. Mainz, 1511; facsimile reprint 1936, 1938.

SUMNER, W. L. S. *The Organ, its evolution, principles of construction and use*. London, 1952.

WHITWORTH, R. *The Electric Organ*, London, 1948.

*Note:* of the above, W. L. S. Sumner's book is the most comprehensive and up-to-date in covering every aspect of the subject, including the science of registration.

WILLIAMS, P. *The European Organ* 1450–1850. London, 1966.

### CLAVICHORD

BACH, C. P. E., transl. MITCHELL, W. J. *Essay on the True Art of Playing Keyboard Instruments*. New York, 1949.

GOEHLINGER, F. A. *Geschichte des Klavichords*. Basel, 1910.

GUMPEL, K.-W. 'Das Tastenmonochord Conrads von Zabern' in *Archiv für Musikwissenschaft*, XII, 143, 1955.

JEANS, S. 'The Pedal Clavichord and other practice instruments of organists' in *Proceedings of the Royal Musical Association*, LXXVII, 1952.

NEF, K. 'The Polychord' in *Galpin Society Journal*, IV, 23, 1951.

NEUPERT, H. *Das Klavichord*. Kassel, 1950. Engl. transl. 1965.

WORSCHING, J. *Die historischen Saitenklaviere*. Mainz, 1946.

### HARPSICHORD, SPINET, AND VIRGINAL

BOALCH, DONALD H. *Makers of the Harpsichord and Clavichord, 1440–1840*. London, 1956.

DENT, EDWARD. 'Notes on Continuo-playing' in *Musical Monthly Record*, Vol. 79, No. 106, 1949.

HUBBARD, FRANK. *Four Centuries of Harpsichord-Making*. Harvard, 1965.

RUSSELL, RAYMOND. *The Harpsichord and Clavichord*. London, 1959.

### PIANOFORTE

HARDING, ROSAMUND, E. M. *The Pianoforte, its History traced to the Great Exhibition*, 1851. Cambridge, 1933.

HIPKINS, A. J. *The Story of the Pianoforte.* Novello Primer No. 52, London, 1896.

HIPKINS, EDITH J. *How Chopin Played.* London, 1937.

### VIOLIN

BACHMANN, ALBERTO. *An Encyclopedia of the Violin.* New York and London, 1929.

BOYDEN, DAVID. *The History of Violin Playing from its Origins to* 1761. London, 1964.

DUBOURG, G. *The Violin,* London, 1836; 5th edn. 1878.

HART, G. *The Violin.* London. 1875; revised reprint, 1909.

HAYES, G. R. *Musical Instruments and their Music* 1500–1750. 2 Vols., London, 1930.

HERON-ALLEN, E. *Violin-Making as it was and is.* London, 1884; 2nd edn 1889.

HUTCHINS, C. M. 'The Physics of Violins' in *The Scientific American,* Nov. 1962.

OTTO, J. A. *Treatise on the Structure and Preservation of the Violin.* Halle, 1817; Eng. trans. London, 1848.

SAINT-GEORGE, HENRY. *The Bow.* London, 1896; 3rd edn. 1922.

SANDYS, W., and FORSTER, S. A. *History of the Violin.* London, 1864.

SAUNDERS, F. A. 'Recent Work on Violins' in *Journ. Acoustical Society of America,* May 1953.

STRAETEN, E. van der. *The History of the Violin.* 2 Vols, London, 1933.

### Makers and Players

FARGA, F. *Violins and Violinists.* London, 1950.

HILL, W. H., A. F. and A. E. *Antonio Stradivari.* London, 1902.
*The Violin Makers of the Guarneri Family.* London, 1931; New York, 1963.

JALOVEC, K. *Encyclopaedia of Violin-Makers.* 2 Vols. London, 1968.

LUTGENDORFF, W. L. von. *Die Geigen- und Lautenmacher.* 2 Vols, Frankfurt, 1922.

MUCCHI, A. M. *Gasparo da Salò.* Milan, 1940.

PINCHERLE, MARC. *Les Violinistes.* Paris, 1922.

### Of Special Interest to Violinists

BABITZ, SOL. *The Violin, Views and Reviews.* Published by The American String Teachers' Association, n.d.

BOYDEN, DAVID D. 'The Violin and its Technique in the 18th
    Century' in *Musical Quarterly*, Jan. 1950.
GEMINIANI, F. *The Art of Playing on the Violin*. London, 1751;
    facsimile edition, London, 1952.
MOZART, LEOPOLD. *Violinschule*. Augsburg, 1756; Eng. trans.,
    London, 1948, 2nd edn 1951.
TARTINI, G. *Traité des Agréments*. New York, 1961.


DOUBLE BASS

ELGAR, R. *Introduction to the Double Bass*. St Leonards-on-Sea, 1960.
    *More about the Double Bass*. 1963.


LUTE

BARON, E. G. *Historisch-theoretische und praktische Untersuchung des
    Instruments der Lauten*. Nuremburg, 1727; reprint, Amsterdam,
    1962.
BERMUDO, JUAN. *Declaración de Instrumentos Musicales*. Osuna,
    1549, 1550; reprint, Kassel, 1957.
BOETTICHER, W. *Studien zur soloistischen Lautenpraxis der 16ten
    und 17ten Jahrhunderte*. Berlin, 1943.
DOLMETSCH, ARNOLD. 'The Lute' in *The Connoisseur*, April-
    May, 1904.
GILL, DONALD. 'The Elizabethan Lute' in *Galpin Society Journal*,
    XII, 1959.
KOERTE, O. *Laute und Lautenmusik bis zur des Mitte des 16ten Jahrhun-
    derts*. Leipzig, 1901.
LUMSDEN, D. J. 'The Lute in England' in *The Score*, 1953.
MACE, THOMAS. *Musick's Monument*. London, 1676; facsimile edn,
    London, 1958.
REUSSNER and WEISS. 'German Lute Music of the 17th and 18th
    Centuries' in *Das Erbe Deutscher Musik* – Reichsdenkmal 12,
    Brunswick, 1939.


GUITAR

BERMUDO, JUAN. *Declaración de Instrumentos Musicales*. Osuna, 1549,
    1550; facsimile reprint, Kassel, 1957.
DART, THURSTON. 'The Cittern and its English Music' in *Galpin
    Society Journal*, I, 1948.
GILL, DONALD, 'The Orpharion and Bandora' in *Galpin Society
    Journal*, XIII, 1960.

HEARTZ, DANIEL, 'An Elizabethan Tutor for the Guitar' in *Galpin Society Journal*, XVI, 1963.

JAHNEL, F. *Die Gitarre und ihr Bau*. Frankfurt, 1963.

PRYNNE, MICHAEL. 'A Surviving Vihuela de Mano' in *Galpin Society Journal*, XVI, 1963.

PUJOL, EMILIO. *Escuela razonada de la Guitarra*. Vol. I, Buenos Aires, 1934.

SHARPE, A. P. *The Story of the Spanish Guitar*. London, 1954.

TREND, J. B. *Luis Milan and the Vihuelistas*. Oxford, 1925.
*The Music of Spanish History to 1600*. Oxford, 1926.

USHER, TERENCE. 'The Spanish Guitar in the Nineteenth and Twentieth Centuries' in *Galpin Society Journal*, IX, 1956.


## VIOLS

DOLMETSCH, N. *The Viola da Gamba*. London, 1962.

FRUCHTMAN, E. 'The Baryton', *Acta Musicologica*, XXXIV, Basel, 1962.

GANASSI, S. *Regola Rubertina*, Venice 1542; reprint Leipzig, 1924.

HAYES, G. R. *The Viols and other bowed instruments*. London, 1930.


## THE HARP

ARMSTRONG, R. B. *English and Irish Instruments*. Edinburgh, 1908.

FOX, C. MILLIGAN. *Annals of the Irish Harpers*. London, 1911.

RENSCH, ROSLYN. *The Harp*. New York, 1950.
See also LAVIGNAC, *La Harpe*, p. 1892 ff., and GROVE, 5th edn; also BLUME (*Die Harfe*).

RIMMER, JOAN. 'Harps in the Baroque Era' in *Proc. Royal Mus. Assoc.*, 1964. And *Galpin Society Journal*, XVII–XVIII, 1964–5.


## ANCIENT AND FOLK BACKGROUNDS
### (*Also Early Wind Intsruments and Recorder*)

ALEXANDRIU, T. *Instrumentele Muzicale Ale Poporului Romin* (*Les Instruments de musique du peuple Roumain*). Bucharest, 1956.

ANDERSSON, O. *The Bowed Harp*. London, 1930.

BACHMANN, W. *Die Anfange die Streichinstrumentenspiels*. Leipzig, 1964.

BAINES, A. *Bagpipes*. Oxford: Pitt Rivers Museum, Occasional Papers on Technology, 1960.

'Shawms of the Sardana Coblas' in *Galpin Society Journal*, v. 1952.

COCKS, W. A., and BRYAN, J. F. *The Northumbrian Bagpipes*. Newcastle-on-Tyne, 1967.

D'ERLANGER, R. *La Musique arabe*. Paris, 1930.

FARMER, H. G. *The Minstrelsy of the Arabian Nights*. Glasgow, 1945.

GAND, HANNS IN DER. *Volkstümliche Musikinstrumente in der Schweiz*. Basel, 1937.

GANASSI, S. *Opera intitulata Fontegara*. Venice, 1535; reprint, Milan, 1934.

HICKMANN, H. *Catalogue général des antiquités égyptiennes du Musée du Caire: Instruments de musique*. Cairo, 1952.

HUNT, E. *The Recorder and its Music*. London, 1962.

KLIER, K. M. *Volkstümliche Musikinstrumente in den Alpen*. Kassel, 1956.

LAVIGNAC. *Encyclopédie*. See Dictionaries and Encyclopedias; essential for study of Oriental instruments.

MARCEL-DUBOIS, C. *Les Instruments de musique de l'Inde ancienne*. Paris, 1941.

MATOS, M. GARCIA. 'Instrumentos musicales folklóricos de España' in *Anuario Musical*, XI, Barcelona, 1956.

NEW OXFORD HISTORY OF MUSIC, Vol. I, *Ancient and Oriental Music*. ed. E. Wellesz, London, 1957 (with many sections on instruments). And Vol. III ed., A Hughes and G. Abraham, Chaps. 12 and 13 by Y. Rokseth and G. Hayes, London, 1960.

PANUM, H., trans and ed. PULVER, G. *Stringed Instruments of the Middle Ages*. London, 1940.

PETER, H., trans. GODMAN, S. *The Recorder: its traditions and its tasks*. Berlin, 1953.

PIGGOTT, F. *The Music and Musical Instruments of Japan*. London, 1909.

REINACH, T. 'Syrinx', 'Tibia' in DAREMBERG and SAGLIO, *Dictionnaire des antiquités grecques et romaines*. Paris, 1877–1919.

ROWLAND-JONES, A. *Recorder Technique*. London, 1959.

SACHS, CURT. *The Rise of Music in the Ancient World*. New York, 1943.

SCHNEIDER, E. HARICH. 'The Present Condition of Japanese Court Music' in *Musical Quarterly*, XXXIX, New York, 1953.

TINCTORIS, J. see BAINES, A. 'Fifteenth Century Instruments in Tinctoris' *De Inventione et Usu Musicae*' in *Galpin Society Journal*, III, 1950.

WELCH, C. *Six Lectures on the Recorder*. Oxford, 1911.

## THE WOODWIND

BAINES, A. *Woodwind Instruments and their History*. London, 1957.

BATE, P. *The Oboe*. London, 1956.

BOEHM, THEOBALD, trans. MILLER, C. DAYTON. *The Flute and Flute-playing*. Cleveland, 1922; New York, 1964.

CAMDEN, ARCHIE. *Bassoon Technique*. London, 1962.

CARSE, ADAM. *Musical Wind Instruments*. London, 1939.

CHAPMAN, F. B. *Flute Technique*. London, 1936.

DAY, C. R. *Descriptive Catalogue of Musical Instruments at the Royal Military Exhibition, London, 1890*. London, 1891.

FRÖHLICH, J. F. *Vollständige theoretisch-praktisch Musikschule*. Bonn, 1810–11.

GOLDMAN, R. FRANKO. *The Concert Band*. New York, 1946.

HALFPENNY, E. 'The two- and three-keyed English Hautboy' in *Galpin Society Journal*, II, 1949.

'The English Debut of the French Hautboy' in *Monthly Musical Record*, July, 1949.

HECKEL, W. *Der Fagott*. Leipzig, 1931.

KROLL, O. 'Das Chalumeau', *Zeitschrift für Musikwissenschaft*, May, 1933.

*Die Klarinette*. Kassel, 1965. Eng. transl., London, 1968.

LANGWILL, L. G. *An Index of Musical Wind-Instrument Makers*. Edinburgh, 1960.

*The Bassoon and Double Bassoon*. London, 1965.

de LORENZO, L. *My Complete Story of the Flute*. New York, 1951.

MARX, JOSEF. 'The Tone of the Baroque Oboe' in *Galpin Society Journal*, IV, 1951.

RENDALL, F. G. *The Clarinet*. London, 1954.

ROCKSTRO, R. S. *A Treatise on the Flute*. London, 1890, 1928.

ROTHWELL, EVELYN. *Oboe Technique*. London, 1953.

THURSTON, F. *Clarinet Technique*. London, 1955.

VENTZKE, K. *Die Boehmflöte*. Frankfurt, 1966.

WELCH, C. *History of the Boehm Flute*. London, 1883, 1896.

WILLAMAN, R. *The Clarinet and Clarinet Playing*. New York, 1949.

## OLDER BRASS INSTRUMENTS

ALTERBURG, J. E. *Versuch einer Anleitung zur heroisch-musikalischen Trompeter-und Paukerkunst*. Halle, 1795; reprint, Dredsen, 1911; trans. of parts, *Brass Quarterly*, Vol. I, Nos. 3, 4, 1958.

ARNOLD, D. 'Ceremonial Music in Venice at the time of the Gabrielis' in *Proc. Royal Mus. Assoc.*, 1955–6.

BACH, VINCENT. *The Art of Trumpet-Playing*. New York, 1925.

BATE, P. *The Trumpet and Trombone*. London, 1966.

BLANDFORD, W. F. H. 'Bach's Trumpets' in *Monthly Musical Record*, July, 1931. 'The Bach Trumpet', ibid. March–June, 1935.

BRASS QUARTERLY, 1958–1964. Durham, New Hampshire. Continued as *Brass and Woodwind Quarterly*, New York, 1964.

CARSE, ADAM. *Musical Wind Instruments*. London, 1939.

FANTINI, G. *Modo per imparar a sonare di tromba*. Frankfurt, 1638; reprint, Milan, 1934.

GALPIN, F. W. 'The Sackbut' in *Proc. Royal Mus. Assoc.*, 1906.

HALFPENNY, E. 'Musicians at James II's Coronation' in *Music and Letters*, XXXII, 1951. And in *Galpin Society Journal*, 1960, 1962, 1963.

KARSTADT, J. 'Zur Geschichte des Zinken' in *Archiv für Musikforschung*, Leipzig, 1937.

MCCARTHY, A. J. *The Trumpet in Jazz*. London, 1945.

MENKE, W., trans. ABRAHAM, G. *History of the Trumpet of Bach and Handel*. London, 1934.

SACHS, CURT. 'Chromatic Trumpets in the Renaissance' in *Musical Quarterly*, XXXVI, 1950.

WÖRTHMÜLLER, W. 'Die Nürnberger Trompeten- und Posaunenmacher . . .' in *Mitteilungen des Vereins für Geschichte der Stadt Nürnberg*, 46, Nürnberg, 1955.

### HORN

BLANDFORD, W. F. H. Articles in the *Musical Times*:

'The French Horn in England', Aug. 1922.

'Wagner and the horn parts of *Lohengrin*', Sept.–Oct. 1922.

'The fourth horn in the Choral Symphony', Jan.–Feb.–Mar., 1925.

'Some observations on horn chords', Feb., 1926.

'Bach's horn parts', Aug., 1936.

'Handel's horn parts', Oct.–Nov., 1939.

COAR, BIRCHARD. *The French horn*, Ann Arbor, Michigan, 1947. *Nineteenth-century horn virtuosi in France*, De Kalb, Illinois, 1952.

FARKAS, PHILIP. *The Art of French Horn Playing*. Chicago, 1956.

FETIS, F. J., 'Cors à pistons'. *Revue musicale de Fétis*, Vol. 2. 1828.

FITZPATRICK, HORACE. 'The Valveless Horn in Modern Performances of Eighteenth-Century Music', in *Proc. Royal Mus. Assoc.*, 1965.

GREGORY, R. *The Horn*. London, 1961.

JANETZSKY, KURT. *Zum Erscheinen der Bach-Studien für Waldhorn*. Leipzig, 1957.

KARSTÄDT, G. *Lasst lustig die Hörner erschallen*. Hamburg, 1964.

KLING, H. 'Giovanni Punto, célèbre corniste', *Bulletin Français de la S.I.M.*, 1908.

'Le cor de chasse' in *Revista musicale italiana*, XVIII, 1911.

MAHILLON, V. C. *Le cor, son histoire, sa théorie, sa construction*. Brussels, 1907.

MAROLLES, G. de *Essai de monographie de la trompe de chasse*, Privately printed.

*Trois questions relatives à l'historique de la trompe de chasse*, Paris, n.d.
*Monographic abrégée de la trompe de chasse*, Privately printed.

MARX, JOSEF. *Twelve duos for two French horns*. Contains an important and interesting introduction, New York, 1947.

MEIFRED, P. J. 'De l'étendue, de l'emploi et des ressources du cor en général et de ses corps de rechange en particulier'. Paris, n.d. 'Notice sur la fabrication des instruments de musique en cuivre et sur celle du cor chromatique en particulier'. *Annuaire de la société des anciens élèves des écoles nationales des arts et métiers*, Année 1851.

MORLEY PEGGE, R. *The French Horn*. London, 1960.

SCHULLER, GUNTHER. *Horn Technique*. London, 1962.

## OTHER BRASS

CARSE, ADAM. *Musical Wind Instruments*. London, 1939.

DAY, C. R. *Descriptive Catalogue of the Musical Instruments in the Royal Military Exhibition, London*, 1890. London, 1891.

HAMPSON, JOSEPH N. *Besses o' th' Barn Band*. Northampton, n.d.

HIND, HAROLD C. 'The British Wind Band'. Hinrichsen's *Musical Year Book, Vol.* VII, 1952.

KASTNER, G. *Manual général de musique militaire*. Paris, 1848.

MILLER, G. *The Military Band*. Novello's Music Primers, London, 1912.

ROSE, ALGERNON. *Talks with bandsmen*. London, n.d.

RUSSELL, J. F., and ELLIOT, J. H. *The brass band movement*. London, 1936.

## PERCUSSION

BLADES, JAMES. *Orchestral Percussion Technique*. London, 1961.

GOODMAN, SAUL. *Modern Method for Timpani*. New York, 1948.

KASTNER, G. *Méthode de Timbales*. Paris, n.d.

KIRBY, P. R. *The Kettle-Drums*. London, 1930.

MORALES, HUMBERTO. *Latin-American Rhythm Instruments and How to Play Them*. New York, 1949.

SHIVAS. *The Art of Timpanist and Drummer*. London, 1957.

TITCOMB, CALDWELL. 'Baroque Court and Military Trumpets and Kettledrums' in *Galpin Society Journal*, IX, 1965.

# Index

## (NAMES OF INSTRUMENTS IN ITALICS)